Teaching and Learning in and Inclusive Classrooms

C000174197

This accessible text focuses on diversity in education and the inclusion of *all* children and young people in all aspects of the school or college community. It provides an introduction to policy, theory and practical strategies in relation to diversity in education for practitioners, researchers and policy makers.

The fully revised and updated chapters discuss recent debates, research studies and current initiatives, particularly relating to teaching and learning, and conclude with key questions for student reflection. Topics include:

- inclusive education
- ethnic and cultural diversity
- challenging behaviour
- bullying
- gender identity and sexuality
- Gypsy, Roma and Traveller children
- special educational needs
- listening to parents
- religious and cultural diversity
- disability and human rights
- children and young people who are refugees or seeking asylum.

Reflecting on legislative duties, personal values and the importance of listening to the voice of all learners, particularly those who may experience disadvantage or discrimination in educational settings, *Teaching and Learning in Diverse and Inclusive Classrooms* is a key resource for initial teacher training programmes and professional development courses.

Gill Richards is Professor of Special Education, Equity and Inclusion at the School of Education, Nottingham Trent University, UK.

Felicity Armstrong is Emeritus Professor at the Institute of Education, University College London, UK.

Teaching and Learning in Diverse and Inclusive Classrooms

Key issues for new teachers

Second edition

Edited by Gill Richards
and Felicity Armstrong

Routledge
Taylor & Francis Group

LONDON AND NEW YORK

First published 2016
by Routledge
2 Park Square, Milton Park, Abingdon, Oxon OX14 4RN

and by Routledge
711 Third Avenue, New York, NY 10017

Routledge is an imprint of the Taylor & Francis Group, an informa business

First edition published by Routledge, 2010

British Library Cataloguing in Publication Data
A catalogue record for this book is available from the British Library

Library of Congress Cataloging in Publication Data
Names: Richards, Gill. | Armstrong, Felicity.
Title: Teaching and learning in diverse and inclusive classrooms : key
issues for new teachers / [edited by] Gill Richards & Felicity Armstrong.
Description: Second edition. | New York : Routledge, 2016.
Identifiers: LCCN 2015026493| ISBN 9781138919617 (hardback :
alk. paper) | ISBN 9781138919600 (paperback   ) | ISBN
9781315687780 (eBook)
Subjects: LCSH: Inclusive education—Great Britain. | Special education—
Great Britain. | Multicultural education—
Great Britain. | Special education teachers—Training of—Great Britain.
Classification: LCC LC1203.G7 T43 2016 | DDC 371.9/0460941—
dc23LC record available at http://lccn.loc.gov/2015026493

ISBN: 978-1-138-91961-7 (hbk)
ISBN: 978-1-138-91960-0 (pbk)
ISBN: 978-1-315-68778-0 (ebk)

Typeset in Sabon
by Keystroke, Station Road, Codsall, Wolverhampton

Contents

List of contributors

Vikki Anderson has taught in schools, further education colleges and in higher education. She is currently a Learning Support Advisor at the University of Birmingham where she works with a wide range of students with specific learning difficulties and delivers continuing professional development. Her research interests include listening and responding to the voice of the learner, transition to higher education and the inclusive curriculum.

Felicity Armstrong is Professor of Education at the Institute of Education, University College, London. She has a life-long commitment to supporting the development of policies and practices for inclusive education. She is on the editorial board of *Disability and Society* and the *International Journal of Inclusive Education*, and has published numerous books and articles relating to equality, human rights and education.

Steve Bartlett is Professor of Education Studies and currently honorary lecturer at the University of Wolverhampton. He has published in the areas of Education Studies, practitioner research and teacher professionalism and is editor of *Educational Futures*: e-journal of the British Education Studies Association. He chaired the recent QAA Education Studies Benchmarking Committee.

Diana Burton is part-time Professor of Education at the University of Wolverhampton leading education research in the Faculty of Education, Health and Wellbeing. She has held executive leadership positions in a number of universities and has published widely in the areas of Education Studies, practitioner research, learning and teaching and teacher professionalism.

Mano Candappa is Senior Lecturer in Sociology of Education at UCL Institute of Education, University College London, UK. Her research focuses on Childhood, migration and forced migration, and issues around social marginalization and human rights. She has collaborated with EU partners on research on human trafficking and asylum; and directed UK research for a range of funders, including research councils, national and local government and voluntary sector organisations around the experiences of refugees and asylum-seeking children and families. Recent publications include *Education, Asylum* *and the 'Non-Citizen' Child: the politics of compassion and belonging* (with Halleli Pinson and Madeleine Arnot).

Kelly Chambers has been a primary school teacher since 2002 and became a Local Lead on the National Programme for Specialist Leaders of Behaviour & Attendance. She was an Advanced Skills Teacher (AST) from 2008 until 2012 and during this time, much of her focus was on improving inclusive environments in schools across Nottinghamshire. She also ran 'Climate for Learning Networks', an inclusive behaviour initiative, across Nottinghamshire, for three years. Kelly has been an Assistant Head Teacher since 2013. She is currently completing an MA in Special and Inclusive Education and delivering courses for Newly Qualified Teachers.

Chris Derrington is founder and Director of the EQualities Award. Her previous career spans thirty-five years of teaching pupils with learning disabilities, hearing impairment and emotional and behavioural difficulties. In 1990, she established the first Traveller Education team in Northamptonshire and went on to manage a large Race Equality Service. She has also been a head teacher, Ofsted inspector and a senior researcher for the NFER before joining the University of Northampton as a senior lecturer in Inclusive Education. Chris has a PhD in Cultural Psychology & Education and has published widely in the field of Traveller education.

Neil Duncan qualified as a teacher of Art from Bretton Hall College (Leeds University) in 1977. He became a Residential Child Care Officer in a secure unit for young people in Cumbria, then held a number of posts in special residential schools in the North of England, before settling in the West Midlands where he was Head of Year and Head of Behaviour at a local high school. While working as a teacher, Neil gained a PhD with his research into sexualised and gendered forms of bullying. Since then, Neil has appeared on TV and radio, both in the UK and overseas, and published several books and papers, which take a unique view of bullying in schools as an institutional problem rather than an individual child problem. He is currently Reader in Education for Social Justice at the University of Wolverhampton.

Linda Lyn-Cook has had longstanding experience teaching and managing in both mainstream and special schools. Her specialist expertise is in Autism, Special Educational Needs, Inclusion and Teacher Professional Development. She was employed for twelve years as a Local Authority Consultant Teacher leading a team of specialist staff. She is a visiting lecturer at Nottingham Trent University and lectures on the National Award for SENCOs as well as other post-graduate programmes. Linda is an additional school inspector and currently works independently as a school improvement advisor.

Michele Moore is a Professor of Inclusive Education. She is Editor of the world leading journal *Disability & Society* and on the Editorial Board of *Medicine, Conflict & Society*. Her work is concerned with advancing the global agenda for inclusion working with governments, teachers, disabled people, their families and representative organisations most recently in the Middle East and Africa. She works on numerous international projects to develop inclusion in schools and communities.

Johanna Myddleton is a lecturer at De Montfort University and is currently completing her PhD in the area of workplace cyberbullying at the University of Wolverhampton. Her interests lie broadly in the area of cyberpsychology and the implications of computer mediated communications for social interactions.

Michael J. Reiss is Professor of Science Education at UCL Institute of Education, University College London, Visiting Professor at the Universities of Leeds and York and the Royal Veterinary College, Honorary Fellow of the British Science Association and of the College of Teachers, Docent at the University of Helsinki, a Fellow of the Academy of Social Sciences, a Priest in the Church of England, President of the International Society for Science & Religion and President of the International Association for Science and Religion in Schools.

Gill Richards is Professor of Special Education, Equity and Inclusion at Nottingham Trent University. Prior to this, she taught pupils identified as having special educational needs. At NTU, she has designed courses in Special and Inclusive Education and for the National SEN Co-ordination Award; led Government SEN projects in schools and a European project in Greece with teachers; and carried out a longitudinal study of disadvantaged girls. She currently teaches national courses for SENCOs and Head Teachers, and supervises PhDs. Her research, publication and international conference presentations focus on issues of equity and inclusion.

Raphael Richards is a director of a Learning Trust and Chair of Governors at a primary school in Nottingham. He retired in 2014 from Sheffield City Council where he worked for the last 12 years in the Children Young People and Families (CYPF) Department as Head of their Ethnic Minority Travellers Achievement Service (EMTAS). Before that he held senior positions in private, community and voluntary sectors. He attained an MA in Equal Opportunities from the University of Central England in 2002 and has been a visiting lecturer in several universities.

Richard Rieser is a consultant, trainer, advocate, writer and film-maker working on inclusive education of disabled people and disability equality in the UK and internationally. For many years a disabled teacher and then charity director, he now runs World of Inclusion (www.worldofinclusion.com). Richard represented the UK disabled people's movement at the UN when the UNCRPD was being negotiated. He also coordinates UK Disability History Month, is a member of the Special Education Consortium and a Tribunal member of SENDIST. He has written a number of books and many articles and he is a regular contributor to the Alliance for Inclusive Education journal, *Inclusion Now*.

Jackie Scruton has spent most of her career working with children and young people for whom inclusion might be an issue. This has been in a range of settings, from special schools to further education. Her special interest is in communication skills and she is a Makaton regional tutor. She currently works as a senior lecturer at Nottingham Trent University and is a specialist member of the Special Educational Needs and Disability Tribunal (SENDIST).

Marjorie Smith taught throughout the age range and also in special and higher education settings. She was an educational psychologist who worked in teacher education as well as contributing to research on gender and learning. She was a tireless human rights campaigner with a specific interest in young people with issues around their gender identity or sexual orientation, believing that education was key to overcoming homophobia and other discrimination. Sadly, Marjorie died on 9 February 2011.

Foreword

Teaching and Learning in Diverse and Inclusive Classrooms is a twenty-first century book about inclusion and Felicity Armstrong and Gill Richards are to be congratulated for it. This second edition is testament to its relevance and importance.

If you look at many books about inclusion from the 1990s, or about 'integration' (as it was then called) from twenty years ago, you will find something very different from this book. You will find discussion of 'special educational needs' that occludes an understanding of where children and young people lie in relation to the education system: there is almost a disembodiment of the child. The resolute emphasis on 'special educational needs' somehow depersonalises the child.

By particularising the difficulties that children experience at school Armstrong and Richards reintroduce the person to the scene. With an unusually well written collection of contributions they create a tableau of characters whom educators have difficulty dealing with and in doing this they effectively combine the theoretical with the practical – always a difficult task. They offer not only understanding but guidance on learning and teaching for these young people. This second edition contains important new chapters on using evidence and religious issues in relation to diversity and inclusion.

I very much like the idea – running right through the book – of focusing on communities of learners. This is a thoroughly contemporary approach to learning: it is about the ways in which people identify with learning and with what goes on in schools. We all learn every minute of the day but if our identity is not as a member of a community that shares the aspirations and the motivations of others then we fail to share the cultural richness of the wider community of which we are part. This is surely what school is all about. By looking at areas such as ethnicity, gender and sexuality and at Gypsy, Roma and Traveller children the book's contributors show how alienation happens and they point to ways in which participation is possible. In doing this they show how 'diversity' can be more than simply a buzzword. They also implicitly deconstruct 'special educational needs'.

This focus on communities of learning is combined very nicely with a review of important national initiatives and developments for promoting inclusion and diversity and these help the reader to understand what can be done and where to go in seeking help.

I am really pleased to see the publication of this book. It marks a turning point in the way that we think about inclusion, participation and diversity.

Gary Thomas
Professor of Inclusion and Diversity
University of Birmingham

Acknowledgements

We would like to thank Alison Foyle (Senior Publisher) and Rebecca Hogg (Editorial Assistant), and the team at Routledge, for their encouragement and invaluable support in the production of this book. We would also like to thank Michele Taylor, Subject Administrator in the School of Education at Nottingham Trent University, for vital support with the administrative work associated with the final stages of this book.

Introduction

Felicity Armstrong and Gill Richards

This book is dedicated to teachers, head teachers, governors and – in particular – to all those starting out on a career in teaching in challenging times. Our focus is on inclusive education and the particular interpretations and challenges relating to this concept from a number of different perspectives. For us, inclusive education has multiple meanings and reaches into all aspects of education, but it is based on some fundamental principles as outlined by Tony Booth:

> We see inclusion as concerned with reducing all exclusionary pressures in education and society, thus providing a dynamic relationship between the two concepts. We view inclusion in education as concerned with *increasing participation in, and reducing exclusion from, the learning opportunities, cultures and communities of the mainstream.* Inclusion is a never-ending process, working towards an ideal when all exclusionary pressures within education and society are removed.
>
> (Booth 2003: 2)

This approach, far from being *utopian*, recognizes that social and cultural change requires both *ideals* through which to frame it, and an understanding of the breadth, depth and complexity of social relationships and policy making in education. Working towards inclusive education requires a continuous commitment to critical examination of our own values, assumptions and practices, as well as of those of others in the wider context of school and society. It also requires an understanding of the many ways in which children and young people can experience exclusion and discrimination in education and so our book tries to explore some of these and suggest ways in which teachers and schools can try and prevent these from occurring. For us *understanding* must include, where possible, *listening to the voices of 'insiders'* who have direct experience of questions relating to the issues under discussion. We have tried to ensure that the perspectives of insiders are reflected in some of the contributions which make up this book.

Education in all its varied forms, takes place within many different contexts and policy constraints, and we cannot ignore these. On the contrary, an awareness on the part of practitioners of wider policy directives, legal requirements and the in-house guidelines of schools and colleges is necessary in order to understand both the challenges and possible opportunities for developing a community, in which every member is valued equally, based on principles of the right to full access and participation. This does not mean that differences are ignored or overlooked, but it does rest on the belief that differences must not be seen as a reason or justification for unequal treatment or exclusion. The chapters in this book provide opportunities for developing understanding and sensitivity on the part of teachers, to both the uniqueness of each individual, and to possible issues that may arise in relation to particular groups.

Some chapters focus specifically on 'groups' – such as children and young people who are members of the Gypsy, Roma and Traveller communities, or asylum seeking and refugee children.

Other chapters focus on broader areas such as bullying, behaviour and teachers and teaching assistants working together for inclusion. You will also find chapters that raise fundamental issues for inclusive education, such as human rights and the relationship between parents, communities and schools. One of the purposes of the book is to explore questions of diversity and inclusion in relation to teaching and *communities of learners*, rather than focusing on a particular group of learners. Indeed, our concern has been to provide a collection of chapters that challenge the dominant notion that inclusive education is primarily the domain of 'special educational needs'. On the contrary – inclusive education is concerned with all school members, regardless of difference, and with the wider communities that schools are part of. Difficulties in learning and barriers to participation can arise for many different reasons, but the primary cause is the failure of societies and of education systems to respond in positive ways to diversity, not failures or deficits on the part of individual learners.

Tony Booth argues that

> The identification of inclusion with an aspect of student identity such as impairment or ethnicity is self-defeating since students are whole people, with multiple, complex identities. When it is associated with a devaluing label such as 'a child *with special educational needs*' it involves a particular contradiction. The inclusion in education of a child categorized as '*having special educational needs*' involves their de-categorization. Inclusion has to be connected to the recognition to all aspects of diversity.
>
> (Booth 2003: 2)

We agree with this position, and also recognise that some groups in society experience very particular kinds of discrimination and marginalisation, which need to be understood and addressed. So, what we are saying is that inclusive education concerns everybody in and around school communities. *Within* these communities there are some children and young people whose identification with a particular group, their appearance, situation or life style, their prior experiences and aspirations, may be misunderstood or constructed by others in particular ways that may be negative and lead to the creation of barriers to their full participation and sense of well-being and belonging. We believe that teachers need to understand, as far as possible, the perspectives and experiences of all learners as individuals and as members of their communities and we hope this book will prove to be a valuable contribution in developing this understanding.

The chapters in this book represent different interpretations of inclusion, and understandings of the underlying barriers to participation and approaches to overcoming these, reflecting the perspectives of their authors and mirroring some of the differences and even contradictions that are evident in recent policies and practices. We are united, however, in wanting to explore and understand the conditions and processes that contribute to inequalities and marginalisation in the classroom as they affect individuals, groups and school communities. This is not a book that seeks to present a 'unified view' on issues, but represents the diversity of values, preoccupations and experiences that we, as a group of contributors, bring to our writing. We have not used our editorial powers to smooth over differences and impose our own voices on contributions. Nevertheless, during the process of editing this book the question of the use of labels and their effects has arisen frequently. This has led us to an increased awareness of the embeddedness of labels and how they have become a kind of globalizing 'shorthand' in many sectors, which lumps groups of children together on the basis of a defining characteristic as perceived by powerful others. We have had many discussions about this between ourselves as editors and with individual contributors by e-mail, and questions and new insights have emerged about the language we use to describe others, and about why some ways of talking about others have more negative connotations than others.

Contributors were invited to review some important debates, research studies and current initiatives relating to their area, with a focus on developing new teachers' understanding of issues and of classroom practice and considerations for teaching and learning. Each chapter concludes with two or three questions for teachers to reflect upon and a short list of additional resources for further study. We seek to move beyond broad discussions of 'diversity' and inclusive education, to a focus on what these mean for schools and for teachers' practice in the classroom. Diversity and inclusion are not issues that can simply be taught as subjects; they involve reflection on personal values and professional practice.

We hope the book will provide a key resource for teacher education and, in particular provide support for new teachers.

In reading this book, you may find your own prior assumptions challenged – but this can be a positive and fruitful experience in opening up new insights and possibilities for happier and more equitable relationships in the classroom and in the community.

The structure and contents of the book

Teaching and Learning in Inclusive Classrooms is made up of fourteen chapters, which all address different aspects and issues relating to inclusive education, diversity and teaching and learning.

In **Chapter 1** Felicity Armstrong discusses the meanings and principles of inclusive education, and the ways in which these can be translated into school cultures, teaching and learning. She draws out some of the difficulties and constraints that schools and teachers have to negotiate, and considers some core values that are necessary for the development of inclusive thinking and practices.

In **Chapter 2** Marjorie Smith and Kelly Chambers explore sexuality and gender identity in relation to children and young people and their experience of education. Drawing on some examples, they show how this area of inclusion presents special challenges for schools and teachers, yet it is an area where comparatively small shifts in attitude and practice can bring about extraordinary benefits in the achievements and well-being of a significant number of individuals. 'Sexuality' is routinely ignored in debates about inclusive education, and this chapter makes a powerful contribution to addressing this important and invisible subject.

Chapter 3 by Neil Duncan and Johanna Myddleton explore bullying from the perspective that schools are powerful systems that can inadvertently support or even produce bullying behaviours. Neil argues that teachers need to move beyond a common but simplistic way of looking at bullying, which focuses entirely on children as the problem. The chapter considers some of the implications of this and suggests ways to reduce the negative impact of 'schooling' on pupils' social relations.

In **Chapter 4** Chris Derrington introduces questions relating to inclusive education in relation to Gypsy, Roma and Traveller children and young people and their communities. She explains the importance of understanding cultural differences, and explores some of the possible barriers to participation that can arise in schools, particularly in relation to these communities, and suggests ways in which these can be overcome.

Chapter 5 by Steve Bartlett and Diana Burton covers a brief review of research and past initiatives relating to boys' and girls' aspirations and achievement. It explores a range of current gender specific initiatives supported by the Government and the impact these can have on pupils. It reflects on current curriculum and social issues that affect participation and achievement, identifying considerations for teachers as they plan for their learners.

Chapter 6 by Raphael Richards explores the ethnic diversity that exists in classrooms across Britain today. The chapter starts by considering the needs of Black and Minority Ethnic (BME) children and those with English as an additional language, drawing out issues of community and personalisation of lessons. Much of 'Not in my image' is about building positive relationships, so readers are called upon to reflect on what they, as individuals, will bring to the classroom. The chapter seeks to help new teachers enter the classroom ready to be champions for young people from diverse ethnic backgrounds.

Chapter 7 by Mano Candappa is about asylum-seeking and refugee children and their experiences in British schools. The chapter explains how these students are among the most marginalised in our society and even among their peers at school. They are often 'invisible' within schools yet they desperately need the school's support to help them 'get on with their lives', and the challenge for schools is how best to support them whilst not taking agency away from them. The chapter argues that the inclusive school that adapts in order to respond to the diversity of its community, is the most supportive environment for asylum-seeking and refugee students.

Chapter 8 by Gill Richards considers issues of teaching and learning raised by the increasing inclusion of learners identified as having 'special' educational needs in mainstream classrooms. It reviews the need for such labels in inclusive schools and the impact these have on teacher expectations and practice. The chapter draws on recent Government initiatives, reflecting on the impact these have on new teachers and explores strategies for increasing teachers' confidence.

Chapter 9 by Jackie Scruton explores a brief review of research, legislation and policies concerning students that are perceived as challenging within educational settings. It explores barriers that contribute to young people's disenfranchisement and considers the role of teachers and schools within this. The chapter draws on a range of initiatives currently used in schools to respond to behaviour that is seen to be difficult, using these to suggest ways that teachers can work positively with learners and other professionals.

Chapter 10 by Michael J. Reiss examines issues relating to religious and cultural diversity and inclusive practice from the perspective of teachers working in schools. It supports the right of all members of the school community to hold a particular belief, religious or secular, as part of a wider spectrum of rights to equal participation in education, regardless of difference. Inclusive schools welcome the diversity represented by members of their neighbourhood communities and regard differences as sources for enriching teaching and learning and for fostering harmonious and respectful relationships and mutual understanding.

In **Chapter 11** Vikki Anderson and Linda Lyn-Cook briefly trace the historical development of teaching assistants in education settings and explore the current range of roles they undertake in schools. The chapter considers the working relationship between teachers and teaching assistants, focusing on recent studies and current policy initiatives. In particular, it examines how this key relationship may affect the quality of learners' experiences, identifying implications for teachers' roles.

In **Chapter 12** Michele Moore examines the positioning of parents as allies in the new teacher's project of advancing inclusion. She provides an insider perspective by exploring how relationships between parents and teachers can be understood from her own point of view as a parent of two children with impairments. She reflects on her experiences as a parent seeking to work closely with teachers who are willing to see parents as allies, but also writes from the viewpoint of a professional working with teachers on best practice in inclusive education. The approach Michele puts forward in this chapter is, she argues, effective in building positive relationships with parents of *all* children at risk of, and at risk from, exclusion.

In **Chapter 13** Gill Richards explores the requirements for teachers to engage with research as a basis for developing teaching and learning and providing evidence of the impact of interventions to increase pupils' achievement. It reviews key research about diversity and inclusion, identifying issues for teachers to consider as they plan for their diverse learners. The chapter argues that as teachers develop their knowledge of, and skills in, 'evidence-based practice', this will enable them to enhance all pupils' learning through approaches that take account of individualised circumstances.

Chapter 14 by Richard Rieser examines some of the main issues facing teachers in thinking about the values and practices that underpin inclusive education from a global perspective, particularly in relation to disability. However, in adopting a human rights and international perspective, a powerful argument is developed that links all children and young people together as having the shared rights to participation in education in inclusive schools. The chapter explores the relationships of the 'social model' and the 'medical model' of disability to different educational structures and practices, demonstrating that a 'deficit-view' of children has serious consequences in terms of the failure to respect children's rights. The argument is put forward that a firm understanding of the issues involved in responding to, and celebrating, difference is essential to the development effective inclusive teaching.

Reference

Booth, T. (2003) Inclusion and exclusion in the city: concepts and contexts. In P. Potts (ed.) *Inclusion in the City: Selection, schooling and community*, London: Routledge Falmer, pp.1–14.

Chapter 1

Inclusive education

School cultures, teaching and learning

Felicity Armstrong

Inclusive education is one of the most important yet elusive concepts to have emerged in the UK and internationally over the past thirty years (Florian 2014).[1] It is an important concept because, in its full interpretation, it represents a potentially profound shift away from policies and practices based on selections according to perceptions about ability, and which have traditionally sanctioned the exclusion of many learners from mainstream education. Inclusive education rests on the belief that all members of the community have the right to participate in, and have access to, education on an equal basis. However, it is an *elusive* concept because it is the subject of many different interpretations, depending on who is using the term, in what context and for what purpose.

In spite of the wide variations in the use of the term across different contexts, some broad principles underpinning inclusive education have made their way into policy statements, nationally and internationally. UNESCO, working, often at grass-roots level, with representatives from all parts of the world, has headed up the *Education For All* (EFA) movement and produced documents and instruments in support of a particularly powerful interpretation of inclusive education:

> Inclusive education is a process that involves the transformation of schools and other centres of learning to cater for all children – including boys and girls, students from ethnic and linguistic minorities, rural populations, those affected by HIV and AIDS, and those with disabilities and difficulties in learning and to provide learning opportunities for all youth and adults as well. Its aim is to eliminate exclusion that is a consequence of negative attitudes and a lack of response to diversity in race, economic status, social class, ethnicity, language, religion, gender, sexual orientation and ability. Education takes place in many contexts, both formal and non-formal, and within families and the wider community. Consequently, inclusive education is not a marginal issue but is central to the achievement of high quality education for all learners and the development of more inclusive societies. Inclusive education is essential to achieve social equity and is a constituent element of lifelong learning.
>
> (UNESCO 2009: 4)

Inclusive education is interpreted as concerning all learners, and hence of universal importance to school communities, not just the concern of a particular group of students, teachers or 'experts'.

Policy making: a complex process

Policies put in place in support of inclusive education are often sidelined or obscured by other policies that have greater currency (Hardy and Woodcock 2015) such as those concerned with reaching national targets for attainment (Smith and Douglas 2014) or the distribution of resources. There is a persistent mismatch in the UK context between the apparent intentions of one set of policies and what actually happens in practice (Dyson and Gallanaugh 2007). This should not be understood simply as a 'gap between policy and practice', but as an indication of the complex nature of policy making and interpretation, especially in the light of conflicting national and global policy agendas. Enormous changes in policies and practices in relation to all aspects of education, including in relation to historically marginalised groups, most notably to disabled children, have taken place over the past century, reflecting changes in governments (see Norwich 2014) and contrasting values and attitudes in society. Indeed, 'change' must be seen as a never-ending process in education (Ball 2013). These changes are reflected in the evolving and sometimes erratic use of terminology in schools, official documents and in the media. In particular, the term 'inclusion' is used inconsistently and often limited specifically to policies relating to students with 'special educational needs'.

Inclusion, participation and recognition

Tony Booth describes participation in the inclusive classroom in the following terms:

> It (. . .) implies learning alongside others and collaborating with them in shared lessons. It involves active engagement with what is learnt and taught and having a say in how education is experienced. But participation also means being recognised for oneself and being accepted for oneself: I participate with you when you recognise me as a person like yourself and accept me for who I am.
>
> (Booth 2002:2)

Booth emphasises the importance of *recognition* as well as *participation*. Recognition is concerned with '. . .injustices which are understood to be cultural (and) rooted in social patterns of representation, interpretation and communication' (Fraser 1999). *Participation* is about being a part of and belonging to communities, and having equal access and rights with others. Inclusive education demands both – that every child and young person has a right to attend their local school or college (i.e. all *participate*), and that all members of the school and college, and of the wider community, have the right to *recognition* in terms of who they are, their culture and beliefs, appearance, interests, life-style and uniqueness. Inclusion recognises, and is responsive to, diversity and the right 'to be oneself' in an open, shared and democratic community. *Inclusion*, therefore, is a rather different concept from 'integration', which focuses on how individual learners, or a group of learners, might 'fit in' to a school or a class. Inclusive education implies a transformation in the social, cultural, curricular and pedagogic life of the school, as well as its physical organisation. Integration was a dominant term in the past and traditionally, referred to concepts and practices relating to learners labelled as 'having special educational needs'. Confusion arises when 'inclusion' is used simply to replace the term 'integration' (e.g. 'This child is being included 3 afternoons a week' or 'Would you like to visit our inclusion suite for children with special educational needs?'). The terms mean fundamentally different things.

For over 30 years The Centre for Studies on Inclusive Education (CSIE) has made a major contribution to the development of critical debate and materials on inclusion (see the CSIE website http://www.csie.org.uk). CSIE has also promoted the *Index for Inclusion* (Booth and Ainscow 2002, 2011), which provides materials to support schools through an engagement of critically examining their policies and practices, and guides them through a process of development towards inclusive education. It is 'about building supportive communities and fostering achievement for all staff and students' (CSIE 2014). The *Index* is not a 'blueprint' or a 'checklist', but an invitation to schools to engage with *where they are now*, and to move forward in a process of positive change. It describes the processes involved as:

- Valuing all students and staff equally.
- Increasing the participation of students in, and reducing their exclusion from, the cultures, curricula and communities of local schools.
- Restructuring the cultures, policies and practices in schools so that they respond to the diversity of students in the locality.
- Reducing barriers to learning and participation for all students, not only those with impairments or those who are categorised as 'having special educational needs'.
- Learning from attempts to overcome barriers to the access and participation of particular students to make changes for the benefit of students more widely.
- Viewing the difference between students as resources to support learning, rather than as problems to be overcome.
- Acknowledging the right of students to an education in their locality.
- Improving schools for staff as well as for students.
- Emphasizing the role of schools in building community and developing values, as well as in increasing achievement.
- Fostering mutually sustaining relationships between schools and communities.
- Recognizing that inclusion in education is one aspect of inclusion in society.

(CSIE 2014)

The importance of *transforming school cultures* lies at the heart of these processes. In the context of discussions about inclusive education, the notion of 'school culture' refers to the principles and practices that inform relationships, curricula, pedagogy and the organisation of schools and their connections with, and recognition of the communities which they serve.

In addition to a focus on children and schools, CSIE is supportive of families and community organisations. The importance of establishing engagement and dialogue between schools and families, and between children and teachers, cannot be overestimated. This is particularly important in relation to groups who have traditionally been excluded from mainstream society, as Flecha and Soler (2013) have demonstrated in their work on Roma families in the Spanish city of Albacete.

Inclusive practices and values

One of the most deeply embedded expressions of school culture is the ways in which teaching and learning are understood. We need therefore to think about the *values* and *processes* involved in pedagogy and to measure these against the principles of inclusion. This involves asking the questions: to what extent do teaching practices and the curriculum exclude, marginalise or demean any groups of learners or individuals, and to what extent do they recognise and draw on students' own rich 'funds of knowledge' and experience? (Andrews and Yee 2006; Hedges 2015). The notion of 'funds of knowledge' refers to the experience, culture and knowledge children and young people bring into school with them. Their 'funds of knowledge' draw on familiar social and cultural norms and practices, language, their understanding of the nature of the world around them, relationships, the purposes of education, and their experience of creativity. Seeing children as possessing 'funds of knowledge' recognises them as being 'experts in their own lives' (Mason and Danby 2011).

Here it is helpful to think about the meaning of 'pedagogy'. Pedagogy is often used to refer to how teachers transmit a curriculum to learners (Corbett 2001). In contrast, inclusive pedagogy can also refer to the particular teaching strategies teachers adopt in response to different contexts and learning styles. Inclusive pedagogy involves:

- a recognition of individual differences;
- a valuing of cultural diversity;
- a conscious and visible commitment to fostering and promoting inclusive values in all aspects of the life of the school, as well as in the classroom;
- a recognition and celebration of what the local community has to offer in terms of supporting education and inclusion.

Of course, all the terms used above are open to interpretation. Terminology such as 'inclusion', 'participation' and 'citizenship' can be used in very diverse, and often-contradictory ways and for different purposes. It reflects contextual variations and concerns – cultural, geographical, economic and autobiographical. It is the *values* that are at work and that underpin these variations that are important.

Similarly the concept of inclusion will have particular meanings in contexts such as nurseries, special schools, young offenders institutions, inner city schools, fee-paying private schools, asylum detention centres, and rural community colleges. To suggest that 'inclusion' only has meaning in the context of mainstream schools is, in the present social and political context, to marginalise other settings in which many teachers, support staff, children and young people find themselves. The implication of this would be to *exclude* some of the most marginalised groups in society from the wider struggle for inclusion which, by definition, has to encompass all members of society, regardless of the particular settings they attend, or are assigned to.

Inclusive pedagogy and learning theory

Let us now turn to the life of the classroom. Are there any theories of learning or ideas relating to education in general that we can draw on to help us develop understanding about our own teaching practices and attitudes? A possible theoretical framework that may be helpful in thinking about inclusive pedagogy is that of social constructivism. This approach contrasts with theories that are based on a 'transmission' model in which the teacher possesses – or 'owns' – the knowledge, and their task is to transmit some of this knowledge to the learner. This may be reinforced by systems of rewards and disincentives (or 'grades', positive or negative attitude of teacher towards students). Since the 1980s there has been a return to approaches to teaching and learning that focus primarily on content and measurable outcomes rather than process. In constructivist teaching the learner is regarded as

> A self-activated maker of meaning, an active agent in his (sic) own learning process. He is not one to whom things merely happen; he is the one who, by his own volition, causes things to happen. Learning is seen as the result of his own self-initiated interaction with the world: the learner's understanding grows during a constant interplay between something outside himself – the general environment, a pendulum, a person – and something inside himself, his concept-forming mechanisms. . .
>
> (Candy 1989: 107)

The Russian psychologist Vygotsky developed a version of social constructivism as a model of learning in which the existing knowledge, experience and context was of prime importance. Learning was understood as a process of constructing new insights and concepts through the interaction with the environment and the intervention of the 'teacher' who could be a more experienced person, a sibling or play-mate (although in Vygotsky's examples the assumption seems to be that the 'teacher' will usually be an adult). The 'expertise' of the teacher is actively engaged with the learner's own knowledge, experience and thought processes and existing level of competence or 'zone of proximal development – or 'ZPD' (Vygotsky 1962, in Wood 2003). Instructional support, or 'scaffolding' is provided by the teacher to help the learner move on to a different level or kind of understanding (Bruner 1979, in Wood 2003).

> Thus, constructivism in education is concerned with two things: how learners *construe* (or interpret) events and ideas, and how they *construct* (build or assemble) structures of meaning. The constant dialectical interplay between construing and constructing is at the heart of a constructivist approach to education. . .
>
> (Candy 1989:108)

This theoretical framework has a number of possible implications and opportunities for developing an inclusive pedagogy – or, rather, 'inclusive pedago*gies*' since there is no suggestion that one model or approach – however flexible and learner centred – will necessarily 'fit' all circumstances. Indeed, no theory should be taken as providing a blueprint for teaching and learning. Social constructivism does, however, provide a possible theoretical framework within which the potentially awkward mismatch between the knowledge, experience and expectations of the teacher and those of the learner may be resolved.

While some of Vygotsky's ideas may seem to us rather formulaic and counter-intuitive in terms of the assumptions made about how much teachers can fully understand the learner's 'internal course of development', his work does open up some really important principles for exploration and interpretation. 'Theories' can be seen as getting in the way of innovative transformation of practice if we let them work as straitjackets on our thinking, but they can also be used as catalysts for creativity if we are prepared to interpret them imaginatively so that they are sensitive and relevant to particular contexts and issues. A number of researchers and teachers have developed Vygotsky's ideas. Bruner, for example, insists on the importance of understanding the *cultural influences* that are involved in the process of learning (Bruner 1990 in Pollard 2002).

The approaches suggested by this framework can be extended and reinterpreted to encompass peers working together in groups in a process of collaborative co-construction of learning, creating active and vibrant communities of learners in the classroom. An openness on the part of teachers to collaborate with others and draw on shared knowledge and experience is fundamental to the development of inclusive teaching and learning (Florian and Linklater 2010).

And what about the perspectives of students themselves on their own experiences and interests in relation to their learning? How can teachers engage with students' 'funds of knowledge', which are an integral part of their experience of learning? It is difficult to imagine a commitment to developing an inclusive school in which little value is placed on the voices of learners themselves. In order to understand students' perspectives on their learning and experience, schools need to listen to their voices and try and learn from these (Keddie 2015). This requires a willingness on the part of teachers to listen respectfully to students (Fielding 2004) and reflect critically on their own practices as part of a commitment to developing teaching and learning (Nind 2014).

If we put together some of these ideas, the process of teaching and learning involves understanding both the uniqueness of the individual, their history and existing knowledge *and* the collective cultural knowledge and practices of the social context of the learner. A learner, then, is an *individual in a social world*. Communities of learners are made up of individual learners who exchange knowledge and experiences, collaborate and hypothesise, argue, build and create, to develop understanding and knowledge.

Building on, summarising and interpreting some of the ideas we have touched on, there are a number of positive implications for developing inclusive approaches to teaching and learning which we might consider:

- Learners are all individuals with their own unique histories and experiences.
- Learners bring with them to the learning process particular kinds of socially and culturally constructed knowledge, which will interact with the curriculum and teaching practices of the school (i.e. learners are not 'blank slates' or 'empty vessels').
- This knowledge has the capacity to transform, re-interpret or expand on what is being taught.
- Learning is a two-way or collaborative process in which the 'teacher' seeks to understand and take into account prior learning, preferred learning style, and social context.
- Collaborative exploration in the classroom in which students share knowledge as a means of problem solving and hypothesizing is a form of 'scaffolding'.
- 'Pedagogy' cannot be separated from 'curriculum' in that approaches to teaching and learning reflect what is recognised and valued as 'knowledge'.
- Inclusive pedagogy rests on recognition of the uniqueness of every student and of the importance of social and cultural factors in influencing responses to curriculum and pedagogy.

Understanding institutional cultures and practices

When carrying out research or a critical analysis of a school or other setting, researchers and practitioners who focus first on issues relating to processes of inclusion and exclusion, will usually try to understand its social and cultural nature and explore how this is translated into classroom practice. We could describe this as starting at the 'macro' level and moving into the 'micro' level to see how broad contours and features translate into rich details – rather like using the 'Google earth' navigation engine. At the micro level there is a need to critically examine how the values that are apparently espoused at the *macro* levels are translated and communicated at the level of the classroom, and their impacts on the relationships and opportunities available to individual learners. We also need to ask questions that explore inclusive values from a number of different vantage points. The following section presents examples taken from case studies of two schools, based on research in an inner city, in which an apparent commitment to inclusive education and equal opportunities is confronted by a number of contradictory policies, values and practices. These two small studies illustrate how pressures and constraints at work at the macro level *outside* the school can work their way through to different levels of school life.

Acorn Community School

Acorn School is a large comprehensive school that prides itself on being an inclusive community school with an 'open door' policy for all learners. It is situated on a large, economically deprived housing estate on the edge of an industrial city. The buildings are accessible to disabled people. In response to being put under 'special measures' following an Ofsted inspection, the school introduced a finely graded system of setting across subjects, based on selection according to attainment, in an attempt to 'raise standards'. There is an active policy of 'including' students who are seen as having behaviour problems in their attainment group and ensuring that the lowest sets don't become receptacles for those who disturb lessons. Examination results are improving in the 'A–C' band. A group of eleven and twelve year olds spoke about their learning. Some in the group complained that only the 'top' sets in Science 'got to do experiments'; if you were in a lower set, you watched the teacher carry out the experiment or copied notes and diagrams from the board (surely, a more abstract and, therefore, demanding mode of learning than the 'hands-on' approach, for children of this age). One child who was in a 'top' set commented: 'I like Science practical. You work in a group and it's fun and you want to do it. Anything that's not fun, you don't learn because it's boring.' In the same school, it emerged that students in the top sets in their final GCSE year were given course texts so they could study at home; these were not provided for students in lower sets. Are these practices 'inclusive' and what are the reasons that underlie disparities and inequalities that may impact on students' learning?

I raised some of these questions with a member of the senior management team who explained that if children were allowed to do practical experiments in Science, they had to be 'highly responsible' and 'careful' or 'valuable materials could be wasted or damaged'. A similar explanation was put forward for the policy on the provision of course texts for home study: these are expensive and there was 'always a risk of books getting lost or damaged at home' but, he added, perhaps in the future more students would be able to take books home. Embedded in these arguments are a number of factors that need to be critically examined, including the possible effects of under-resourcing and pressure to increase the numbers of A–C grades at GCSE on approaches to teaching and learning and the strategic rationing of resources. But are these constraints ever a justification for abandoning principles of fairness and equity? A further element in the justifications provided for the unequal distribution of resources in the school is attitudinal; there is an implicit assumption that students who are not in 'top sets' will be less careful with equipment or, even, that their homes are more likely to be conducive to 'losing or damaging' books. This raises questions about the way student identities are formed on the basis of assumptions made about students' home life linked to their academic performance.

These examples may be fairly typical of the kinds of contradictory attitudes and practices that occur routinely in schools in which policies at the 'macro' level, which are apparently 'inclusive' in terms of stated policies on equality issues, are contradicted at the less visible 'micro' levels of teaching and learning and the provision of learning resources. These contradictions raise difficult and uncomfortable questions, but the purpose of raising them is not to vilify schools, which are often struggling to develop more equitable policies and practices within an increasingly competitive and unforgiving system. On the contrary, it is to shed light on some difficult issues that arise as a result of the profound social inequalities and conflicting values that work their way through schools and communities.

Sharrow School, Sheffield

In England, schools that claim, and demonstrate, a serious commitment to inclusion and equality and do not operate formal or informal selection policies are often to be found in the least economically advantaged areas and they tend to perform poorly in national tests, in comparison with schools in wealthier areas. Inclusive schools such as Sharrow Primary School in Sheffield, England (Abram et al. 2009), have an 'open door' policy and welcome all members of the community regardless of disability or level of attainment. Its population includes children 'in transition' who are refugees, seeking asylum, or living in temporary accommodation, and reflects the diversity of the area, with only 8 per cent of children in the school who speak English as a first language. The increase in cultural and linguistic diversity, especially in towns and cities, is one of many outcomes of globalisation that are transforming schools and colleges in towns and cities in the UK.

Sharrow School is fully accessible and there is a serious engagement with transforming curricula and pedagogical practices so that every child receives a meaningful education. Scores in national tests are lower than the average and, although Ofsted (Office for Standards in Education) has praised the school for its inclusive response to diversity and its close links with the local community, this praise is overridden by criticism of the school's performance in national tests, which are regarded in public reports as the only 'real' indicators of 'achievement'.

The school building is entirely accessible to disabled children and adults, both from the outside and internally, with a central lift area and careful gradations between levels making ramps unnecessary.

The school places an important emphasis on equal opportunities policies, including anti-racism policies, and runs regular pupil-led campaigns on, for example, bullying and healthy eating, which all members of the school community are involved in. There is a school council run by elected representatives from each class, which meets regularly and reports back to their 'constituents'. One campaign run by the council concerned complaints about the quality of school dinners, which are provided by a private company, and children organised protests against the poor quality of the food and small portions. The practices of inclusion and equity are embedded in the daily life of the school. For example, there is a system of 'playground friends' to ensure that children are not 'left out' or victimised in the playground or in other aspects of school life.

Disabled children are welcomed into the school as a matter of course and there are policies and practices in place to ensure that *all* children are able to participate fully in learning and in every aspect of the life of the school. These include developing supportive collaborative learning practices between groups of children. There is a teacher with special responsibility for inclusion in the school, although it is clear that all members of the school are *collectively* and *individually* 'responsible' for inclusion.

Schools such as Sharrow Primary School develop creative responses to diversity in their local communities, which, while enhancing opportunities for participation and the creation of equitable school cultures, sometimes come into conflict with the demands of national attainment and assessment agendas. Research studies have shown how pressures to improve scores on national tests have distorted the work of schools, especially those seeking to promote inclusive policies and practices (Florian and Rouse 2005; Ainscow *et al.* 2006). This is, perhaps, an important indication of the ways in which schools themselves are left to develop strategies in response to government policies which are potentially contradictory – some of which appear to support 'inclusion' while others are driven by a more powerful agenda – that of performance in the global arena.

Conclusion

In this chapter I have introduced some issues and questions for consideration within a wider set of concerns relating to the nature and culture of schools and teaching generally, rather than in terms of some 'special' conditions and qualities.

In seeking to gain a more informed understanding of such factors and their inter-relationship, we support the use of a framework in which a critical engagement can take place in terms of what we say we do and what we actually do as practitioners, and the tensions and dilemmas that this raises in relation to specific encounters in schools and classrooms or other institutional contexts. Arenas such as schools, colleges and universities reflect the wider social conditions and relations, including the inequalities, of the society in which they are placed in overt, subtle, complex and often-contradictory ways. Schools are involved in important political and social functions involving the support of particular values and the encouragement of specific forms of thinking and behaving. How schools and teachers engage with the contradictory pressures from external forces, including governments, is a crucial question for inclusive education.

Reflection on values and practice

Think about the context in which you work, or a context you are familiar with, and ask yourself the following questions:

- Does your school or college have active policies on equal opportunities that challenge racism, sexism, sexuality, bullying, disablism and discriminatory practices of all kinds and what action does the school take when these policies are disregarded by pupils or staff?
- Do teachers seek to understand the perspectives of students on their learning and experience?
- What is the relationship between the school and the wider community, including minority groups?

Further resources

Booth, T. and Ainscow, M. (2011) *The Index for Inclusion*, Bristol, CSIE, http://www.csie. org.uk.

Armstrong, F. and Moore, M. (eds) (2004) *Action Research for Inclusive Education: changing places, changing practices, changing minds*, London: Routledge.

Useful websites

Alliance for Inclusive Education (ALFIE) http://www.alphie.org.uk
Centre for Studies on Inclusive Education (CSIE) http://www.csie.org.uk
Enabling Education Network www.eenet.org.uk

Note

1 You will find a full discussion of the emergence of inclusive education as a global movement, and related policies, in the final chapter of this book, *Global approaches to education, disability and human rights: why inclusive education is the way forward*.

References

Abram, E., Armstrong, F., Barton, L. and Ley, L. (2009) 'Diversity, democracy and change in the inner city: understanding schools as belonging to communities', in Lavia, J. and Moore, M. (eds) (2009) *Decolonizing Community Contexts: Cross-cultural Perspectives on Policy and Practice*, London: Routledge, pp.132–148.

Ainscow, M., Booth, T. and Dyson, A. (2006) *Improving Schools, Developing Inclusion*, London: Routledge.

Andrews, J. and Yee, Wan Ching (2006) 'Children's 'funds of knowledge' and their real life activities: two minority ethnic children learning in out-of-school contexts in the UK', *Educational Review*, 58(4): 435–449.

Ball, S. (2013) *Policy Paper: Education, justice and democracy: the struggle over ignorance and opportunity* (Policy Paper), Centre for Labour and Social Studies (CLASS), London.

Booth, T. (2002) Inclusion and exclusion in the city: concepts and contexts. In Potts, P. (ed.) (2003) *Inclusion in the City*, London: Routledge, pp.1–14.

Booth, T. and Ainscow, M. (2002, 2011) *The Index for Inclusion*, Bristol: CSIE http://www.csie.org.uk.

Bruner, J. (1979) *On Knowing, Essays for the Left Hand*, London: Belknap Press of Harvard University.

Candy, P. (1989) Constructivism and the study of self-direction in adult learning, *Studies in the Education of Adults*, 21(2): 95–116.

Centre for Studies on Inclusive Education (CSIE) (2014) 'Developing learning and participation in schools', http://www.csie.org.uk, http://www.csie.org.uk/resources/inclusion-index-explained.shtml. Accessed 4/08/14.

Corbett, J. (2001) *Supporting Inclusive Education: a connective pedagogy*, London: RoutledgeFalmer.

Dyson, A. and Gallanuagh, F. (2007) National policy and the development of school practices: a case study, *Cambridge Journal of Education*, 37(4): 473–488.

Fielding, M. (2004) Transformative approaches to student voice: Theoretical underpinnings, recalcitrant realities. *British Educational Research Journal*, 30: 295–311.

Flecha, R. and Soler, M. (2013) Turning difficulties into possibilities: engaging Roma families and students in school through dialogic learning, *Cambridge Journal of Education*, 43(4): 451–465.

Florian, L. (2014) What counts as evidence of inclusive education?, *European Journal of Special Needs Education*, 29(3): 286–294.

Florian, L. and Linklater, H. (2010) Preparing teachers for inclusive education: using inclusive pedagogy to enhance teaching and learning for all, *Cambridge Journal of Education*, 40:4, 369–386.

Florian, L. and Rouse, M. (2001) 'Inclusive practice in English secondary schools: lessons learned', *Cambridge Journal of Education*, 31:3, 399–412.

Florian, L. and Rouse, M. (2005) 'Inclusive practice in English secondary schools: lessons learned', In Nind, M., Rix, J., Sheehy, K. and Simmons, K. (eds) Curriculum and Pedagogy in Inclusive Education: Values into Practice, London: RoutledgeFalmer.

Fraser, N. (1999) 'Social justice in the age of identity politics: redistribution, recognition and participation', in Ray, L. J. and Sayer, R.A. (eds) *Culture and Economy After the Cultural Turn*, London: Sage, pp.25–52.

Hardy, I. and Woodcock, S. (2015) Inclusive education policies: discourses of difference, diversity and deficit, *International Journal of Inclusive Education*, 19:2, 141–164.

Hedges, H. (2015) Sophia's funds of knowledge: theoretical and pedagogical insights, possibilities and dilemmas, *International Journal of Early Years Education*, 23(1): 83–96.

Keddie, A. (2015) Student voice and teacher accountability: possibilities and problematics, *Pedagogy, Culture & Society*, 23(2): 225–244.

Mason, J., & Danby, S. (2011) Children as experts in their lives, *Child Indicators Research*, 4: 185–189.

Nind, M. (2014) Inclusive research and inclusive education: why connecting them makes sense for teachers' and learners' democratic development of education, *Cambridge Journal of Education*, 44:4, 525–540.

Norwich, B. (2014) Changing policy and legislation and its effects on inclusive and special education: a perspective from England, *British Journal of Special Education*, Volume 41(4): 403–425.

Pollard, A. (2002) *Readings for Reflective Teaching*, London: Continuum.

Smith, E. and Douglas, G. (2014) Special educational needs, disability and school accountability: an international perspective, *International Journal of Inclusive Education*, 18(5): 443–458.

UNESCO (2009) *Policy Guidelines on Inclusion in Education*, Paris: United Nations Educational, Scientific and Cultural Organization.

Vygotsky, L. (1962) *Thought and Language*, Cambridge: M.I.T. Press, Massachusetts Institute of Technology.

Wood, D. (2003) *How Children Think and Learn: The Social Contexts of Cognitive Development*, Oxford: Blackwells.

Chapter 2

Half a million unseen, half a million unheard

Inclusion for gender identity and sexual identity

Marjorie Smith and Kelly Chambers

Who matters?

The 'Equality Act' (2010) states that,

> Schools and other public bodies have to be more pro-active and go beyond non-discrimination by advancing equality.
>> (Stonewall (n.d.) What The Law Says, available at
>> http://www.stonewall.org.uk/at_school/what_the_law_says/default.asp)

But this is not the experience of many young people. They are children and young people with gender identity and sexuality issues, most of whom will eventually come out as lesbian, gay, bisexual or transgender[1] (LGBT). There are about half a million of these young people in our schools, two or three in every class of thirty[2] and Poteat and Russell (2013) have found that these young people are coming out at an earlier age than previous generations.

Compared with others, these young people are more likely to:

- self-harm; consider or attempt suicide; experience mental health problems such as anxiety or depression (Department of Health 2007; Strudwick 2014);
- experience domestic abuse from either parent or even siblings (Yip 2004; Wilson and Rahman 2005);
- have been bullied at school (Stonewall 2006);
- take time off school (Rivers 2000);
- choose to leave full-time education at 16, despite having the qualifications to stay on (Rivers 2000).

This list is a terrible indictment. Until we do more to nurture the well-being of these young people, they will continue to pay for our society's shortcomings with their happiness, their health and their lives.

Despite the efforts of some, parts of our education system remain '. . . eerily unresponsive. . .' to the needs of LGBT young people (DePalma and Jennett 2007: 22). This is in spite of 'The Education and Equalities Act' (2006) stating that,

> Teachers have a legal duty to ensure homophobic bullying is dealt with in schools.

Inclusion, based on human rights, seeks to ensure that all young people feel a sense of belonging in their educational settings. This involves challenging the way that society and its schools construct gender and sexuality. Schools and classrooms are not gender-neutral places. Stereotypical gender norms ensure that only certain expressions of gender are acceptable, and gender atypical behaviour is noticed and regulated. Including those young people whose gender expression is unusual means challenging gender norms and providing educational spaces where all children feel comfortable. The view of human relationships presented in our classrooms is almost exclusively heterosexual (Epstein *et al.* 2003). Where there is a presumption that everyone is heterosexual and this is the norm, it is called heterosexism (Stonewall 2014). Poteat and Russell (2013) talk about the need for an inclusive curriculum 'that represents LGBT issues and individuals' (Poteat and Russell 2013: 268). This acknowledges the reality of sexual diversity and teaches that non-heterosexual relationships have the same legitimacy as heterosexual ones. An inclusive approach also recognises the educational and social needs of LGBT people and their families.

Introducing

Many of the 'half a million' will remain hidden and silent throughout their school careers, but some will be noticed. These are young people I have encountered through my work and their experiences raise issues for teachers to consider:

Aysha

Aysha is 16. She became withdrawn in school and started to avoid eating lunch. A teacher, concerned that Aysha might be anorexic, talked to her. Aysha eventually admitted that she thought she was a lesbian but that she was frightened of telling anyone. The school helped her to come out to her parents, who were very supportive.

It is common for young people to be fearful of coming out to their families. Many also react badly to the realisation of their sexuality. This troubled young woman found a way to harm herself, but there are many ways in which young people express their distress, including withdrawal, anger and acting out behaviour.

Question: The school played a significant part in helping resolve the problem, but what could it have done to support the developing sexuality of its LGBT students in years 7–11?

Ben

Ben is 12. He has a wide range of interests, including classical music and ballet. At primary school he was often on his own at playtimes because he did not like football. When he started at secondary school and it became known that he did ballet, he experienced some gay name-calling. He was followed home by other boys and on one occasion was knocked to the ground.

Ben is vulnerable in a number of ways. He has unusual interests, which leads others to make assumptions about his sexuality. He is also more prone to bullying because he is quite solitary (Crowley *et al.* 2001).

Question: What could the primary school have done to support Ben at break times? What could the secondary school do to help Ben in forming positive relationships with other students?

Charlie

Charlie is 4. He is a popular little boy who loves drawing and make-believe play. He plays exclusively with girls and ignores boys completely. When he arrives at nursery, he goes straight to the dressing up rail, puts on his favourite pink bridesmaid's dress and wears it all day. This behaviour has persisted throughout four terms in nursery and is accepted both by nursery staff and by Charlie's parents.

There is absolutely nothing wrong with Charlie. He is happy, sociable and in a context where he is completely accepted. Given the persistence of his behaviour, he could be said to be displaying gender identity issues, which are a normal part of human diversity. Nevertheless, life could be hard for Charlie in contexts that are not as inclusive as his nursery.

Question: The nursery supports Charlie's behaviour. What do you think this means in terms of everyday actions? What might the nursery do to ease Charlie's transition into school?

Danielle

Danielle is 10. She dresses like a boy and all her friends are boys. She is very competitive with them, wanting to be better at the things that boys do than all her friends. Danielle is causing problems in her class. She has a strong personality and is the ringleader of some gay name-calling.

Like Charlie, Danielle also has gender identity issues. In her bullying of gentle, quiet boys, she is drawing attention to her own masculinity.

Question: What could Danielle's class teacher do in this situation? Who could she turn to for help and ideas?

Elliott

Elliott is 13. He stopped attending his dance and drama group without explanation. Eventually, he told a learning support assistant at school that his father made him stop because it was 'gay'. Elliott also disclosed that his father has hurt him and that he is frightened of him. As a result, Social Services became involved.

Most parents are supportive of their child's sexuality, but some (both mothers and fathers) find it hard to accept gender-atypical behaviour or homosexuality. LGBT and gender-atypical young people are likely to need close monitoring and schools need to be alert to possible abuse at home as well as in school.

Question: How can school staff (including non-teaching staff) be supported in carrying out their responsibilities towards this vulnerable group of young people?

Finn

Finn is 16 and was assigned female at birth. At the age of 15 he told his mother that he did not feel like his assigned birth gender, and instead felt male. He approached his school and asked if he could attend wearing male uniform after his 16th birthday, when Finn changed his name by deed poll. The school agreed to the uniform change and he now uses the disabled toilet, which he finds easier, as it is private and also gender neutral. Finn has friends who have stood by him, but he has nevertheless been subjected to name-calling and harassment from other pupils who are ignorant of gender identity issues.

While the number of young people who transition from one gender to another is very small, that number is increasing as parents and young people become more aware of the availability of psychological and medical help.

Question: The school was supportive in agreeing to practical arrangements. How might this school address the issue of the behaviour of other students?

Gender identity and sexual orientation

Some children and young people do not conform to gender norms. Even a boy who dislikes football or a girl who refuses to wear a skirt may need backup in a context where only stereotypical expressions of masculinity and femininity are considered acceptable. More significant gender identity issues can be apparent from an early age, or may become more pronounced later on. Charlie's behaviour, where he chooses the 'girliest' dress to almost 'outgirl' the girls, is fairly typical. Gender identity issues may disappear as a child gets older but they may persist, as with Danielle, or take different forms as time goes on. Some people feel a mismatch between the gender they feel themselves to be and the gender they were assigned at birth. Medical help may be sought where this causes extreme unhappiness. A small number, four times as many boys as girls, will be diagnosed with 'gender dysphoria' (Brill and Pepper 2008; Memon 2014). Some will make the decision to transition, which is not necessarily a permanent course of action in younger children.

Gender identity is different to sexual orientation, which refers to sexual attraction. There is an overlap between the two groups, in that some young people with gender identity issues will eventually come out as LGBT (Wilson and Rahman 2005), although this is by no means invariably the case. Some LGBT adults will report having experienced gender identity issues as children, but the majority will not. Despite the overlaps, these are two different groups with some individuals in both. Conflating the two ignores the experiences of children with gender identity issues, who tend to encounter prejudice earlier in their lives (Airton 2009). It also leads to confusion about the roots of negative reactions. A little boy may be called 'gay' because he wants to play with girls, but the reason for this name-calling is his gender atypical behaviour, not his sexuality. LGBT young people are more likely to encounter discrimination based on assumptions about sexual activity or religious bigotry. Inclusive schools will be challenging both sources of discrimination.

Creating diversity-friendly environments

Starting young

Groundbreaking work by the 'No Outsiders' research project began in 2006 (DePalma and Atkinson 2009) and has explored ways of addressing LGBT rights at age-appropriate levels in primary schools. This project gave us our first taste of what effective work in primary schools might look like. Through discussion, literature, drama and visitors, children were taught the correct meanings of terms and encouraged to recognise and think about gender stereotyping and hetero-normativity. This early work was essential in developing diversity-aware, diversity-friendly cultures in schools. Groups like 'Out In Education' are now working in schools in their local areas to educate young people, including those of primary age, to challenge homophobia. Homophobia does not appear overnight, and secondary schools cannot take effective action without building the foundations at the primary level.

Nurseries and primary schools cater for children with same-sex parents or LGBT family members, and need to find ways of openly acknowledging and welcoming these children's families. Materials, such as the 'Different Families, Same Love' pack, have been produced by Stonewall (see suggested resources) to help schools to deliver a positive message to young children.

Some LGBT adults report that they were aware of their difference at primary school age, and 6 per cent of children who call 'ChildLine' about sexual orientation or homophobic bullying are under eleven (NSPCC website 2010). Those who realise their difference at an early age may not communicate their feelings for several years: '. . .the gap between self-realisation and disclosure' (DePalma and Jennet 2007: 24). Without the vocabulary or the concepts to help them, these troubled children are silenced. Schools and nurseries need to develop the age-appropriate language, policies, curricular responses and resources, which will ensure that these children experience a growing awareness of their identities.

The professional development of staff

Including those with gender identity and sexuality issues is an important aspect of the continuing professional development of all adults who work with children and young people. For schools, the best approach is whole-school training involving everyone who works in the school, including school governors. Stonewall (2009) discovered a range of attitudes in school staff, suggesting that senior managers should provide an unambiguous steer on respect for pupil identities. Class teachers and subject teachers need to provide a firm lead to adults who work in their classrooms. However, Stonewall (2014) found that only 8 per cent of primary teachers and 17 per cent of secondary teachers had received specific training on tackling homophobic bullying. This is in spite of an expectation by Ofsted that schools will challenge and tackle any form of bullying, including the use of homophobic language.

Some teachers may feel a tension between their religious beliefs and their professional responsibilities in the context of same-sex relationships. Teachers have every right to their views. Expressing beliefs in school, however, must be consistent with the guidance provided on religious education (RE) and sex and relationships education (SRE). It would not be inclusive, or professional, to voice political, moral or religious beliefs in ways that might cause distress to any young person or exploit their vulnerability. A study by Stonewall (2008) showed that many people of faith are accepting of lesbian and gay people and co-exist with them in harmony. Schools, especially faith schools, can build on these expressions of hope. Most of the major religions now have followers who are working towards a more respectful approach to homosexuality. These groups are an important resource to teachers of faith and faith schools.

Many LGBT young people are people of faith themselves and may be seeking ways of rationalising their sexuality with their spirituality. Unfortunately, in this instance, religion can be: 'a source of conflict rather than solace' (NSPCC website 2010). As educators, we must rise to the challenge of helping these young people cope with the diverse and often contradictory messages they will be receiving from their faith communities.

The formal and informal curriculum

The introduction of a statutory Personal, Social and Health Education (PSHE) programme in secondary schools in 2012, and a new primary curriculum in 2014, should mean that some age-appropriate work on diversity is now undertaken in all maintained schools as part of the National Curriculum. Faith schools are required to educate pupils about homosexuality, but the legislation includes a clause allowing them to apply their 'values' and 'ethos'. However, stating that homosexuality is sinful would contravene General Teaching Council guidelines, guidelines produced by the Equality and Human Rights Commission (EHRC 2014), so faith schools need to establish inclusive ways of teaching about homosexuality within their faith perspective. This balance can be, and has been, achieved by many faith schools.

Sex and Relationships Education (SRE) is a statutory component of PSHE. Homosexuality could be pathologised where it is taught as a 'one-off' lesson along with social ills like drugs and STIs (Ellis and High 2004). Buston and Hart (2001: 100) identified inclusive practice in lessons where diversity in sexual orientation was: '. . .recognised and normalised', and information for same-sex relationships was provided alongside that for heterosexual relationships.

Some young LGBT people grow up in ignorance, thinking that they are the 'only one'. Others, brought up in homes or communities where homophobic attitudes prevail, may be repeatedly exposed to negative views about their identity.

It is important that *all* young people regularly encounter positive LGBT images. LGBT people have achieved in a multitude of areas, including the arts, science and sport – but they can only be role models where their sexuality or gender identity is acknowledged and discussed as part of a lesson. Positive images can also be provided through posters, Pride notice boards, speakers in assemblies and 'out' teachers in school. Providing images of LGBT people from the black and ethnic minority community, and those with disabilities, is particularly important.

Young LGBT people are not sure what they can aspire to in later life because of the invisibility of role models and may opt for careers traditionally seen as 'safe'. They, and other students, would benefit from encountering examples that challenge assumptions, such as gay police officers, lesbian MPs and transgender lawyers.

LGBT History Month is recognised by the DCSF and is an opportunity for schools to focus attention on gender identity and sexuality as whole-school themes. Assemblies can be used to inform pupils, to raise important issues for discussion, or to invite in external contributors. Some secondary schools have successfully encouraged LGBT young people to present assemblies themselves. However, it is important that LGBT month does not become a token gesture and issues of sexuality ignored for the remainder of the year.

There is an increasing selection of books for primary age children that challenge gender stereotypes and provide images of families with same-sex parents. Secondary school libraries, too, could include an LGBT section with appropriate fiction, non-fiction and information books.

Language is an important part of the informal curriculum and, as responsible adults, we must reclaim the words: 'gay', 'lesbian', 'bisexual' and 'transgender' which are taboo precisely because children do not hear us using them in a positive way. Atkinson (2007) suggests that teachers tend to wait until an opportunity arises to discuss these issues and as 89 per cent of secondary teachers say that they hear the term 'you're so gay' being used as an insult (Stonewall 2014), it is vital to *make* those conversations happen in order to persistently underline the legitimacy of gender and sexuality difference.

The school's response to bullying

Homophobic bullying (regardless of the actual sexuality of the victim) is one of the most prevalent forms of bullying in British schools. Schools have been required to record all incidents of homophobic bullying since 2010. Anti-bullying policies should specifically include homophobic and transphobic bullying. Reasons for bullying can be a reflection of society's prejudices. Punishing an act of bullying is a hollow exercise where there is no work done to address the ignorance and misinformation that underlies it. Successful schools have worked hard, not only to educate the entire school community, but also to empower their LGBT pupil population by creating an environment where they feel safe to speak up and speak out. Policies written by the pupils themselves can help them to feel acknowledged and valued.

Relationships with parents and the wider school community

The principle of including young people with gender identity and sexuality issues can conflict with attitudes held in the wider school community. Schools need to take parents with them on their journey, starting with the clear message that children and young people who do not conform to gender stereotypes, and those with sexuality issues, will be positively supported using a wide range of strategies in school. For nurseries and primary schools, this also means communicating a firm message to parents and carers that homo/transphobic language will not be accepted in the playground. Schools should be proud of the work they undertake in this field. Routinely informing parents about policies and practice through the school prospectus and the school website underlines the legitimacy of this work.

Support for individuals

Sometimes schools have to manage life-changing events. A young person coming out or transitioning may not happen every day, but every teacher in every school needs to plan to manage such a situation thoughtfully and sensitively and to establish in advance where to go for guidance.

When a young person comes 'out' in school, it is not the job of the school to inform his or her parents. Even though young LGBT people are more resilient in tackling the difficulties they have to face if they have the unconditional support of their families, this support will not necessarily be forthcoming. However, opportunities may arise for the school to support a young person in coming out to parents. Some parents will be aware of what their child is facing and may welcome contact with their son or daughter's school, but few will have had any preparation for this responsibility (Smith 2008). Schools are uniquely placed to help them.

Whilst many young people can and do keep their gender identity or sexuality issues secret, camp boys and butch girls are not in a position to hide (Crowley *et al.* 2001). Part of including the diversity of gender expressions and sexualities means accepting these young people as they are, and not pressurising them to conform (Rogers 1994). A school's public recognition of a 'different' student, or its handling of a transition, can contribute to the normalisation of gender identity and sexuality issues in school.

Young LGBT people need access to LGBT-*specific* information on local youth groups, websites and guidance on how to keep themselves safe (Douglas *et al.* 1997). This information could be made available on the school website so that young people and their parents can access it privately. LGBT young people with disabilities may require help in accessing the information they need. The firewalls in some schools prevent young people from accessing legitimate LGBT websites and may need to be adjusted.

LGBT young people come from a range of cultures and religions and will need access to information that meets their specific cultural and religious needs. Schools need to be aware of the extreme nature of the homophobia that exists in some communities and to be watchful of pupils who are vulnerable.

A significant number of gender-atypical or LGBT young people suffer from social isolation and ostracism. Some studies suggest that this is a more prevalent problem than homophobic bullying (Ellis and High 2004). Being without friends has profound effects on a young person's well-being and can affect mental health in later life. Sometimes young people withdraw from social contact when they realise that they are different, or they fear exposure. A young person with gender identity or sexuality issues may find little in common with same-sex peers or may not be accepted in the friendship groups they seek to join. Schools can tackle social isolation proactively in a number of ways. All adults can provide good role-models of acceptance and friendliness. Teachers can use seating plans, move pupils around to sit with a range of different classmates and provide plenty of pair-work and group-work in lessons. Schools can provide a 'diversity-friendly' range of activities at lunchtimes and after school. Older students can be trained to act as 'befrienders'.

Some situations pose particular difficulties. Areas like toilets and changing rooms can feel unsafe to LGBT young people and need good supervision. All schools need to be alert to difficulties that may be posed by residential school trips. Children with gender identity issues may be vulnerable for unexpected reasons, like a boy who arrives with pink pyjamas. Many young LGBT people find sharing a bedroom challenging and may avoid going on trips for that reason. Schools can help by discussing arrangements in advance with students, or their parents, where this is appropriate.

Finally

This area of inclusion presents special challenges for schools and teachers, yet it is an area where comparatively small shifts in attitude and practice can bring about extraordinary benefits in the achievements and well-being of a significant number of individuals. Young people with gender identity and sexuality issues can be remarkably strong, articulate and resilient but, time and again, we fail to realise how much they have to contend with. We need to let them know in every way we can that they are valued for who they are, and that they all matter.

Reflection on values and practice

A group of potential students have come to visit your school. Amongst them is a young person who is questioning their sexual identity and another who is questioning their gender identity. How are those people reflected back at themselves as they walk around your school? What do they see that makes them feel welcome, supported and celebrated as individuals? Or are they simply invisible? If this is the case, what needs to change?

Suggested further reading

No Outsiders Project Team (2010) *Undoing homophobia*. Stoke on Trent: Trentham Books.
Stonewall (2014) *The Teachers Report*, London: Stonewall.

Resources

Families Together London www.familiestogetherlondon.com: support and information for parents; information on education resources, information on culture and religion.

Out for Our Children www.outforourchildren.co.uk: Foundation Stage pack and books that reflect family diversity.

School's Out www.schools-out.org.uk.

Stonewall www.stonewall.org.uk/at_school/education_for_all/quick_links/8634.asp: 'Free' resource aimed at teaching primary children about difference, diversity and respect.

Stonewall http://www.stonewall.org.uk/at_school/education_for_all/quick_links/education_resources/5737.asp: 'Different Families, Same Love' resource ensuring that all families are celebrated.

Terrence Higgins Trust www.ygm.org.uk: Teaching pack for Key Stage 4, ideas for different subject areas.

Notes

1 'Transgender' is an umbrella term that covers a range of gender-related issues.
2 Assuming Britain's LGB population is 5–7 per cent (Stonewall website 2015) and the transgender population is about 1 per cent (Reed et al. 2009).

References

Airton, L. (2009) From sexuality (gender) to gender (sexuality): the aims of anti-homophobia education, *Sex Education* 9(2): 129–139.

Atkinson, E. (2007) Speaking with small voices: voice, resistance and difference. In Reiss, M., DePalma, R. and Atkinson, E. *Marginality and Difference in Education and Beyond*, Stoke on Trent: Trentham Books, pp.15–29.

Brill, S. and Pepper, R. (2008) *The Transgender Child: a handbook for families and professionals*. San Francisco, USA: Cleis Press.

Buston, K. and Hart, G. (2001) Heterosexism and homophobia in Scottish school sex education: exploring the nature of the problem, *Journal of Adolescence* 24: 95–109.

Crowley, C. Hallam, S. Harre, R. and Lunt, I. (2001) Study support for young people with same-sex attraction – views and experiences from a pioneering support initiative in the north of England, *Educational and Child Psychology* 18(1): 108–124.

DePalma, R. and Atkinson, E. (2009) Putting queer into practice: problems and possibilities. In DePalma, R. and Atkinson, E. (eds.) *Interrogating Heteronormativity in Primary Schools: the work of the 'No Outsiders' project*, Stoke on Trent: Trentham Books, pp.1–16.

DePalma, R. and Jennett, M. (2007) Deconstructing heteronormativity in primary schools in England: cultural approaches to a cultural phenomenon. In van Dijk, L. and van Driel, B. (eds.) *Challenging Homophobia: teaching about sexual diversity*, Stoke on Trent: Trentham Books, pp.19–32.

Department of Health (2007) *Reducing Health Inequalities for Lesbian, Gay, Bisexual and Trans People (Briefing Papers 1–13)*, London: Department of Health.

Douglas, N., Warwick, I., Kemp, S. and Whitty, G. (1997) *Playing it Safe: responses of secondary school teachers to lesbian, gay and bisexual pupils, bullying, HIV and AIDs education and Section 28*, London: Health and Education Research Unit, Institute of Education.

EHRC (Equality and Human Rights Commission) (2014) The Equality and Human Rights Implications for the Provision of school Education. Available at www.equalityhuman rights.com. Accessed 22/05/2015.

Ellis, V. with High, S. (2004) Something more to tell you: gay, lesbian or bisexual young people's experiences of secondary schooling. *British Educational Research Journal* 30(2): 214–225.

Epstein, D., O'Flynn, S. and Telford, D. (2003) *Silenced Sexualities in Schools and Universities,* Stoke on Trent: Trentham Books.

Memon, M.A. (2014) Gender dysphoria. Available at http://emedicine.medscape.com/article/2200534-overview#a0156. Accessed April 2015.

NSPCC website www.nspcc.org.uk (accessed February 2010).

Poteat, V. & Russell, T. (2013) Understanding homophobic behaviour and its implications for policy and practice, *Theory Into Practice* 52 (4): 264–271.

Reed, B., Rhodes, S., Schofield, P. and Wylie, K. (2009) *Gender Variance in the UK: prevalence, incidence, growth and geographic distribution,* London: Gender Identity Research and Education Society.

Rivers, I. (2000) Social exclusion, absenteeism and sexual minority youth, *Support for Learning* 15(1): 13–18.

Rogers, M. (1994) Growing up lesbian: the role of the school. In Epstein, D. (ed.) *Challenging Lesbian and Gay Inequalities in Education,* Buckingham: Open University Press, pp.31–48.

Smith, M. (2008) *Including Lesbian and Gay Youth in School – Parents find a voice.* London, Institute of Education. Unpublished dissertation.

Stonewall (2006) *The School Report: the experiences of young gay people in Britain's schools,* London: Stonewall.

Stonewall (2008) *Love Thy Neighbour: what people of faith really think about homosexuality,* London: Stonewall.

Stonewall (2009) *The Teachers' Report: Homophobic bullying in Britain's schools,* London: Stonewall.

Stonewall (2014) *The Teachers' Report,* London: Stonewall.

Strudwick, P. (2014) *Nearly half of young transgender people have attempted suicide – UK survey* [online] Available at: http://www.theguardian.com/society/2014/nov/19/young-transgender-suicide-attempts-survey (accessed April 2015).

Wilson, G. and Rahman, Q. (2005) *Born Gay: The psychobiology of sex orientation,* London: Peter Owen.

Yip, A. K. T. (2004) Negotiating space with family and kin in identity construction: the narratives of British non-heterosexual Muslims, *The Sociological Review* 52(3): 336–350.

Chapter 3

What we know about bullying

Neil Duncan and Johanna Myddleton

From the earliest times of public schooling 'the bully' has been a recognisable figure in popular culture and common knowledge. However, until the late 1980s there were no books available in English with 'bullying' in the title; now there are literally hundreds. Unfortunately, these books mostly say the same things: a mixture of knowledge based on narrow research mixed with folk wisdom. This chapter takes a very different approach to the topic of bullying and is intended to provoke consideration of alternative thinking to help professionals as they develop their inclusive practice.

So, what do we really know about bullying? Everything, it would seem; apart from how to actually stop it.

Neil once carried out a bullying questionnaire survey in a high school where he was shocked to see that one year 7 boy reported he was hit, kicked pushed and spat upon on an almost daily basis. Despite having the highest score for being a victim, he ticked the 'I don't think I get bullied' box! He explained the person doing these things to him was his big brother. Neil asked him why he didn't feel bullied. He replied, 'Everyone gets it from their older brother, don't they? I do it to my little brother too.'

This boy's idea of bullying prevented him from thinking of himself as a victim. He didn't like the beatings, but accepted them as inevitable and not unfair. On the other hand, some pupils ticked none of the boxes for being attacked, but then ticked that they worried all the time about being bullied and avoided certain places *in case* they were attacked.

Would you say these children suffered because of bullying even if it had not (yet) happened to them? If the presence and fear of bullying made them permanently scared and miserable, couldn't they be called victims? All this is complicated and depends more on social relationships and feelings rather than simple acts and behaviours.

Whilst we do need a consensus understanding of the key terms used in bullying so that discussion is meaningful, we also need to avoid being too dogmatic that any single definition is correct. One widely accepted example comes from Olweus (1993) who states that bullying is an aggressive act with an imbalance of power, has some element of repetition and can be physical, verbal or indirect (hate texts, socially shunning). One element often missed is the sense of entrapment. There is something special about bullying that includes being stuck in a relationship or situation with your tormentor. It is hard to be comprehensive in a short definition, but one operational definition of bullying might be 'an interpersonal abuse of power.'

Prevalence of bullying in schools

In terms of victimisation, the Tellus4 Ofsted survey (Chamberlain *et al.* 2010), indicated 29 per cent of respondents claimed to have been bullied in the past year. Research for ChildLine and the Department for Education and Skills (DfES) found that just over half (54 per cent) of both primary and secondary school children thought that bullying was 'a big/quite big problem' in their school. Distribution and frequency of bullying varies with school phase, with a general tendency for this to decrease with age (Oliver and Kandappa 2003). A quarter of children bullied by their peers reported that they suffered long-term harmful effects lasting into adulthood (Cawson *et al.* 2000: 30), with some tragic cases ending in suicide.

Smith and Shu (2000) found in 2,300 pupils aged 10–14 that 30 per cent did not tell anyone when they had been bullied; the percentage for boys and older children being higher, and higher still in cases of online bullying (Smith *et al.* 2008). Other studies (Katz *et al.* 2001) found around a third of boys and a quarter of girls admitted they personally had bullied other children 'a little' or 'a lot'. A total of 15 per cent of primary school students, and 12 per cent of secondary school students said that they had both bullied other children and been bullied themselves in the last year (Oliver and Kandappa 2003).

Characteristics of bullies

Most of us are capable of unfairly dominating other people given the wrong circumstances, and we might have bullied other children but then stopped under correction. Would we be happy with the label sticking? Our preference is for the term 'aggressor' to replace bully, and 'target' instead of victim. But why bother changing words that we all know and are comfortable with? One reason is exactly that, we have become comfortable about using the concept 'bully', so we stop thinking carefully about how we use it. If we didn't reconsider and refresh our language, we'd still be using terms such as *moron* and *cretin* without any sense of embarrassment. However, as the term 'bully' is so prevalent, we must use it to discuss the work of other people.

Olweus (1997) believes that bullies act without thinking too much about the consequences, and typically resort to violence to get what they want. Often they are more physically powerful than peers and have a greater mental toughness and lower empathy.

More significantly, it has been shown that bullies who engage in non-physical aggression have unusually high social intelligence (Sutton *et al.*1999). They are experts in causing great pain and hurt in subtle ways, manipulating and entrapping their targets without adults being aware of what is happening. New technology has made this so much easier in many cases.

Characteristics of victims

Like the term 'bullies', the label 'victims' might raise the idea of a fixed condition. Often research will categorise these children as either passive or provocative. Passive victims may be viewed as displaying vulnerability that 'encourages' bullies to attack them. They put up no effective resistance and therefore bullies repeatedly abuse them without being punished. Provocative victims don't aggress others, but are thought to 'wind people up', and their response to aggression is said to inflame that aggression further. You need to make up your own mind as to whether that is just an excuse to hit someone who is irritating! Whilst we might find them annoying, bullies respond to them with violence.

If these categories were so simple, then why do so many children report being bullied? Nearly 45,000 children contacted ChildLine about bullying in the 2012/13 period, and countless other cases go unreported (ChildLine Review 2013). Applying this figure to the categories makes it sound like most of our children are either too provocative or too passive! This discrepancy suggests that what has been described by the researchers is too simplistic to give us the kind of understanding that would be helpful in dealing with the problem. If we recall a time when we were bullied, would we be happy with that analysis – we were either too soft, or we wound the aggressor up?

Effects of bullying

One thing is certain about bullying: its effects can be long term, and, in some cases, deadly. In addition to suicide, self-inflicted injury and the direct damage of physical abuse, there are many lasting problems suffered by targets of bullying. These include loneliness, depression, panic attacks, anxiety, guilt, shame and low self-esteem (Schäfer et al. 2004). Less obvious perhaps but just as important an effect of bullying is truancy. It is impossible to know exactly how many school days are lost each year by pupils who are too frightened to come into school. The true figures of this effect are obscured by children's excuses, sometimes supported by unwitting parents telling the school that they are sick or otherwise unable to attend.

Alongside these outcomes, the way that bullying creates a general atmosphere in schools should not be underestimated. Unhappy or anxious children are not performing their best academically. It is hard to concentrate on your studies if you are worried about being attacked, or sweating about being ridiculed on social media. If we want to establish an inclusive environment within our schools, we must create an ethos in which bullying has no place.

How schools deal with bullying

There is a plethora of different approaches to management of bullying, but one could categorise them into pre-emptive or preventative, and responsive or remedial categories. As a teacher, one can embed pre-emptive measures in the curriculum at any level of study, though it is less awkward to adapt the curriculum for the younger age range where the teaching is perhaps more child-centred than subject-centred. In PSHE, preventions include directly discussing bullying in the classroom, thereby promoting a 'telling school' to combat a culture of 'not grassing'.

You would need to use your own professional awareness of how realistic such a project for a 'telling' school was. But the culture of not 'grassing' is a deeply embedded one, not just in schools but also in communities and in the families of the children themselves. Teachers can inadvertently fuel 'anti-grassing' behaviour by dismissing pupils' righteous but trivial indignation over rule-breaking with 'don't tell tales' or 'mind your own business.'

Another pre-emptive strategy used by some schools is a 'buddy' system to match up vulnerable pupils with older protectors. These older pupils monitor the safety of their younger partners and support them if there is a problem. Apart from the inter-year buddy-work, some schools use a version of circle time where all the children in the same class are involved in formally organised social activities that raise empathy, improve pro-social behaviour and increase peer support (Smith 2004).

Responding to bullying incidents after they have happened depends to a great extent on the particular school's anti-bullying policy, and how assiduously the adults follow its guidance. Frequently, anti-bullying responses mirror the processes found in the courts of law. Unfortunately, the investigative resources at schools' disposal are not of the quality or rigour required to serve such legalistic processes. This can lead to protracted denials and lack of conclusive evidence where all parties feel aggrieved and slighted. Where the burden of proof is only on probability, it can do serious damage to the children's sense of justice and their faith in the system.

Another unwanted outcome of trying to take a judicial line in bullying sanctions is the increased likelihood of retaliation by the accused or his/her friends against the complainant. Retaliation is a realistic fear of many pupils who desperately want intervention to end their suffering, and this means that staff should be proactive but sensitive. Rather than interrogate the target of the bullying and elicit evidence from them against the perpetrator, it is safer to couch accusations thus:

> I have not spoken to Kim, but if you have been threatening her, you need to sort yourself out now before you get into real bother with me. I'll check up on this in a couple of days, and if I think you have continued, I'll be back to see you.

By doing this you are depersonalising the spat between the pupils and taking the adult role on your own initiative.

Some schools reduce these problems by operating a 'no-blame' anti-bullying policy (Maines and Robinson 1992). In this seven-step programme, the adult concerns themselves with making the target feel better about things, and getting the perpetrators to stop their attacks, even getting them to befriend or support the target. Anti-bullying initiatives across the world testify to the effectiveness of the strategy, and particularly appreciate the way it attempts to break the cycle of aggression and hurt that abides in bullying. However, as the no-blame approach takes time and skill to apply, it can be unpopular. Recently, this approach has been reinvigorated by Ken Rigby's book (Rigby 2011).

Why bullying happens in schools

A view linked with the punitive approach is that some people bully because they are just horrible people. If that was really the case one might expect that once the bullies had been kicked out of school then bullying in that school would cease.

We might also consider, if bullying was only the fault of a few nasty kids, then why do schools of similar sizes and intakes report very different rates of bullying? Are there simply more nasty kids there or is it something else? One clue to solving this puzzle comes from researchers Yoneyama and Naito (2003), who were struck by the powerful differences between school cultures in Australia and Japan. In the Western school systems they noted bullying tended to be one or two pupils causing fear and harm to a larger group of pupils. In the Japanese school system, the situation was almost reversed with the whole class picking on one child and making their life unbearable.

Their analysis is worth reading in full, but suffice to say that their theory is that bullying is not just a personality flaw, but conditioned by the way adults run schools and local cultures. Their message is clear: if you want to stop school bullying, begin with how schools operate.

Bullying ethos in institutions

Though schools might seem to be primarily about academic education, they are equally important in the social education of children. Schools train people in cultural norms to enable a life where that generation can get along with each other and enjoy what the community has to offer. Usually we only hear about the first purpose of schooling, but schools are often criticised for not shaping pupils' behaviour effectively enough.

Some school rules need to be modelled rather than written, and how the staff do this, the nuanced way we interact and communicate our values to each other and to the pupils, creates an ethos peculiar to each individual school (see Rutter *et al.* 1979 for the enormous impact of ethos on school achievement, pupil behaviour and quality of institution). These modelled behaviours reflect a power structure based on a hierarchy. At the top is the head teacher, then the senior management team, followed by middle management staff such as heads of year. Beneath this are the teaching staff followed by classroom assistants, mid-day supervisors and cleaning staff. At the bottom, are the pupils – even though they may be classified as being the *raison d'être* for the school in the first place.

Of course, within the pupil culture there are even more differentiated power levels driven by many factors – ability, strength, size, age, intelligence, and popularity. Pupils are influenced by what they see demonstrated by adult examples elsewhere in the school (and at home and the community as well as the ubiquitous influence of the mass media).

In those schools where the ethos is one of fear of authority rather than warm human relationships, where personal feelings come second to goal-achievement, bullying amongst pupils is more likely to thrive. These signs of the cultural values of the leadership are very difficult to challenge by the staff – they can be subtle and seemingly innocuous or natural. This illustrates to us as professionals involved in anti-bullying just how tough the task is to get children to confront, resist or avoid being bullied if we ourselves find it a problem to be treated fairly and respectfully.

How schools can bully children

This section aims to challenge your assumptions as professional educators about the universal benefits of schooling. We are brought up to believe that schools are wholly benign institutions, designed with pupil welfare at the centre and with an aim to provide an enjoyable learning experience. But many people look back on their schooldays with a shudder at the unpleasant experiences they had, and think of schools as places where they were humiliated and disempowered. Most people who go into the teaching profession had a good experience – they were rule-abiding, friendly, popular with their peers, and schools fitted their needs very well.

However, compulsory schooling for some children often means being deprived of liberties that adults take for granted. We demand they attend the institution for six hours a day, five days a week. There they are worked in minute detail for no extrinsic reward, or even for realistic future gains – deferred gratification does not work for them. The micro-control extends to speaking only with permission; performing activities they have no interest in, and being harassed for not trying hard enough. It also entails being measured and set against their peers as competitors. It includes the control of their appearance, when to eat and where to drink. It extends so far as controlling their visits to the toilet. It is in schools where such conditions exist in an *oppressive* ethos, bullying can become a real problem amongst pupils.

Everyone needs some control over basic areas of their lives or else they maladapt in different ways. Some children do this by seeking unfair and cruel control over their peers. They bully.

Some schools have much higher rates of bullying despite strong similarities otherwise (Xin Ma *et al.* 2001; Roland and Galloway 2004). It is highly improbable that those schools have a higher number of nastier kids, and high exclusion rates in those schools don't appear to improve the problem (Ball and Hartley 2003). Whilst we should accept that schools have to maintain discipline, and all schools need some form of hierarchy in order to run smoothly, we must take care to be fair and humane in the eyes of the children.

Most children are happy within a hierarchical structure as long as they perceive it to be fair, but if they are abused, ridiculed in public, shouted at, punished as a group, or treated with sarcasm and disdain, they resent it (c.f. Ross-Epp and Watkinson 1996). In the eleven year-long competition that is compulsory schooling, there are winners and losers. Some children rarely succeed in that competition, and so bossing someone else about can be the release they crave from failure. Their predicament is described in studies of oppressed groups in other situations as *horizontal violence* (Freire 1972; Leymann 1996).

Most teachers are caring and intelligent people doing a difficult and demanding job, but when occasional lapses occur in their high professional standards, and these prove effective, i.e. they achieve the right results in the wrong way, others might emulate the same undesirable behaviours. Effectively, they are bullying to enforce discipline.

So what advice would be helpful to new teachers in managing discipline in schools? One strategy Neil came up with was to imagine that students' parents were present in every exchange he had with them. Can you justify your words, your tone and your body language? If so, then you can be pretty sure that you are not bullying them. We must retain a professional level of dignifying children equivalent to that which we would use when dealing with other adults. In my practice in secondary schools, pupils were quick to complain (when they felt safe to do so) about what they perceived as double standards. Those teachers seen as hypocrites were disliked and resented. Power without justice is always noted, such as a whole class being punished for the misdemeanours of one pupil.

Although they might seem petty 'injustices', to some pupils they signal a strong message of 'might is right': if you are powerful enough, you can get away with anything.

Cyberbullying

The term 'cyberbullying' is a relatively new one, and it has garnered a lot of media attention. Put simply, cyberbullying can be defined as bullying conducted via technological media (Hinduja and Patchin 2010), although there may be some justification for considering cyberbullying as a separate phenomenon due to unique characteristics such as the wide public audience and ability to act anonymously. In the 2012–13 period ChildLine saw an 87 per cent increase in reports of online bullying (ChildLine 2013), a worrying trend that seems to be repeated across the research, with approximately 1 in 5 students cyberbullied (Hinduja and Patchin 2010).

You may be wondering why cyberbullying is relevant to this chapter, if it is conducted using technology such as mobile devices and the Internet, so many of which are banned on school grounds. Well, despite the majority of cyberbullying occurring outside of school hours, it is thought that around 25 per cent of victims and cyberbullies attend the same school (Slonje and Smith 2008) and victims' academic achievement often suffers as a result (Beran and Li 2007). Neither is cyberbullying confined to pupils; teachers themselves are targeted by their students and parents for appalling abuse (The Guardian 2015).

Whereas targets may have once been able to escape bullying by removing themselves from school grounds, the increase in mobile technologies and personal computers has allowed bullying to invade the students' homes and given 24-hour access to targets. In turn, there seems to be an indication that this inability to escape the bullying may have an even more drastic impact on victims with suicidal ideation, depression and social withdrawal all at higher levels in those who are cyberbullied compared to those who experience 'traditional' bullying (Hinduja and Patchin 2010).

Whilst much 'traditional' bullying has always had a sexual edge to it, mobile phones and social media have seen an explosion in 'sexting', or sexually offensive communications, frequently with compromising photographs or movie clips of the victim with captions and comments derogating or threatening them (see ASBAE for more information and help http://www.asbae.eu/).

So, why don't students simply turn off their phones or down their computers? In the modern age this is the same as asking students to reject their friends and segregate themselves, which can have additional severe consequences as it isolates them from much needed peer support. It seems fear of this type of reaction from adults, along with a perception that they won't be able to understand or prevent the bullying anyway, is one of the main reasons why children fail to report online bullying (Smith *et al.* 2008). This is an important notion for teachers to understand, as removing students' access to websites such as Facebook, makes them feel they are being punished for being victimised whilst the bullies themselves are not. The 'just ignore it' approach seems to students as if their teachers do not understand the seriousness and negative impact cyberbullying has: and they may be right. Research suggests that teachers treat physical bullying more severely than they do verbal and relational bullying and that, worryingly, cyberbullying as a whole is responded to as a lower priority (Boulton *et al.* 2014).

What further complicates this situation is aggressors' ability to appear anonymous online. This may not only increase anxiety, fear and undermine victims' trust in friends (Smith *et al.* 2008), but may encourage cyberbullying by those who would not usually take part in offline bullying for fear of punishment, retaliation or due to inferior physical strength.

Despite apparent anonymity, cyberbullies *are* traceable online, and with appropriate evidence, extreme cases can be successfully prosecuted under:

- Communications Act 2003 (use of technology specifically);
- Offences Against the Person Act 1861 and Protection from Harassment Act 1997 (when credible threats are made);
- Section 28–32 of the Crime and Disorder Act 1998 and section 145 of the Criminal Justice Act 2003 (when involving discrimination).

However, the crown prosecution service actively advises against prosecuting children, and police do not have the resources to investigate every case. Pair this with parents who are seemingly ill equipped to prevent their children from cyberbullying due to a lack of understanding and technological ability, and there is a worrying gap in ability to protect children from cyberbullying.

An obvious cyclical issue with this problem is that if students do not report incidences of cyberbullying then no punitive action can be taken, so the soundest advice for teachers is to prevent their students from taking part in cyberbullying in the first place. Perhaps this is best approached through change in organisational culture, where cyberbullying is not tolerated; 'online bystanders' are expected to support victims; reporting is encouraged; and clear consequences are stated for cyberbullying and are consistently applied (Perren *et al.* 2012). Whilst unfortunately it is unrealistic to prevent all incidences of bullying, schools can gain excellent advice on serious sexting and related cyberbullying issues from the IWF (https://www.iwf.org.uk/hotline/report-process).

Summary

Bullying is often seen as the fault of particular children. We would argue that labels such as 'bully' are not helpful as they prevent us from looking to what we *could* and *should* change (relationships with children, professional standards we consider important, and punitive rules we set in our classrooms). This would have a greater impact than focussing on things we are *unlikely* to change, such as children's personalities. We would suggest that interventions to reduce bullying should be preceded by discussions on improving school ethos and culture. Whilst it may be more comfortable and acceptable to consider bullying as purely a pupil problem, any attempt to make a lasting impact will be unsuccessful until adults engage with their own role in creating and maintaining a pro-social, non-oppressive, inclusive environment.

Additional resources

ASBAE (addressing sexual bullying across Europe) for very up to date information and support relating to sexual bullying (see http://www.asbae.eu/). Ken Rigby is a leading academic from Australia who has revisited some of the more interesting and inclusive approaches to bullying in his recent work. In particular, he has re-configured the Common Concern Method pioneered by Anatol Pikas, and the No Blame method, proposed by Maines and Robinson (see http://www.kenrigby. net). One of the most helpful things to aid our better understanding of bullying, is to study other cultures and note the differences in the way their children bully. In Japan, for example, there are profound differences, such as the tacit acceptance by teachers of whole classes bullying a scapegoat. It is important not to lapse into moral superiority in these cases, but to consider why these phenomena are allowed. You can start by visiting this site for a look inside a different world of bullying. See http://thisjapaneselife.org/2013/06/12/japan-ijime-bullies/.

Reflection on values and practice

1   Defining bullying. Instead of using common definitions of bullying, listen to the range of things that pupils do to other pupils that they say they don't like. What

really bothers them? What can you do to address this in your classroom and beyond?

2   Developing fairness and justice. If you have a pupil who is involved in bullying others, how can you encourage them to rethink occasions when s/he was treated unfairly, drawing out a sense of empathy from this experience and a recognition that s/he is emulating the unfair person? How could this practice be incorporated into your teaching and learning practice?

3   The acid test. You are a role model to the children in your class, and must avoid any signs of bullying practice. Reflect on your own interpersonal exchanges with pupils. Think back to an incident when you were disciplining a pupil. How would you feel if you had to watch a video of this with the child's parents? If you would not feel comfortable, then consider how you should conduct yourself, think too about how you speak to people online. Many pupils' behaviour does change when they realise you treat them with dignity and professionalism.

References

Ball, C., and Hartley, M. (2003) *Zero Tolerance to Bullying*, Alberta: Mentone Education Centre.

Beran, T. and Li, Q. (2007) The relationship between cyberbullying and school bullying. *Journal of Student Wellbeing*, 1(2): 15–33.

Boulton, M. J., Hardcastle, K., Down, J., Fowles, J. and Simmonds, J. A. (2014) A comparison of preservice teachers' responses to cyber versus traditional bullying scenarios: similarities and differences and implications for practice. *Journal of Teacher Education*, 65(2): 145–155.

Cawson, P., Wattam, C., Brooker, S., & Kelly, G. (2000) *Child Maltreatment in the United Kingdom: a study of the prevalence of child abuse and neglect*, London: NSPCC.

Chamberlain, T., George, N., Golden, S., Walker, F. and Benton, T. (2010) *Tellus4 National Report* (DCSF Research Report 218). London: DCSF.

ChildLine Review (2013) Can I tell you something? What's affecting children in 2013. Found online http://www.nspcc.org.uk/globalassets/documents/research-reports/childline-review-2012-2013.pdf. Accessed 31 March 2015.

Freire, P. (1972) *Pedagogy of the Oppressed*, Penguin Education: England.

Hinduja, S. and Patchin, J. W. (2010) Bullying, cyberbullying and suicide. *Archives of Suicide Research*, 14(3): 206–221.

Katz, A., Buchanan, A. and Bream, V. (2001) *Bullying in Britain: testimonies from teenagers*, East Molesey Surrey: Young Voice.

Leymann, H. (1996) Psychological terrorization – the problem of the terminology. In *The Mobbing Encyclopaedia*. Available at http://www.leymann.se/English/11130E.HTM 1996. Accessed 18 December 2006.

Ma, X., Stewin, L.L. and Mah, D.L. (2001) Bullying in school: nature, effects and remedies. *Research Papers in Education*, 16(3): 247–270.

Maines, B. and Robinson, G. (1992) *Michael's story*. Video cassette recording, Bristol: Lucky Duck Publishing.

Oliver, C. and Kandappa, M. (2003) *Tackling Bullying: listening to the views of children and young people. Summary report*, London: DfES and ChildLine.

Olweus, D. (1993) *Bullying at School. What We Know and What We Can Do*, Oxford: Blackwell.

Olweus, D. (1997) Bully/victim problems in school: facts and intervention. *European Journal of Psychology of Education*, 12: 495–510.

Perren, S., Corcoran, L., Cowie, H., Dehue, F., Garcia, D. J., Mc Guckin, C., Sevcikova, A., Tsatsou, P. and Völlink, T. (2012) Tackling cyberbullying: review of empirical evidence regarding successful responses by students, parents, and schools, *International Journal of Conflict and Violence*, 6: 283–292.

Rigby, K. (2011) *The Method of Shared Concern: a positive approach to bullying in schools.* Camberwell: ACER.

Roland, E., and Galloway, D. (2004) Professional cultures in schools with high and low rates of bullying, *School Effectiveness and School Improvement: An International Journal of Research, Policy and Practice*, 1744–5124, 15(3):241–260.

Ross-Epp, J., and Watkinson, A. (1996) (eds.) *Systemic Violence: how schools hurt children*, London: Falmer Press.

Rutter, M., Maughan, B., Mortimore, P. and Ousten, J. (1979) *15000 Hours: secondary schools and their effects on children*, London: Open Books.

Schäfer, M., Korn, S., Smith, P. K., Hunter, S. C., Mora-Merchán, J. A., Singer, M. M., and Van der Meulen, K. (2004) Lonely in the crowd: recollections of bullying. *British Journal of Developmental Psychology*, 22 (3): 379–394.

Slonje, R. and Smith, P. K. (2008) Cyberbullying: another main type of bullying? *Scandinavian Journal of Psychology*, 49: 147–154.

Smith, C. (2004) *Circle Time for Adolescents: a seven session programme for 14 to 16 year olds*, London: Paul Chapman Sage.

Smith, P., Mahdavi, J., Carvalho, M., Fisher, S., Russell, S. and Tippett, N. (2008) Cyberbullying: its nature and impact in secondary school pupils. *The Journal of Child Psychology and Psychiatry*, 49(4): 376–385.

Smith, P. and Shu, S. (2000) What good schools can do about bullying: findings from a survey in English schools after a decade of research and action. *Childhood*, 7(2): 193–212.

Sutton, J., Smith, P. K. and Swettenham, J. (1999) Social cognition and bullying: social inadequacy or skilled manipulation? *British Journal of Developmental Psychology*, 17: 435–50.

The Guardian (2015) Huge rise in online abuse of teachers by pupils and parents, says union. Found online http://www.theguardian.com/education/2015/apr/02/huge-rise-in-online-abuse-of-teachers-by-pupils-and-parents-says-union. Accessed 14 April 2015.

Yoneyama, S., and Naito, A. (2003) Problems with the paradigm: the school as a factor in understanding bullying (with special reference to Japan). *British Journal of Sociology*, 24(3): 315–330.

Chapter 4

Supporting Gypsy, Roma and Traveller pupils

Chris Derrington

Introduction

Gypsy, Roma and Traveller children attend every type of school and early years' setting throughout the UK. They are all different and individual but, historically, they have been recognised as the group most 'at risk' in the education system in terms of their attendance, engagement and attainment (Ofsted 1999: 7). National data show that the pattern continues and their attainment and attendance still fall well below that of all other groups at every Key Stage. For example, in 2013, only 13.8 per cent of Gypsy/Roma pupils nationally gained five or more GCSE grades at A* to C, including English and mathematics, compared with 60.6 per cent of all pupils (DfE 2013; 2014a; 2014b; 2014c). So who are these children, and why are they underperforming so dramatically in our schools?

The Department for Education (DfE) uses the generic term 'Gypsy, Roma and Traveller,' (GRT) to embrace a number of different communities. Some families from these communities no longer travel and have settled permanently in one place; others maintain a nomadic lifestyle and travel almost continuously or on a seasonal basis between different parts of the country. Children from the most highly mobile communities (for example, those who move around frequently because they have no legal place to stay) typically experience a fragmented education which, not surprisingly, impacts negatively on their attendance and attainment at school. They might attend many different schools, each for a short period of time, provided there are places available. Others might spend considerable periods (months or even years) out of school altogether. Children who travel on a seasonal basis due to their parents' work patterns (for example Fairground families) are often enrolled at a 'base' school all year round even though they only attend physically during the winter months. Some of these children then continue to receive their education when they are travelling by means of distance learning materials provided by their base school.

Most Gypsy, Roma and Traveller families these days, however, live permanently on authorised sites or in houses, either by choice or because there is no other legal option available to them. This may surprise you. Some people, for example, assume, wrongly, that you can't be a Traveller if you live in a house. Furthermore, if the majority of Gypsy, Roma and Traveller children now live in housing or on a permanent site, then why should they have the lowest educational outcomes at all Key Stages?

This chapter aims to help you understand and address the particular needs of this diverse group of children and young people.

Who are Gypsies, Roma and Travellers?

The term GRT represents a diverse collection of communities including Romany Gypsies, Travellers of Irish heritage, European Roma, Fairground and Circus Showmen and New Travellers. Whilst it is fair to say that these communities have some shared cultural characteristics, there are also some important distinctions to make. The main one is that some, but not all, are recognised in law as constituting a minority ethnic group. In considering whether a community is an ethnic group (as opposed to a social group), a number of criteria must be met. Two essential characteristics are:

- ancestry and a long shared history of which the group is conscious as distinguishing it from other groups and the memory of which it keeps alive, and;
- a distinct cultural tradition including social customs and manners, often but not necessarily associated with religious observance.

Let's explore this further by looking at the various communities included under the generic term 'Gypsy, Roma and Traveller'. The first three groups described below are recognised in law as having a distinct ethnicity.

Romany Gypsies

The largest group of Travellers in the UK is often referred to in the literature as Romany Gypsy, although other terms such as Gypsy Traveller, English or Scottish Gypsy, Romany and Romanichal may also be applied. Increasingly, the term Roma (see below) is adopted. It should be recognised that people have the freedom to describe themselves in whatever way they wish and teachers therefore should take the lead from parents and pupils rather than make assumptions about 'correct' terminology.

Regardless of the preferred term, this community is believed to have descended from North West India. Around a thousand years ago, groups of nomadic migrants fled the Indian sub-continent during clashes between invading warriors and settled in almost every region from Persia to the Balkan states, eventually arriving in the UK in the fifteenth century. With their dark skin, it was assumed that they were pilgrims from Egypt and so they were called Egyptians (from which the word 'Gypsy' is derived). Linguistic evidence, however, supports the theory of their Indian origins and, although it is not widely known, Romany Gypsies have retained elements of a language known as Romanes or Romani, which has its roots in ancient Sanskrit (the language used in northern India around the ninth century). A hybrid version of this language is commonly spoken by Romany families and a number of words have been incorporated into common English usage (e.g. cushti, bloke, pal, gaff).

Many Romany Gypsies today live in houses; others might live in trailers (caravans) or mobile homes. Regardless of where they live, they are Romany Gypsies by birthright and are therefore recognised in law as being a legitimate ethnic group, protected by equality legislation.

European Roma

This diverse sub-group, believed to number around ten million globally, also constitutes a minority ethnic group in the UK. The largest numbers continue to live in Eastern Europe, particularly in Romania, Bulgaria and Hungary. However, since the incorporation of countries from Eastern Europe into the European Union (EU) in 2004, more Romanian, Czech and Slovak Roma families have settled in the UK. Each Roma group has its own national identity and language and families will often identify themselves first in national terms and then as Roma, for example 'Czech Roma'.

Travellers of Irish heritage

As the name suggests, these Travellers are indigenous to Ireland and are believed to be descendants of travelling entertainers, itinerant craftsmen and metal workers. The derogatory term 'tinker' refers to the traditional occupational status of tinsmith. Travellers of Irish heritage have retained aspects of a Celtic language that has its roots in Gaelic. Although their historical roots are different, their customs and traditions have similarities with those of Romany Gypsies, partly due to pragmatic reasons associated with a nomadic way of life and partly due to intermarriage between the communities.

It is important that teachers and schools understand that all the groups described above are legitimate minority ethnic communities and are therefore protected by the Equality Act 2010. Statutory ethnic monitoring of Gypsy, Roma and Traveller pupils in schools has only been in place since 2003, when 'Gypsy/Roma' and 'Travellers of Irish heritage' were included for the first time as two distinct ethnicity group categories within the School Census. Consequently, all maintained schools are now required to include these categories as part of the data collection reported in School Census returns. Unfortunately, many Traveller parents and children choose not to disclose their identity for fear of bullying and prejudice. This impacts significantly on the accuracy of statistical data available and led to government guidance for schools to encourage wider practice in self-ascription (DCSF 2008a).

The School Census does not explicitly identify pupils from Fairground or Circus (Showmen) communities, 'New Travellers' or those dwelling on the waterways, unless they also belong to one of the above groups. These communities are recognised as Occupational Travellers or social groups as opposed to minority ethnic groups. However, it is very important to mention these other Traveller groups within this chapter as they experience many of the same educational challenges.

Fairground showmen

Fairground communities have a distinctive culture and lifestyle that stretches back many centuries. Their ancestral links date back to the travelling merchants and entertainers of the Charter Fairs in the Middle Ages and possibly beyond that to pagan times when seasonal gatherings were held for trade and festivity. Today, Fairground showmen families tend to own or rent land, which serves as their base during the winter months, but spend the majority of the year following a circuit of meticulously planned events both in the UK and, increasingly, on the continent. Children from these communities tend to be enrolled at a 'base' school near their winter quarters and, in many cases, remain in contact with their teachers and engage in distance learning programmes during periods of travelling. However, in 2013, the Government consulted on a proposal to repeal legislation that currently protects travelling parents from being prosecuted for failing to present their children at school on a daily basis. Depending on the outcome, this could have serious implications for the 20,000 or so showmen families in the UK.

Circus communities

Like Fairground showmen, circus communities may describe themselves as Occupational Travellers, although some performers may also be Gypsies. Circus groups are usually diverse, typically comprising a troupe of international performers, some of whom will have children. The frequency of movement between venues can make access to school difficult for them and although some benefit from distance learning programmes organised by their base school, other circuses employ tutors who travel and live as part of the community.

New Travellers

New Travellers (commonly referred to in the past as 'New Age Travellers') are, by definition, a more recent cultural phenomenon. Groups of younger people (known as 'hippies') opted for a nomadic lifestyle during the 1960s but the phenomenon grew during the 1970s and 1980s with the emergence of the free festival movement as more young people bought large vehicles to transport themselves and their possessions between the summer festivals. In the late 1980s, cut-backs in social security and housing benefits, made by the Thatcher government, had a particular impact on young people between the ages of 16 and 25, leading to a surge in youth homelessness and young economic refugees taking to the road and an alternative travelling lifestyle (Martin 1998).

Key considerations for teaching and learning

Having provided a brief overview of the various Traveller communities in the UK, let's now consider the key implications for teachers and schools. National initiatives aimed at narrowing the achievement gap are particularly targeted at these groups because there has been so little progress recorded over recent years. In the past, the educational underachievement of Gypsy, Roma and Traveller pupils was associated with problems around practical access to school due to a mobile lifestyle. Later, as planning law became more restrictive, and families began to settle on permanent sites or into housing, cultural influences were assumed to be largely responsible for non-registration, poor attendance and progress. Subsequent research, however, has identified 'push' factors as well as 'pull' factors that can impact on GRT pupils' attendance and engagement in school (Derrington 2007). Push factors can be either subtle or overt school-based effects, which deter some Traveller pupils from achieving their educational potential. In order to help address this inequality, teachers and schools need to:

- Be alert to and challenge racism.
- Be aware of and respect cultural influences.
- Maintain and communicate high expectations.

Racism

Children from Gypsy, Roma and Traveller families have exactly the same rights to education as any other child and it is unlawful for schools to discriminate on the grounds of lifestyle, culture or ethnicity. Under the Equality Act (2010), schools have a general duty to promote equality of opportunity, eliminate racial discrimination and promote good relationships between people from different racial backgrounds. This applies to all schools regardless of whether there are pupils from different ethnic groups on roll. It is important that all schools remember to include Gypsy, Roma and Traveller communities in their work on inclusion and diversity in order to challenge the negative stereotypes that abound in the media.

People and groups that do not conform to or fit neatly into our own perception of 'normality' tend to be stigmatised and rejected. Some people have a mental image of a 'true' Gypsy; the exotic and romanticised version which is deemed more acceptable than the alternative, criminalised Gypsy; associated with theft, deception and mess. Both of these are unhelpful stereotypes generated and fuelled by reports and images in the media and consolidated through a lack of awareness. Travellers are as diverse as any other group of people and, if left unchallenged, such stereotyped attitudes will affect our behaviour towards and expectations of Traveller children in our schools, resulting in unprofessional practice.

Gypsy, Roma and Traveller pupils probably endure more racist name-calling than most teachers realise. Research studies reveal this to be a very common problem that can discourage these children from attending school regularly (Warrington 2006; Fremlova and Ureche 2011; Foster and Norton 2012). In a six-year longitudinal study (Derrington and Kendall 2004), it was observed that around one in three Traveller students dealt with racist name-calling by retaliating physically, often with the encouragement of their parents. Unfortunately, this way of coping attracted negative attention from teachers. What's more, it was found that teachers were likely to attribute the retaliating behaviour to cultural traits rather than emotionally fuelled responses to racial harassment. Other studies also found that teachers were inclined to believe that GRT pupils were the initiators of conflict between peers (Wilkin *et al*. 2009a; D'Arcy 2014a).

Awareness of Traveller culture

Although it can be detrimental to generalise cultural characteristics (particularly as these communities are diverse) some insight can help teachers to gain a better understanding of Gypsy, Roma or Traveller pupils and their families. It is important to appreciate, for example, that Traveller parents do tend to be very child-centred and highly protective and it may take time and effort for a trusting relationship to develop between home and school. It is important to remember that Gypsies and Travellers have endured a long history of persecution and rejection by the settled community and many parents continue to express anxiety about the physical, moral and psychological welfare of their children in school (Derrington and Kendall, 2004; Bowers 2004; Padfield 2005; Wilkin *et al*. 2009b; D'Arcy 2014a, 2014b). Older siblings and cousins may be under strict instructions from home to 'look out' for and protect younger ones in the playground and there may be reluctance from parents to allow their children to take part in school trips and extra-curricular activities. Not all Traveller parents will have attended school as children themselves. Those parents may not be able to read and write well or may be confused by educational jargon used in school. Some Traveller parents may have had unhappy personal experiences of school making them wary of, or intimidated by, the school environment. Events such as pupil progress consultations, review meetings and curriculum information evenings may be avoided by anxious parents, perhaps giving teachers the impression that they are unsupportive or uninterested in their child's education (Derrington and Kendall 2004).

Traveller parents' anxiety about secondary school (in particular) is sometimes driven by the generalised belief that non-Traveller society is corrupt and lacking in moral standards. Strict moral codes are generally upheld in the community and consequently, Travellers tend to marry at a young age. Widely publicised reports in the media of mainstream social problems related to drugs, alcohol and promiscuity are often cited by young Travellers and their parents in discussions about secondary education (Derrington 2007). These also feature strongly among the concerns that Traveller parents articulate when opting for Elective Home Education (D'Arcy 2014a and 2014b). Consequently, Traveller parents are likely to be attracted by the prospect of small schools, culturally diverse schools, single sex secondary schools, faith schools and those that are genuinely 'welcoming'; where staff are perceived as having knowledge of, and respect for, Traveller culture and where they believe their children will be safe (Parker-Jenkins and Hartas 2002; Ureche and Franks 2007; Wilkin *et al*. 2009b). This said, opposing concepts of safety and danger are socially constructed and there may be cultural differences that are difficult for schools to understand. As mentioned previously, young Travellers are usually afforded a high level of protection by their families and it is not uncommon for them to be forbidden to go on residential trips, parties or school discos for their own safety. Young children tend to be perceived and treated as 'babies' for several years, and it can be difficult to persuade some parents of the benefits of early years provision. However, paradoxically, once they reach middle childhood, Traveller children tend to assume 'adult' responsibilities such as taking care of domestic and childcare duties, gaining financial independence, using tools and learning to drive. Most Traveller children are therefore quite used to working and socialising alongside adults and tend to display a level of maturity that sets them apart from peers. They are often confident communicators and their conversational style with adults can be direct and may even be perceived in school as outspokenness (Lloyd *et al.* 1999; MacNamara 2001).

Traditional gender roles are also promoted in some Traveller families and girls may be discouraged from pursuing further education and a career (Ofsted 2014). Another potential source of frustration for teachers is that strongly upheld values linked to family and community loyalty can take priority over education. This is gradually changing, as more parents realise the impact of irregular school attendance on academic progress, but opportunities for gatherings to celebrate birthdays, anniversaries and traditional horse fairs may still take precedence over anything that is happening at school.

Traveller pupils should be encouraged to be proud of their culture and it is important that it is recognised within the curriculum. In schools where there is a lack of recognition, or denial of cultural difference, it can perpetuate 'the continuing ignorance of individual teachers' (Lloyd and McCluskey 2008: 10). An enhanced awareness of some of these cultural influences should enable teachers and schools to respond more empathically and flexibly to the needs of Traveller pupils and their families. However, maintaining high expectations and providing consistent messages to *all* pupils in terms of their behaviour, attendance, effort and attainment is fundamental.

Maintaining high expectations

Low expectations are often manifestations of generalised, stereotyped beliefs and we develop them when we are unwilling or unable to obtain all the information we would need to make fair judgements about people or situations. These generalised beliefs may have their roots in our own limited experiences ('I got tricked once by a Gypsy') or those that have been relayed to us by relatives, friends or colleagues ('I had his brother in my class last year – good luck!'). They are also generated from stories we read in newspapers or what we see on TV and film and, as already mentioned, these are likely to be less than positive. Teachers' expectations of their pupils therefore tend to be based on limited evidence gleaned before they have even met the pupil(s) in question. Teacher expectations (whether high or low) also tend to be self-fulfilling.

A number of studies have noted that teacher expectations in relation to Gypsy Traveller pupils can be unreasonably low (Ofsted 1999; Bhopal *et al.* 2000; Derrington and Kendall 2007). Low teacher expectations may be expressed in conscious or unconscious, overt or subtle ways in the classroom and they may even be well-intentioned. Consider the following examples:

- A reception class teacher removes the shared reading record card from a Gypsy pupil's book bag because she has been told that the parents are illiterate.
- A Traveller pupil new to the school is placed in the lowest literacy and numeracy groups because it is assumed that he will have gaps in his learning.
- A pupil tells the teacher that her parents won't allow her to transfer to secondary school because 'Gypsy girls don't go to high school'. When no transfer form is returned, the school makes little attempt to follow this up.
- A Traveller pupil is absent from school most Fridays and this is marked in the register with the code T.[1]
- A fight breaks out in the playground and it is assumed that the Traveller boys started it.
- A part-time vocational course aimed especially at Traveller students is set up at the local college.

Even though some of these actions might have been implemented with the best interest of the child and his/her family at heart, what message might each one convey? The chances are, even the most subtle expression of low expectation will be internalised by pupils and their parents. For example, if absence from school is not followed up rigorously in the same way that it is for other pupils, this may be interpreted as an act of passive condoning that encourages further disengagement (self-fulfilling prophecy).

Conclusions

Despite official guidance aimed at raising outcomes for Gypsy, Roma and Traveller pupils over the past fifteen years or so (Ofsted 1996, 1999, 2003, 2014; Bhopal et al. 2000; DfES 2003; DCSF 2008a, 2008b; DCLG 2012) the achievement of these groups remains unacceptably low. Some commentators argue that the predominant data-driven approach to raising educational standards has failed to take account of the complex and holistic needs of individual Gypsy Roma Traveller pupils (Foster and Walker 2009). A systematic review of the literature (Wilkin et al. 2009a) concluded that a history of low expectations and negative attitudes (on the part of teachers, parents and pupils), a lack of cultural awareness in schools, racist bullying and discriminatory policies and practices have collectively been associated with the longstanding record of poor educational outcomes for these pupils.

A major longitudinal research project, commissioned by the former Labour Government (Wilkin et al. 2009b) explored the phenomenon in great depth and identified a number of recurring inter-woven conditions that impact positively on educational outcomes for these groups of learners. These include the establishment of parental trust in the school as a perceived place of safety, evidence of mutual respect between pupils and staff and between parents/carers and staff, flexibility of school and teacher responses to cater for individual needs and the communication of consistently high expectations for GRT pupils. The research team emphasised the importance of achieving a balance between each of these. If the set of conditions is out of balance, then things can go wrong. For example, a school might uphold very high expectations for GRT pupils but show little evidence of flexibility, leading to a higher incidence of exclusions and drop-out. A different school might reflect the opposite scenario where exceptions are made on the basis of culture but expectations are low, resulting in low attainment.

The analytical model that Wilkin *et al.* devised also drew attention to the impact of contextual influences, acknowledging that every school is different and that external variables may or may not lie outside the immediate influence of the school and these can either support or obstruct the raising of outcomes for GRT pupils. Because of this diversity, specific interventions may lead to quicker results in some schools than others that are operating under very different circumstances.

Nonetheless, every teacher has a professional duty to help close the attainment gap for all groups of pupils. The provision of high quality teaching underpinned by a commitment to inclusive education and equality issues is likely to benefit all pupils including those from Gypsy, Roma and Traveller backgrounds. Furthermore, it has been suggested that the experiences and achievements of Gypsy, Roma and Traveller pupils in the classroom can be said to represent the 'litmus test' of inclusive education (Foster and Walker 2009).

Reflection on values and practice

1   A Gypsy, Roma or Traveller pupil in your class is reported for fighting in the playground. He defends his actions by saying he was called 'Gyppo'.
    What would your response be a) in the immediate term b) as a follow up to the incident?

2   You have never had an opportunity to talk with the parents of a Traveller child in your class. They sit in the family vehicle rather than wait at the school gate with other parents and they have never been to a parents' evening.
    How do you interpret this behaviour? What could you do to encourage dialogue and build a relationship?

Suggested further reading

Bhopal, K. and Myers, M. (2009) Gypsy, Roma and Traveller pupils in schools in the UK: inclusion and 'good practice', *International Journal of Inclusive Education*, 13(3): 219–314.

National Association of Teachers of Travellers and Other Professionals www.NATT.org. uk

O'Hanlon, C. and Holmes, P. (2004) *The Education of Gypsy and Traveller Children: towards inclusion and educational achievement,* Stoke on Trent: Trentham Books.

Tyler, C. (ed.) (2005) *Traveller Education: accounts of good practice,* Stoke on Trent: Trentham Books.

Danaher, A., Coombes, P. and Kiddle, C. (2007) *Teaching Traveller Children: maximising learning outcomes*. Stoke on Trent: Trentham Books.

Note

1 The 'T' code may currently be used when Traveller families are known to be travelling for occupational purposes and have agreed this with the school.

References

Bhopal, K. with Gundara, J., Jones, C. and Owen, C. (2000) *Working Towards Inclusive Education for Gypsy Traveller Pupils* (RR 238), London: Department for Education and Employment.

Bowers, J. (2004) *Prejudice & Pride: The Experience of Young Travellers*, Ipswich: Ormiston Children & Families Trust.

D'Arcy, K. (2014a) *Travellers and Home Education: safe spaces and inequality*, Stoke-on-Trent: Trentham Books.

D'Arcy, K. (2014b) Home education, school, Travellers and educational inclusion, *British Journal of Sociology of Education*, 35(5):818–835.

DCLG (2012) *Progress Report by the Ministerial Working Group on Tackling Inequalities Experienced by Gypsies and Travellers*, London: Department for Communities and Local Government.

DCSF (2008a) *The Inclusion of Gypsy, Roma and Traveller Children and Young People*, London: Department for Children, Schools and Families.

DCSF (2008b) *Raising the Achievement of Gypsy, Roma and Traveller Pupils*, London: Department for Children, Schools and Families.

DfE (2013) *Phonics Screening Check and National Curriculum Assessments at Key Stage 1 in England 2012/13 (National Statistical First Release SFR 37/2013)*, London: Department for Education.

DfE (2014a) *Pupil Absence in Schools in England 2012/13 (National Statistical First Release SFR 09/2014)*, London: Department for Education.

DfE (2014b) *GCSE and Equivalent Attainment by Pupil Characteristics in England 2012/13 (National Statistical First Release SFR 05/2014)*, London: Department for Education.

DfE (2014c) *National Curriculum Assessments at Key Stage 2 in England 2014 (National Statistical First Release SFR 05/2014)*, London: Department for Education.

DfES (2003) *Aiming High: raising the achievement of Gypsy Traveller pupils: a guide to good practice*, London: Department for Education and Skills.

Derrington, C. (2007) Fight, flight and playing white: an examination of coping strategies adopted by Gypsy Traveller adolescents in English secondary schools. *International Journal of Educational Research*, 46(6):357–367.

Derrington, C. and Kendall, S. (2004) *Gypsy Traveller Students in Secondary Schools: culture, identity and achievement*, Stoke-on-Trent: Trentham Books.

Derrington, C. and Kendall, S. (2007) Still in school at 16? Conclusions from a longitudinal study of Gypsy traveller students in English secondary schools. In Bhatti, G., Gaine, C., Gobbo, F. and Leeman, Y. (eds.) *Social Justice and Intercultural Education: an open ended dialogue*, Stoke on Trent: Trentham Books, pp.17–31.

Foster, B. and Norton, P. (2012) Educational equality for Gypsy, Roma and Traveller children and young people in the UK. *The Equal Rights Review*, 8: 85–112.

Foster, B. and Walker, A. (2009) *Traveller Education in the Mainstream: the litmus test,* Corsham: Hopscotch Educational Publishing.

Fremlova, L. and Ureche, H. (2011) *From Segregation to Inclusion: Roma pupils in the UK. A pilot research project.* Budapest: Roma Education Fund. Available at http://equality.uk.com/Education_files/From%20segregation%20to%20integration_1.pdf. Accessed 17 February 2015.

Lloyd, G. and McCluskey, G. (2008) Education and Gypsies/Travellers: 'contradictions and significant silences'. *International Journal of Inclusive Education*, 12(4): 331–45.

Lloyd, G., Stead, J., Jordan, E. and Norris, C. (1999) Teachers and Gypsy Travellers. *Scottish Educational Review*, 31: 48–65.

Martin, G. (1998) Generational differences amongst New Age Travellers. *Sociological Review*, 46(4):735–756.

MacNamara, Y. (2001) Education on the move, *ACE Bulletin*, 104 (December):13.

Ofsted (1996) *The Education of Travelling Children,* London: Office for Standards in Education.

Ofsted (1999) *Raising the Attainment of Minority Ethnic Pupils: school and LEA responses,* London: Office for Standards in Education.

Ofsted (2003) *Provision and Support for Traveller Pupils*. HMI Ref: 455. London: Ofsted.

Ofsted (2014) *Overcoming Barriers: ensuring that Roma children are fully engaged and achieving in education.* Manchester: Office for Standards in Education.

Padfield, P. (2005) Inclusive educational approaches for Gypsy/Traveller pupils and their families: an 'urgent need for progress?' *Scottish Educational Review*, 37(2):127–144.

Parker-Jenkins, M. and Hartas, D. (2002) Social inclusion: the case of Travellers' children, *Education 3–13*, 30(2):39–42.

Ureche, H. and Franks, M. (2007) *This is Who we Are: a study of the views and identities of Roma, Gypsy and Traveller young people in England.* London: The Children's Society.

Warrington, C. (2006) *Children's Voices: changing future – the views and experiences of young Gypsies and Travellers,* Ipswich: The Ormiston Children and Families Trust.

Wilkin, A., Derrington, C. and Foster, B. (2009a) *Improving Outcomes for Gypsy, Roma and Traveller Pupils: a literature review,* London: DCSF.

Wilkin, A., Derrington, C., Foster, B., White, R. and Martin, K. (2009b) *Improving Outcomes for Gypsy, Roma and Traveller Pupils: what works? Contextual influences and constructive conditions,* London: Department for Children, Schools and Families.

Chapter 5

The influence of gender in the classroom

How boys and girls learn

Steve Bartlett and Diana Burton

Introduction

All of us are affected in some way by issues of social class, ethnicity and gender. In this chapter we look specifically at the influence of gender on the achievement of pupils in our education system to raise the implications for inclusive ways of working. We consider how, for much of the twentieth century, research concentrated on the inequality of opportunity for girls and the social changes that have attempted to rectify this. We then look at the current debates surrounding the now apparently poor achievement of boys and the culture of underperformance accompanying this. We conclude by suggesting that any examination of the self perception, motivation and achievement of children and young people needs to include a consideration of social class and ethnicity as well as gender. It is only by being aware of such factors that policies promoting social inclusion can have any hope of success. All teachers need to understand these significant forces in pupils' lives in order to make their practice more effective.

Sex and gender

Before we consider the impact of gender on pupil achievement it is important to examine the terminology that is used in such debates. The term sex is usually used when referring to our biological make up. It identifies us as male or female. Biological differences include chromosomes, hormones and physical sexual characteristics such as sexual organs, body hair, physique etc. Gender refers to the social construction of masculine and feminine. It is what we expect males and females to be 'like' in terms of behaviour, appearance, beliefs and attitudes. There is a continuing debate as to how much of our maleness and femaleness is biologically determined and how much is socially constructed.

A biological determinist position holds that our biological sex is significant in determining us as individuals. Our biological make up plays the major part in deciding how we behave. Thus mothering and caring are presented as female traits, whilst aggression and protecting are male. This biological base can be seen as underpinning many explanations for the structure of families and the conjugal roles within them. An alternative view is that though there are certain biological differences between males and females it is society and the culture that we live in that creates the notions of masculinity and femininity.

Early feminist writers such as Oakley (1975) wished to highlight the significance of cultural as opposed to biological factors in explaining the ongoing socially inferior position of women in society. Their argument was that it was the social constructions of gender and sexuality that led to the oppression of women. The biological accounts were seen as part of male social control that perpetuated the myth of male superiority. The whole notion of masculinity and femininity from this perspective was socially determined.

There are physical differences between males and females and these become more obvious as we grow up and move through adolescence and into adulthood. However, there is a wide variation both within and across the genders in terms of individual physical characteristics. What is deemed as attractive to the opposite sex is different from society to society and changes over time with fashion. Clothing, diet and body building/reducing exercises to change our appearance are all used and with advances in medical science people can radically alter their physical characteristics and even biological sex. In modern societies and across a range of cultures any presentation of a clear uncomplicated sexual divide is rather an over simplification.

Masculinities and femininities

Harber (2014) suggests that whilst there are many forms of male identity or masculinities, there are some 'dominant or hegemonic forms of male identity internationally which have traditionally preserved patriarchal power and privilege' (p.162). These promote perceptions and so reinforce realities of male dominance and female subordination in many societies.

Marshall (2014) points out that many girls in the developing world face significant barriers in accessing education resulting from traditional cultural beliefs linked at the same time to economic poverty. Key factors adversely affecting girls are things such as boy's education being more valued, girls being kept at home for household chores, married at a young age and being perceived as having a home-based future and not worth educating. In some regions girls report violence and sexual harassment on the way to and from school and also in school and so are more likely to stay at home. For such reasons Marshall (2014) suggests that girls in various geographical areas are unlikely to receive an education equivalent to boys and in some cases any significant formal education at all.

However, Harber (2014) does note that in a number of areas, Honduras for example, it is the boys who are more likely to drop out of school as they are needed to earn a wage to supplement the family income, whilst girls are not expected to work outside the home. As Harber (2014) points out, once again poverty is a key factor in influencing gender and schooling.

In the developed world, such as the UK, Swain (2004) and Connell (2006) speak of a range of masculinities and femininities thus allowing for greater variation. As teenagers strive to be independent from their elders they are also subject to strong peer pressures. Gender characteristics that stereotype appropriate physical appearance and behaviour can cause pressure to conform, particularly on young people who are coming to terms with themselves as they develop. To be identified as different or 'other' can have a significant effect upon the self-image of young people. Pupil interaction and perceptions are significant in the 'othering' process. Labels become attached to pupils and some are more difficult to resist or counter than others. Language plays a very powerful part in this process and use of sexual insults such as 'gay', 'queer' or 'slag' may have lasting repercussions on the identities, future interactions and sexual behaviour of the young people involved (see Vicars 2006).

Stereotypical images of boys in school include loud, boisterous behaviour, lack of interest in studying and generally taking a rushed and untidy approach to work. Images of stereotypical girl behaviour include being quiet, hard working, neat and careful in appearance. If we look at real groups of young people and consider the broad range that exists in terms of behaviour, beliefs, values and appearance, we see how inappropriate it is to use such stereotypes. One should beware of using too rigid a definition of what constitutes female or male behaviour of young people.

Swain (2004) says that pupils live within the context of their own communities and that these wider contexts influence the individual school policies and cultures. Thus schools are influenced by local employment opportunities, housing type, religious and ethnic mix of the area. Within this Swain says that each school also has its own *gender regime*. This 'consists of individual personnel expectations, rules, routines and a hierarchical ordering of particular practices' (p.182).

It is worth considering the integral part that gender relationships play in school life and how these vary depending upon the ethos of the school (see Liu 2006 and Mellor and Epstein 2006). School uniform, lining up in the playground or outside the classroom, class lists that separate boys and girls, and how pupils and teachers are addressed are all instances where gender may or may not be highlighted in formal school procedures. Gender is also part of informal school processes e.g. the arrangement of each individual classroom and where pupils sit, who children play with at break times and what they play, the number of pupils choosing different subjects at secondary school, the number of male and female adults employed by the school and their positions of responsibility. Since schools are a key part of the wider socialisation process they both influence, and are influenced by, gender relationships.

A historical view of recent developments in gender relations in Britain

How the roles of men and women and their relationships to each other vary over time can be illustrated by considering the period from Victorian England to the present day. In the early 1800s Britain was very much a patriarchal society. Women were not able to vote, own property or obtain a divorce. Within the middle classes women were effectively either under the control of their father or their husband. It was men who governed the empire and the society, ran businesses and supported the family. Women did not work and were confined to a life that revolved around the home. Boys from the more affluent classes would be educated at public and grammar schools but the education of girls would be primarily left to governesses, conducted in the home, based upon the knowledge suitable for a lady. For the working classes life was much harder and both men and women worked, though women did the more menial factory work and were paid less than men. In the early educational provision for the working classes girls were able to attend school as well as boys, though both were taught appropriately to the social expectations of the time.

It has taken many years of political and social pressure for women to achieve legal equality with men. They gained the right to divorce, they won the vote and the Sex Discrimination Act of 1975 outlawed discrimination on the grounds of gender. From this date women, legally at least, had equality with men. However, there were still economic and social differences that were strongly influenced by gender. In employment terms women remained underrepresented in many, usually more highly paid, professions and the average earnings of women remained well below that of men.

In many areas of employment the position of women has improved. Changes in attitude have continued to take place and over the years women have increasingly taken up careers in many areas that previously they did not. However, in spite of progress employment is still an area where there remain significant differences between men and women. These are likely to take a long time to change in spite of the Equality Act of 2010. Women's employment is still shaped by family and domestic responsibilities with mothers more likely to leave work or go part time on having children or choose jobs where the hours fit into child care. These factors result in many women taking jobs with lower pay and fewer prospects. Women in professional jobs are more likely to miss out on promotions during their enforced 'career breaks'.

Education reflects social and political attitudes. State education has been provided throughout the twentieth century to all pupils regardless of gender. In the early part of the 1900s the elementary schools were co-educational. Whilst primary schools have always been co-educational, the introduction of a selective secondary system saw the development of single sex secondary schools. It was the development of new large comprehensive schools from the 1960s onwards that saw boys and girls taught together in their secondary education.

Gender and achievement

Being taught in the same school did not remove the impact of gender upon a pupil's experiences. In the 1970s and 80s much feminist research in education was concerned with the perceived underachievement of girls and how the education process worked to maintain this through discrimination and marginalisation (Oakley 1975; Whyte 1983; Spender 1982). Gender differences were maintained and highlighted through the processes of schooling, which involved the separation of the genders through school uniform, differential expectations of behaviour and a gender-specific curriculum e.g. needlework and typing for girls and metalwork and technical drawing for boys. This was further enforced through the attitude of teachers, peers, parents and later their usually male employers. Thus the ambitions of female students remained low and they were discouraged in a variety of ways from choosing the 'hard' mathematical and scientific subjects so important to future employment prospects in favour of the more 'feminine' arts and humanities.

Raising girls' achievement

In the 1970s and 80s a number of initiatives were designed to improve the achievement of girls by raising awareness, altering attitudes and increasing ambition, for instance The Girls into Science and Technology Project (GIST) and Genderwatch (Myers 1987; Myers *et al.* 2007).

Whilst the raising of awareness and the development work that accompanied it were all based on the belief in the underachievement of girls relative to boys, the reality was not that straightforward. Even in the 1970s girls were outperforming boys in English and modern foreign languages. Also, more girls were achieving five or more 'O' level passes (equivalent to A*–C, GCSE) than boys. However, because these included subjects that were seen as low status such as home economics and because boys were doing better at maths and sciences, regarded as 'hard' subjects of high status, then girls were perceived as underachieving (Francis 2000). Also, the selective system of grammar and secondary modern schools, in operation before the development of the comprehensive system, had favoured boys due to the larger number of places available in boys' grammar schools as opposed to those admitting girls. Thus boys did not need to score as highly as girls in the 11+ to secure a grammar school education. It was not the case then that girls were necessarily underachieving but that their success was not being recognised and that they were not offered the same opportunities or encouragement as boys in order to pursue the more rewarding economic options. Girls' futures were still being perceived as domestically based.

The introduction of the national curriculum in 1988 unwittingly had what is now often regarded as a significant impact on the achievements of girls (Francis 2000). From its inception all pupils were required to study the national curriculum. Thus, it was no longer possible for boys or girls to 'drop' some subjects in favour of others. Along with the new curriculum a system of national assessment for all pupils at different stages in their education was introduced. It was now possible to produce league tables based upon these key stage tests and also GCSE and 'A' level results. These were and are used to judge overall school performance, making the achievements of boys and girls more transparent than ever. They show how the performance of both boys and girls has steadily improved. What has caught the public attention though is that the improvement in the results of girls has been greater than that of boys. Whilst continuing to outperform boys in language subjects, girls have caught up boys in maths and the sciences. Concern now became focused on the performance of boys.

Current performance of boys and girls

We need to be very cautious when interpreting statistics on gender and examination performance. In terms of GCSE performance, DFE figures (www.gov.uk, 2015) show that girls attain a higher percentage of five or more passes at A*–C than boys. They outperform boys in the majority of subjects, the gap being particularly noticeable in English language. There is, however, little statistical difference between the performance of boys and girls in the areas of maths and science. 'A' level pass rates and grades are comparable for boys and girls but what still remains significant is that apart from biology far fewer girls are taking the STEM (science, technology, engineering and maths) subjects than boys.

Along with the increasing number of students taking 'A' levels, higher education has expanded over the last thirty years and become more accessible to a wider proportion of the population. As the number of students has steadily increased women now make up the largest proportion of those studying for both undergraduate and post graduate degrees. In 2013/14 women made up 54.7 per cent of full time undergraduate students (HESA 2015), a significant change from when university study was largely the preserve of a minority of privileged males. Women entrants outnumber men now in the majority of undergraduate courses, including medicine and dentistry, subject areas previously dominated by males. However, men remain over-represented in most STEM subjects, most notably engineering. Adams (2015) suggests that the success of female applicants into higher education mirrors the trend in GCSE and 'A' level, with girls performing well but still being underrepresented in the STEM subjects. Thus whilst this expanding education participation creates the possibility of wider career access for women, this is still not the case in areas such as construction and engineering that require high level qualifications in STEM. Even with the comparable academic performance of females gender may still be having an impact upon behaviour, subject and ultimately career choices. Francis, Burke and Read (2014) noted that many students, male and female, still tended to use stereotypical constructions of gender difference even whilst rejecting the notion that gender and other structural differences impact upon their experiences.

It is important for teachers to realise that the difference in performance between boys and girls is not that great. To see all boys as underachieving is misleading as some groups of boys do achieve highly, whilst some groups of girls do not. Richards and Posnett (2012) notice, for instance, that whilst overall girls' academic achievement appears to be better than or equal to boys, low aspirations continue to affect the performance of working class girls. Thus within both boys and girls there is a wide range of achievement with many young people continuing to experience academic and behavioural difficulties at school. It is these pupils that need the support of education professionals.

Explanations for boys' underachievement

Recent industrial and economic changes have meant that the male is now no longer the only, or even the major 'breadwinner' in the family. Thus the traditional masculine image in working class communities is not as applicable as it was even 20 years ago and it is suggested that many working class boys see no particular role for themselves. The debate has thus shifted from being about the creation of equal opportunities and improving the educational experiences of girls to concerns about male underachievement and disadvantage.

The panic surrounding the underachievement of boys has been rather an over-reaction. The media has portrayed boys as falling behind and homed in on an apparent growth of a 'laddish' culture among teenage boys that is anti-study, against school values and leads to underachievement. Calls for developing strategies that focus on the motivations, attitudes and performance of boys have resulted (Smith 2012). Arnot and Miles (2005) suggest that the increasing emphasis on a performative school system has led to greater resistance from working class boys who have a history of low achievement. This, they say, is being misinterpreted as a new development, termed 'laddishness'. Significantly, Connolly (2006: 15) says that masculinities and femininities are not just about gender alone but must be seen as combining with social class and ethnicity to 'produce differing and enduring forms of identity'. It is this complex mix that teachers need to be aware of.

It is important to consider some of the explanations for the achievement of both boys and girls if only to 'identify and dispel some of the current and unhelpful myths about gender and education' (DCSF 2009a, now DFE).

Explanations involving genetic differences

A biologically determinist view may look for mental differences between males and females to help explain any subject preferences or difference in achievement. However, there is little neurological evidence to suggest that boys have different cognitive ability or ways of learning than girls (DCSF 2009a). In fact, DCSF (2009a) suggested any learning practices or preferences that are gendered are likely to be due to social pressures rather than biological. Feminist analysts would suggest that the 'moral panic' that has accompanied this perceived failure of boys and the demand to rectify the situation is a reflection of the fear within the male-dominated political establishment.

Explanations involving school culture

It has been assumed that assessment regimes have developed to favour girls with more emphasis on coursework rather than final exams. However, this trend in assessment has reversed to final course exams in recent years with no significant falling back of girls' performance. Girls appear to do well in examinations as well as coursework assignments (Elwood 2005).

The curriculum is said by some to favour girls with little to excite boys. This point does ignore the many areas of the curriculum where the content has been specifically chosen to attract boys. DCSF (2009a) suggested that there is no evidence that the content of the secondary curriculum reflects particularly gendered interests, though it does warn that girls still remain underrepresented in science, technology and maths subjects at university. Changing the curriculum to make it 'boy friendly' appears to have little effect on boys' achievements; in fact, such changes may involve gender stereotyping that could actually limit the choices that boys and girls make (Keddie and Mills 2008).

Beliefs about identity can inform teachers' perceptions and Elwood (2005) says that for many teachers and policy makers boys are now seen as 'poor boys' or that 'boys will be boys' or as 'problem' boys. This labelling process may contribute to the low expectations of boys, thus creating a self-fulfilling prophecy. It is these expectations that are perhaps part of the problem.

It is also a myth that boys prefer a competitive environment. In fact, if they are not succeeding, an emphasis on competition may actually be counterproductive. It also appears to be a fallacy that introducing single-sex classes is a way to improve achievement in secondary schools. Whilst in some cases single sex classes may benefit girls, the evidence for boys is much more mixed.

Strategies for raising achievement

As achievement of pupils is based upon a number of interrelated factors, it would be expected that strategies to raise attainment would not just focus on gender. Both boys and girls want teachers who are able to motivate through exciting and challenging lessons regardless of whether they are male or female. The overall quality of the curriculum is more significant than whether some parts are gender biased. DCSF produced guidance for teachers seeking to improve boys' and girls' achievement (DCSF 2009b). It suggests that tackling gender differences that have a negative impact on achievement should be done at a whole school level. The guidance borrows a number of key components from Warrington *et al.* (2006) and suggests that the following contribute to the establishment of an inclusive school ethos:

- High expectations of behaviour from all pupils with emphasis on the development of self-discipline.
- Valuing diversity in all areas of school life. Intolerance, and discrimination are challenged.
- Encouraging pupils to have a pride in their work and achievements.
- Pupils are able to become fully involved in the life of the school.
- The values of inclusion and opportunity are an integral part of school life and are continually emphasised.

(Taken and adapted from Warrington *et al.* 2006)

DCSF (2009b) suggests a number of gender-related strategies that can be used when developing an equitable and inclusive school ethos. These include:

- Creating a gender equitable school culture by tackling gender stereotypes in behaviour.
- Deconstructing and challenging stereotypes in the content of the curriculum.
- Applying expectations of high achievement for all pupils.

Each of these strategies involves a process of reviewing current positions, deciding appropriate actions and monitoring changes. They will involve teachers, other adults working in the school and also pupils.

Conclusions

In summarising the arguments concerning gender and achievement we can say that the performance of boys and girls overall has improved throughout the 1990s and the 2000s, that girls have been improving faster than boys and that they are now performing at least equally to boys in all subjects and outperforming them in some. However, to portray girls as achieving and boys as underachieving is too simplistic a view (Elwood 2005; Smith 2012; Richards and Posnett 2012). It should be noted that the differences in overall performance of boys and girls are not that great. It is the improvement in performance of girls from the more middle class backgrounds in all subjects that has caused the rise in girls' performance overall. Boys from middle class backgrounds continue to generally perform well. Boys and girls from the lower socio-economic groups continue to underperform when compared to their more affluent peers. Thus, as Connolly (2006) points out, whilst gender does exert an influence on attainment, this may be overshadowed by the effects of social class and ethnicity. Effective teachers must take account of these factors whilst endeavouring to treat pupils as the individuals they are. We should not focus on gender alone. Good teaching aims to empower all pupils.

Reflection on values and practice

1   Draw an organisational chart for your school. Identify whether each position is occupied by a male or female. Compare your results with colleagues working in other schools. What conclusions can you draw from the results of this exercise in terms of gender and employment in schools? Do your findings have any policy implications?
2   Conduct a gender audit of one area of the curriculum. Consider content, teaching approaches, resources used such as worksheets and text books. What conclusions do you draw about the gendered nature of the curriculum? Do you need to make changes or not? What can you do to develop and improve this curriculum for all pupils?
3   Observe pupils working in class. Consider how different groups and individuals work differently over a period of time. Look particularly at the characteristics of the groups – how long is spent on task, cooperative behaviour and quality of work produced. Is gender a factor in any of the variations you notice? How might you intervene to change things?

Suggested further reading

Gender and Education. Routledge: London.
This is an academic journal that is available in printed copy and online having seven
   editions per year. It is important for all studying at higher levels to refer to specialist

journals in their field. This journal publishes articles on global perspectives on education, gender and culture and aims to promote discussion across this broad area. As such, it provides access to the most current developments in theory and debate in this field.

DCSF (2009) *Gender and Education – Mythbusters*, www.dcsf.gov.uk

and DCSF (2009) *Gender issues in school – What works to improve achievement for boys and girls*, www.dcsf.gov.uk.

These two short booklets are clearly written, explain the current position, provide many current academic sources and give practical advice. They should be read together.

Oakley, A. (1975) *Sex, Gender and Society*, London: Temple Smith.

Though now rather old this is still a classic feminist text on gender relationships in society. A very interesting account that encourages the reader to reflect upon how things have changed, or not, since its publication.

References

Adams, R. (2015) Gender gap in university admissions rises to record level, *The Guardian*, Wednesday 21 January 2015.

Arnot, M. and Miles, P. (2005) A reconstruction of the gender agenda: The contradictory gender dimensions in New Labour's educational and economic policy, *Oxford Review of Education*, 31(1): 173–189.

Connell, R.W. (2006) Understanding men: gender sociology and the new international research on masculinities. In Skelton, C., Francis, B. and Smulyan, L., *The Sage Handbook of Gender and Education*, London: Sage, pp.18–30.

Connolly, P. (2004) *Boys and Schooling in the Early Years*, London: RoutledgeFalmer.

Connolly, P. (2006) The effects of social class and ethnicity on gender differences in GCSE attainment: a secondary analysis of the Youth Cohort Study of England and Wales 1997–2001, *The British Educational Research Journal*, 32(1): 3–21.

DCSF (2009a) *Gender and education – Mythbusters. Addressing gender and achievement: Myths and realities.* Available at http://dera.ioe.ac.uk/9095/1/00599-2009BKT-EN.pdf.

DCSF (2009b) *Gender issues in school – what works to improve achievement for boys and girls.* http://dera.ioe.ac.uk/9094/1/00601-2009BKT-EN.pdf.

Elwood, J. (2005) Gender and achievement: what have exams got to do with it? *Oxford Review of Education*, 31(3):373–393.

Francis, B. (2000) *Boys, Girls and Achievement. Addressing the classroom issues*, London: Routledge.

Francis, B., Burke, P. and Read, B. (2014) The submergence and re-emergence of gender in undergraduate accounts of university experience, *Gender and Education*, 26:1, 1–17.

Gov.uk (2015) Accessed 19/04/2015. Available at https://www.gov.uk/government/statistics/revised-gcse-and-equivalent-results-in-england-2013-to-2014. Accessed 19 April 2015.

Harber, C. (2014) *Education and International Development: theory, practice and issues.* Oxford: Symposium Books Higher Education Statistics Agency (HESA) (2015) Available at https://www.hesa.ac.uk/stats. Accessed 19 April 2015.

Higher Education Statistics Agency (HESA) (2015) Available at https://www.hesa.ac.uk/stats. Accessed 19 April 2015.

Keddie, A. and Mills, M. (2008) *Teaching Boys*, Crows Nest, NSW: Allen and Unwin.

Liu, F. (2006) School culture and gender, in Skelton, C., Francis, B. and Smulyan, L., *The Sage Handbook of Gender and Education*, London: Sage, pp.425–438.

Marshall, J. (2014) *Introduction to Comparative and International Education*. London: Sage.

Mellor, D., and Epstein, D. (2006) *Appropriate behaviour? Sexualities, schooling and hetero-gender*, in Skelton, C., Francis, B. and Smulyan, L., *The Sage Handbook of Gender and Education*, London: Sage, pp.378–391.

Myers, K. (1987) *Genderwatch: self-assessment schedules for use in schools*, London: Schools Curriculum Development Council.

Myers, K., Taylor, H. with Adler, S. and Leonard, D. (eds.) (2007) *Genderwatch – still watching*, Stoke-on-Trent: Trentham.

Oakley, A. (1975) *Sex, Gender and Society*, London: Temple Smith.

Richards, G. and Posnett, C. (2012) Aspiring girls: great expectations or impossible dreams?, *Educational Studies*, 38(3): 249–259.

Smith, E. (2012) *Key Issues in Education and Social Justice*, London: Sage.

Spender, D. (1982) *Invisible Women: the schooling scandal*, London: Writers and Readers.

Swain, J. (2004) The resources and strategies that 10–11-year-old boys use to construct masculinities in the school setting, *British Educational Research Journal*, 30(1): 167–185.

Vicars, M. (2006) Who are you calling queer? Sticks and stones can break my bones but names will always hurt me, *British Educational Research Journal*, 32(3): 347–361.

Warrington, M., Younger, M. and Bearne, E. (2006) *Raising Boys' Achievement in Primary Schools: towards a holistic approach*, Maidenhead: Open University Press/McGraw Hill.

Whyte, J. (1983) *Beyond the Wendy House: sex-role stereotyping in primary schools*, York: Longman.

Chapter 6

Not in my image

Ethnic diversity in the classroom

Raphael Richards

Introduction

Over 28 per cent of pupils aged 5–16 in maintained schools are from a black and minority ethnic (BME) background, while less than 9 per cent of teaching staff are of similar background. Now, imagine spending five to six hours each day in lessons doing History, Geography, Science and English, without seeing or hearing from adults who look like you or reflect you as a Black, Asian or Muslim young person. When we reflect on our schooling experience, there are often two or three teachers who stand out, mostly because they took an interest in our learning. They may have helped us to develop a sense of who we were, provided us with new learning experiences or believed we were talented and capable of achieving in their classroom and beyond.

Data from the January 2014 'Schools, Pupils, and their Characteristics' and November 2012 'School Workforce in England' show that:

- In state-funded primary schools 29.5 per cent of pupils and 25.3 per cent in secondary schools (of compulsory school age and above) were classified as being of minority ethnic origin (DfE 2015).
- In state-funded schools, 91.7 per cent of teaching staff were of White British or Other White Background, the two largest groups in the remaining 8.3 per cent of teachers were of 'White-Irish' background (1.6 per cent) and 'Indian' background (1.3 per cent) (DfE 2013).

In this chapter I want to explore the varied characteristics that make up the diversity of our classrooms, with a focus on black and minority ethnic (BME) children and young people, linking them to the 'closing the [achievement] gap' (Kendall *et al.* 2008) through a more personalised approach. By highlighting some of the key issues around education in an ethnically diverse classroom and how 'Targeted Intervention' can help respond to these issues, I hope that you will reflect on your own development and practice in our increasingly ethnically diverse classrooms. As we explore 'Not in my image' you will see that the debate is increasingly about us, as individuals and the relationships we are able to build with children and young people, their parents and our understanding of the families we serve and their communities.

The key tenor of my chapter is that to be successful, teachers and other educators must consider what knowledge and experience they bring to the classroom and how that influences or impacts on the children and young people's culture, languages and social development. A targeted approach to supporting individual BME pupils and groups, which is designed to raise their achievement, improve progress and educational experience will enhance our collective success and well-being in schools and local communities. However, for us to be successful, each and every pupil's characteristics need detailed consideration and attention from teachers who understand their lived experiences. I aim to leave readers with a basis from which to expand their role by taking a Targeted Intervention approach to ethnic diversity in raising the achievement of children and young people.

Ethnicity and diversity in schools

The UK has become much more ethnically diverse. In the 2011 census, over 7.0 million people in Great Britain were from ethnic minorities. Of these, 4.5 million (equivalent to 8.1 per cent of the total population) were from non-white minority ethnic groups. Around half of the non-white population described themselves as Asians of Indian, Pakistani, Bangladeshi or other Asian origin. Most minority ethnic groups in England have a younger age structure than the white British population (Office for National Statistics 2011).

The National Census provides the official ethnographic data for the UK. In the 1951 Census the ethnographic measures were 'White' and 'None White' of which there was reportedly less than 1 per cent (Peach 1996). Over time, the ethnographic categories have expanded to reflect the changing population of Britain. In the main, schools today are educating second or third generation British born children, whose heritage is from the West Indies, India, Pakistan, Somalia, Poland and who speak over 360 languages. Some examples of key events covering the last two Census (20 years) that contributed to the rich ethnic diversity of schools today are described below.

- Since 2004, there have been more than 1 million Eastern European (EU) migrant workers from the EU accession countries entering the UK to work. This was extended further in 2014 when restrictions on Romanians and Bulgarians rights to migration and employment was lifted in the UK. (Kausar 2011)
- The schools' population is measured yearly through the Pupil Level Annual School Census (PLASC). The Schools Census, as it is now commonly known, captures information about children, provided by their parents. When a child enters a school, his or her parents or legal carer complete a form declaring the child's ethnicity, first language and other characteristics. While most BME populations can be found in the urban areas of England, few schools have no BME or pupils with English as an Additional Language (EAL). Most BME pupils are born in the UK and are of second or third generation.

- The 2011 Census shows the BME population is growing fastest in rural areas of England. In contrast, the ethnic diversity of the teaching workforce has not significantly changed in the last 10 years.

Within the context of ethnicity and diversity teachers often ask for clarification of terms used to describe groups. It is important to be explicit and clear about what one means when using such terms. Below, I set out a working definition of key terms used, however, it is important that readers review and contextualise diversity, ethnicity, race and home language within their own school and local community:

- *Culture* encompasses the learned traditions and aspects of lifestyle that are shared by members of a society or community, including their habitual ways of thinking, feeling and behaving. The use of this term is often based on an assumption that there is cultural cohesion and homogeneity in the society or community (Fredrickson and Cline 2002).
- *Ethnicity* is a label that reflects perceived membership of, and a sense of belonging to, a distinctive social group. The crucial distinguishing features of an ethnic group vary between different contexts and changes over time. They may include physical appearances, first language, religious belief and practices, national allegiance, family structure and occupation (Phinney 1990). Ethnicity may be self-defined or assigned by how others categorise individuals or groups.
- *Race* was originally a concept that categorised a group of people who are connected by common descent or origin and have some common physical features. However, there is no single characteristic, trait or gene that distinguishes all members of one 'race' from all members of another. Race is a construct created by society to describe people according to their outward appearances. Race is a powerful marker that has often been used for monitoring purposes.
- *BME*, the term 'black and minority ethnic' refers to all people in the UK who self-identify as being in a group other than White British heritage. These include people of Irish heritage, those of mixed parentage where one parent is White and another from predominantly non-white countries. Other groups include Black, Pakistani, Gypsy Traveller, and Mixed Black African. The Pupil Level Annual School Census (PLASC) uses 18 named categories.
- *English as an Additional Language (EAL)* refers to the teaching of English to speakers of other languages. Current statistics indicate that significant numbers of pupils in maintained schools are learning English as a second, third, or indeed fourth, language (Arnot *et al.* 2014).

The terms and concepts that are used to describe society's diversity are relevant in our schools as they are micro reflections of local communities (Corbett *et al.* 1998; Ryan 1999). In many cities the minority ethnic school population is greater than 30 per cent (for example, London, Birmingham, Leicester, Leeds, Manchester). In other areas such as Cumbria, Norwich and Plymouth the minority ethnic school population is less than 6 per cent. Regardless of the setting, the support needs of minority ethnic pupils must be met (Knowles and Ridley 2006). At some point in their careers, the majority of teachers and teaching assistants across Britain are likely to work with minority ethnic pupils. This then makes the case outlined by Cambridge University researchers of the importance of 'improving teachers' general knowledge about countries of origin (e.g. geographical, economic, social, educational, key words) through teacher education and specialist local courses relevant to the school community' (Arnot et al. 2014: 14).

Minority ethnic attainment characteristics

The key purpose of schooling is to ensure that all children make maximum progress and achieve their full potential. This may suggest that the need for targeting and focussing on specific groups has become unnecessary, particularly when schools are being encouraged to focus on the needs of the whole child, using a personalised approach. I would argue that ethnic experiences are an integral part of individual pupils and that it impacts to varying degrees on how they view their environment. More importantly, they react to the way teachers and other adults in school interact with them on a range of levels including verbal, non-verbal, active and inactive. Some educators talk about not 'seeing' colour; others see cultures and social class as barriers to BME pupils achieving. These views are often manifested in the way teachers interact with BME pupils in the classroom and wider school community.

There are high achievers in all minority ethnic groups, with Chinese and Indian pupils generally out performing all groups at all Key Stages. In my experience, high achieving pupils regularly cite supportive teachers, parents or other significant adults, including mentors. They tell of people inspiring them and believing they would achieve and also describe wanting to attain a particular goal. Some talk about overcoming adversity and defying teachers and other adults who told them they would not achieve. Successful BME children and young people usually have an understanding of the academic challenges, are aspirational and have their pastoral needs met by school and at home. They are also often part of a supportive community of self-sufficient, informed and engaged, high-achieving young people. It is important to note that education outcomes for different BME groups vary significantly across local authorities.

Since ethnicity data became more readily available throughout schools, it has highlighted the reality of BME pupils' progression and outcomes in maintained schools: while some minority ethnic groups are out performing their White counterparts, pupils of Caribbean, Pakistani, Bangladeshi and Travellers and other heritages are significantly under-performing. The availability of ethnicity data nationally shows that regional and local outcomes vary significantly. For example, Caribbean pupils do well in a few cities at GCSE, while in others their progress is slow throughout secondary schooling. However, the topical attainment debate since 2008 has been on White working class boys' progress in secondary schools compared with minority ethnic pupils' progress. This reflects the complex interconnectedness of issues of attainment and progression when comparing and reviewing groups by either class or ethnicity. Pupils starting from a very low base can make above average progress without reaching average attainment. For a number of BME groups this is the case.

English as an additional language

'English as an Additional Language' is the expression used in the UK to refer to the teaching of English to speakers of other languages. Current statistics indicate that one in six primary school pupils and one in eight secondary pupils in maintained schools are learning English as a second, third, or indeed fourth, language, in addition to the language spoken within their families and homes. There are more than a million children between 5 and 16 years old in UK schools who speak in excess of 360 languages between them in addition to English (NALDIC 2014). In some ethnic groups, the majority of pupils are registered as EAL pupils: over 90 per cent of Bangladeshi and Pakistani pupils are registered as EAL, 82 per cent of Indian, 75 per cent of Chinese and 65 per cent of Black African. This compares with less than 2 per cent of White pupils and less than 7 per cent of Black Caribbean pupils.

The objectives of teachers are to help EAL pupils beyond being able to communicate fluently in English and to help them acquire sound academic language as appropriate to their curriculum levels. As with all learners, pupils learning EAL should be encouraged to become increasingly independent in their learning. If a pupil appears fluent in social English it is still important to plan carefully for language development so that the pupil can manage the literacy demands of curriculum subjects. Bearing this in mind, English language teaching (ELT) is vital to an inclusive curriculum: it is essential that teachers in schools with a high percentage of bilingual pupils develop their ELT skills and utilise the number of existing specialist roles to support EAL, such as Specialist Language Support Teachers, Bilingual Teaching Assistants, Higher Level Teaching Assistants and EAL Coordinators.

National Curriculum Statutory Guidance (DfE 2014a: 9) proposes that:

> Teachers must also take account of the needs of pupils whose first language is not English. Monitoring of progress should take account of the pupil's age, length of time in this country, previous educational experience and ability in other languages.

For teachers, the challenge is to identify how their individual actions and continued professional development can be shaped to impact positively on individuals and groups in their classroom, particularly those from minority ethnic communities that are learning English as an additional language.

Targeted Intervention and ethnic diversity

Targeted Intervention puts children and their needs first. All children should be supported to make good progress and no child should be left behind. This means close attention is paid to learners' knowledge, skills, understanding and attitudes. Learning is connected to what pupils already know (including from outside the classroom).

The Canadian example forwarded by Hébert and Hartley (2006: 498) is that change will occur through societies shaped by moral and socio-economic influences. They consider that 'these sociological and historical perspectives are important in relation to the personalisation [targeted] agenda. What counts is not fixed but highly bound by cultural and historical factors'. Therefore, educators are called upon to see beyond broad social representations of children and young people so as to support their strengths, legitimacy, diversity and vitality.

In 2014, the Pupil Premium resources provided schools and teaching staff with the opportunity to be creative in responding to the needs of disadvantaged groups that were underperforming, some of whom were from minority ethnic communities. School leaders are now required to monitor and evaluate the impact of their Pupil Premium spending on narrowing the gap between these pupils and their peers. This is monitored by Ofsted judgement, whose judgement of good now requires schools to demonstrate that 'Pupils and particular groups of pupils have highly positive educational experiences at school that ensure that they are well prepared for the next stage in their education, training or employment' (Carpenter *et al.* 2013: 101).

Targeted Intervention begins with the teacher and his or her aspirations for individual pupils. Gary Howard, in his book *We Can't Teach What we Don't Know* (1999), suggests that teachers need to know themselves very well in order to take on 'knowing' others in an open and respectful way. He advocates teachers spending time getting to know the backgrounds of children they are teaching. When we explore ethnic diversity we are mostly talking about people with origins in significantly different lifestyles and cultural experiences from us. Research shows that as significant adults in the classroom, teachers rarely do explore who they are, how they came to believe the things they take for granted and use to inform their assumptions, intuitions and decisions.

The curriculum and ethnic diversity

In reviewing the changes to the National Curriculum and Initial Teacher Training, researchers identified that Government policies, training institutions and school leaderships, provide little support to teachers grappling with the structures of schooling, and its effects on reproducing and widening racialised, gendered, social class-based inequalities (Hill 2007; Gillborn 2010; Smith 2012). Sir Keith Ajegbo (2007) identified that schools, through their ethos, through their curriculum and through their work with their communities, can make a difference to the way children and young people experience learning. However he, like others, identified persistent barriers:

- Not all school leaders have bought in fully to the imperative of education for diversity for all schools and its priority is too low to be effective.
- There is insufficient clarity about the flexibility within the curriculum and how links for diversity can be made.
- Some teachers lack confidence in engaging with diversity issues and lack the training opportunities to improve in this area.
- The notion of racial hierarchies has not altogether disappeared and stereotypes still abound in society.

While citizenship is now limited in the curriculum to secondary age pupils we must consider how we impart 'Fundamental British Values' and 'British Identity' (DfE 2014b). The lived identity/ies and community experiences of children and young people cannot be left at the school gate each morning.

The importance of getting our approaches right is not new, however, often when I raise with head teachers the prospect of taking a targeted approach to impact positively on BME teaching and learning, I am challenged and directed to 'quality first teaching'. As new teachers, high quality teaching must be your priority, and 'yes' in an ideal world all pupils in lessons delivered to a 'quality first' standard would benefit. The reality, however, is different. We can see that the curriculum impacts differently on individual pupils. We are also aware that their characteristics vary and our need to connect as teachers. The result is that, with all the allowances for deprivation and socio economic standing, certain groups benefit less than their peers (Strand 2008). The schools self-evaluation form (SEF) coupled with the Ofsted framework for inspection of maintained schools are key drivers in helping us to think about how the curriculum is meeting the needs of groups of children. This is supported by other researchers who have also drawn attention to the low average achievement and deteriorating position through secondary school of low-income boys from Black Caribbean, Black African and Pakistani backgrounds (Cassen and Kingdon 2007; Strand and Demie 2007; National Equality Panel 2010).

Quality first teaching must respond to the makeup of the classroom and be aware of pupils' learning preferences and what works well for our children. The curriculum is now viewed as flexible and dynamic enough for teachers to bring in cultures, textures and histories from the local, national and international perspectives. The National Curriculum inclusion statement outlines how teachers can modify, as necessary, the programme/content of lessons to provide all pupils with relevant and appropriately challenging work at each key stage. It sets out three principles that are essential to developing a more inclusive curriculum by:

- setting suitable learning challenges;
- responding to diverse learning needs and overcoming potential barriers to learning;
- assessment for individuals and groups of children.

Taking positive action to identify role models that reflect the diversity of your city and choosing people that are relevant can inspire children and young people. When developing an inclusive curriculum it is really important to make choices that reflect the pupils' own experiences, where they can see something of their identity and culture reflected in what they are being taught. It is equally important to give key roles in activities (for example, in drama, the director, narrator, main character, could be pupils who are not necessarily in the highest literacy groups) in order to develop their self-esteem. Further examples of this could include:

- 'culture and identity' incorporated into geographical teaching and learning. These can be incorporated into studies that cover the full range and content, supporting the diverse 'Curriculum Opportunities' and 'Key Processes' of the new Geography Programme of Study;
- mathematics taught as a universal human language, used in different cultures and societies;
- African and Asian number systems explored (including historical references), such as the Islamic contribution to mathematics in Europe;
- all tasks, materials and activities reflect the multi-ethnic nature of modern societies.

Conclusion

The teaching profession must have the capacity to reflect the full spectrum of cultural and social traditions and systems in their collective professional practice. Each individual teacher brings to her or his work a set of cultural norms and expectations. Good teachers are self-critically aware of this, but none of us can recognise all the culturally and socially determined mores that we carry. However, the teaching profession as a whole should be able to match and respond to the range of cultural and social varieties that our society contains. In today's globalised information rich societies the wide range of cultures, customs, languages, faiths and beliefs are easily accessible and acquirable.

Current research indicates that many pre-service teachers are not prepared well to work with a rapidly changing student population that includes an increasing number of immigrant students with limited proficiency in English (Janzen 2008; Latta and Chan 2011). With the changing demography of the pupil population in our schools it is vital that all staff in schools feel confident about working in a culturally and ethnically diverse school environment. The classroom must be an inclusive environment, where difference does not displace or undermine each individual's sense of self. Significant adults within the classroom have a duty to ensure equality of opportunity and outcome for all pupils, regardless of race, gender, ethnicity, ability or sexual orientation.

Knowing what we bring to the classroom helps us to shape pupils' experiences. The debate today is not limited to individual or institutional racism: through critical race theory, it is more focussed on one's level of self-awareness and our ability to take ownership and responsibility for our day-to-day engagement with our environment (Delgado and Stefancic 2001). This should lead to us never making assumptions, instead treating each student first and foremost as an individual and personalising our response to maximise their progress and outcomes. Pupils who are enthusiastic and engaged with and through the curriculum are more likely to become confident, independent learners who are able to articulate what they are learning.

Given the growing opportunities for teachers to engage with increasing numbers of minority ethnic groups of pupils, their training and continuing professional development must include greater emphasis on what can be done to maximise the outcome for minority ethnic children and young people in the school environment. Targeted Intervention provides a greater opportunity for teachers to get to know individual children. There are extended networks available to them in the local community and nationally, that can be called on for support.

It's important to acknowledge that there is an ongoing debate about where underachievement is most significant and where responses such as Pupil Premium and Closing the Gap should be targeted. Amongst the drivers of this discussion are the National College for Teaching and Leadership and the Department for Education. They believe that by focussing on socio-economic issues as represented through the free school meals data, all relevant groups are captured (National Equality Panel 2010). However, Targeted Intervention allows for a much broader focus on young people operating 'under the radar' or 'coasting' and through this, high achievers with cultural support needs can be more actively engaged in the classroom and beyond.

The Targeted Intervention agenda is very much about how we contribute individually to collective networks that will help individual children stay safe, enjoy, achieve and maximise their life chances. Working with pupils from diverse backgrounds is about taking a holistic approach to pupils, an approach that regards them as multi-faceted and complex individuals. It is about recognising the fact of 'hidden' or not visible 'identities' amongst pupils. It is also about exploring your own assumptions and attitudes, and recognising and working with the assumptions and attitudes of others within the classroom.

There are many opportunities now available to teachers to review learning, undertake small research projects within their classrooms and acquire the knowledge and experiences necessary to meet the needs of BME children and young people coming into the classroom. We need to engage with these opportunities to provide an education that is targeted to make a difference to young people's outcomes and lives.

Reflection on values and practice

1   Reflect on successfully targeted interventions. How does listening, empathy, monitoring beyond raw data, design of a dynamic curriculum help provide an inclusive setting?

2 Often we achieve success with children through building an effective rapport and just getting on well with them. Reflect on what helps you to make such relationships with children of diverse backgrounds.
3 What would it mean to challenge yourself to overcome any barriers to building good relationships with, and enhancing teaching and learning for, minority ethnic students?
4 Take time to find out about the ethnic and cultural diversity of your school's pupil and staff population, particularly, how it is changing over time (3–5 years) and analyse how planning in classrooms and across subject areas are meeting new and emerging needs.

Suggested further reading

Commission for Equality and Human Rights: www.cehr.org.uk

Runnymede Trust: www.runnymedetrust.org/projects/education/resourcesForSchools. html

Teachernet English as an Additional Language: www.teachernet.gov.uk/teachingand learning/library/EALteaching/

NALDIC (the National Association for Language Development in the Curriculum) provides information and resources, and campaigns for greater recognition of the role of English language teaching in the UK: http://www.naldic.org.uk/research-and-information.

References

Arnot, M., Schneider, C., Evans, M., Yongcan Liu, Y., Welply, O. and Davies-Tutt, D. (2014) *School Approaches to the Education of EAL Students*, University of Cambridge: Bell Foundation.

Ajegbo, K. (2007) *Diversity and Citizenship Curriculum Review*, Nottingham: DfES.

Carpenter, H., Papps, I., Bragg, J., Dyson, A. Harris, D., Kerr, K., Todd, L., and Laing, K. (2013) *Evaluation of Pupil Premium: Research Report*. Manchester: DfE.

Cassen, R. and Kingdon, G. (2007) *Tackling Low Educational Achievement*, York: Joseph Rowntree Foundation.

Corbett, N.L., Kilgore, K.L., and Sindelar, P.T. (1998) Making sense of a collaborative teacher education program, *Teacher Education and Special Education*, 21(4): 293–305.

Delgado, R. and Stefancic, J. (2001) *Critical Race Theory: an introduction*. New York and London: New York University Press.

DfE (2013) *National Statistic: workforce in England: November 2012*, London: Department for Education.

DfE (2014a) *National Curriculum in England: framework for Key Stages 1 to 4*, London: Department of Education.

DfE (2014b) *Promoting Fundamental British Values as Part of SMSC in Schools*, London: Department for Education.

DfE (2015) *National Statistic: Schools, Pupils, and their Characteristics January 14*, London: Department for Education.

Fredrickson, N. and Cline, T. (2002) *Special Educational Needs, Inclusion and Diversity*, Buckingham: Open University Press.

Gillborn, D. (2010) The White working class, racism and respectability: Victims, degenerates and interest-convergence, *British Journal of Educational Studies*, 58(1): 3–25.

Hébert, Y. and Hartley, W. J. (2006) Personalised learning and changing conceptions of childhood and youth, *Canadian Journal of Education*, 29(2): 497–520.

Hill, D. (2007) Critical teacher education, New Labour, and the global project of neoliberal capital. *Policy Futures in Education* 5(2): 204–25.

Howard, G. (1999) *We Can't Teach What We Don't Know – White teachers, multicultural schools*, New York: Teachers College Press.

Janzen, J. (2008) Teaching English language learners in the content areas. *Review of Educational Research*, 78(4): 1010–1038.

Kausar, R. (2011) *Identifying Social and Economic Push and Pull Factors for Migration to the UK by Bulgarian and Romanian Nationals*, London: DCLG Publications.

Kendall, S., Straw, S., Jones, M., Springate, I. and Grayson, H. (2008) *Narrowing the Gap for Vulnerable Groups. A review of the research evidence*, Slough: NFER.

Kitchen, M. (1996) *The British Empire and Commonwealth: a short history*, Basingstoke: Macmillan.

Knowles, E. and Ridley, W. (2006) *Another Spanner in the Works – challenging prejudice and racism in mainly White schools*, Stoke-on-Trent: Trentham Books.

Latta, M. M., and Chan, E. (2011) *Teaching the Arts to Engage English Language Learners*, Abingdon: Routledge.

NALDIC (2014) National audit of English as an additional language training and development provision. Available at www.naldic.org.uk/resources.

National Equality Panel. (2010) *An Anatomy of Economic Inequality in the UK*. Government Equalities Office. Available online at: ww.equalities.gov.uk/pdf/NEP%20 Report%20bookmarkedfinal.pdf. Statistical annex available online at: www.equalities. gov.

Office for National Statistics, 2011 Census: Aggregate data (England and Wales) [computer file]. UK Data Service Census Support. Downloaded from: http://infuse.mimas.ac.uk.

Peach, C. (ed.) (1996) *Ethnicity in the 1991 Census: Volume Two: the ethnic minority populations of Great Britain*, London: HMSO.

Phinney, J. S. (1990) Ethnic identity in adolescents and adults: review of research, *Psychological Bulletin*, 108(3): 499–514.

Ryan, J. (1999) *Race and Ethnicity in Multi-ethnic Schools*, North York, Canada: Multilingual Matters Ltd.

Smith, H. J. (2012) A critique of the teaching standards in England (1984–2012): discourses of equality and maintaining the status quo, *Journal of Education Policy*, DOI: 10.1080/02680939.2012.742931.

Strand, S. and Demie, F. (2007) Pupil mobility, attainment and progress at secondary school, *Educational Studies*, 33(3): 313–331.

Strand, S. (2008) *Minority Ethnic Pupils in the Longitudinal Study of Young People in England. DfES Research Report RR-002*, London: Department for Children, Families and Schools.

Chapter 7

Invisibility and Otherness

Asylum-seeking and refugee students in the classroom

Mano Candappa

This chapter is about asylum-seeking and refugee[1] children and their experiences in British schools. The refugee experience makes these children resilient, but they are among the most marginalised in our society and the Other among their peers. Paradoxically, these students are often 'invisible' within schools yet they desperately need the school's support to help them get on with their lives. The challenge for schools is how best to support them whilst not taking agency away from them: I argue that the inclusive school is the most supportive environment for asylum-seeking and refugee students. I use the term 'inclusive' to mean including the child with his/her own culture and values in the school, within a culture that celebrates diversity (Corbett 1999; Armstrong 2008). In this model the school adapts to respond to the needs of its students, as against the integrationist model where the student has to fit into the school. It is the right of asylum-seeking and refugee children to be supported to enjoy their right to education under the UN Convention on the Rights of the Child.

Background

A sharp rise in asylum applications in the UK since the 1990s[2] led to perceptions in many quarters of an 'asylum crisis', with applications reaching a peak of 84,130 (excluding dependents) in 2002. This number decreased to 25,710 in 2005 and to under 18,000 in 2010, before rising each subsequent year to reach 23,507 in 2013 (excluding dependents) (Blinder 23.07.2014). However, wars in Syria, Iraq and Somalia today continue to drive people from their home countries to seek asylum in Britain amongst other European countries; many, including families with children, undertake hazardous journeys in overcrowded boats to reach the safety of Europe, many losing their lives in the attempt (The Guardian, 02.06.2014).

The presence of refugees in Britain has attracted aggressive and hostile public attention, making it a politically sensitive issue and giving rise to five major parliamentary Acts since 1990. These saw a progressive reduction in financial and material assistance to people seeking asylum, and their marginalization from mainstream support services. Key among these was the 1999 Asylum and Immigration Act, which witnessed the compulsory dispersal of adults and families seeking asylum away from traditional areas of settlement in London and south-east England to predominantly White areas, mainly in northern England, Scotland, and the Midlands. Many asylum-seeking families were housed in areas where accommodation was available, in many cases in socially and economically deprived areas. Many schools in dispersal areas had little experience of multi-ethnic communities, and were ill-prepared for receiving children with English as an additional language and for diverse religious traditions. Today, people seeking asylum can apply to the Home Office for accommodation and subsistence but they have to accept an offer of accommodation in a 'dispersal' area, which will be outside London and the South East (Refugee Council 2015).

Whilst the UK has a long history of providing asylum and refuge, in the past this had mainly been for White populations, such as Jews facing persecution and dissidents from former Soviet-bloc countries. Today's asylum-seeking and refugee communities by contrast largely originate from Asia, the Middle East and Africa, reflecting countries currently experiencing political conflict. These are more visible populations, bringing with them different languages, religions, customs and traditions, and their presence has significantly increased the UK's Black and minority ethnic (BME) population.[3] It is estimated that refugees represented close to 5 per cent of all international migrants in the UK during 2010 (Vargas-Silva 2011).

Their highly visible presence and aspects of 'difference' that single them out as the Other[4] have been factors in the politics of 'race' being heavily implicated in the country's response to asylum-seeking and refugee communities. They are pathologised in political and media discourses, associated with criminal activity, a drain on the nation's resources, and even with terrorism. The challenge for schools is how to address these negative images and encourage students to celebrate the diversity these students' presence brings.

Rights of the Child[5]

Asylum-seeking and refugee children, as children, are protected under the UN Convention on the Rights of the Child (UNCRC) to which the UK is a signatory.[6] Whilst they are entitled to the same rights as other children, as children seeking refugee status or considered refugees they are given additional protection under Article 22, which states that they should receive 'appropriate protection and humanitarian assistance' in the enjoyment of Convention rights.

The UNCRC gives children protection, provision and participation rights based on four 'general principles': the *right to life*, including the development of the child 'to the maximum extent possible'; the *best interests of the child*; *respecting the views of the child*; and that *no child should suffer discrimination*, stipulating equality of rights for *all* children (Hammarberg 1995). Specific articles *inter alia* give children the right to education: Article 28 recognises the child's right to education on the basis of equal opportunity; Article 29 states among other things that the child's education shall be directed to the 'development of the child's personality, talents and mental and physical abilities to their fullest potential'. Under Article 19 schools need to take appropriate action to protect children from all forms of violence (which includes bullying). Asylum-seeking and refugee children are therefore entitled to a learning environment where their abilities can be nurtured and developed to their fullest without fear of being subjected to violence. These rights are all the more precious to them because the school as a universalist service might be the only statutory agency from which they derive support (Candappa and Egharevba 2000), and as Elbedour *et al.* (1993:812) indicate, for many children 'the school serves as a second security base outside the home, or perhaps their only security base'.

Under the Children Act 2004 the Children's Commissioner oversees the interests of children in relation to (a) physical and mental health and emotional well-being; (b) protection from harm and neglect; (c) education, training and recreation; (d) the contribution made by them to society; and (e) social and economic well-being. The Act also places a duty on local authorities to promote co-operation between agencies to improve children's well-being, and a duty for key agencies (including education departments and schools) to safeguard and protect the welfare of children.

Given their rights under the UNCRC and the provisions of the Children Acts it might be expected that asylum-seeking and refugee children's educational needs can be supported to achieve their full potential, but as we shall see, various factors operate to make this goal more challenging. But let us first consider what these children have had to endure, using evidence from the author's research.

The child as refugee

Many asylum-seeking and refugee children have had extraordinary childhoods (see Candappa and Egharevba 2000; Stanley 2002; Chase *et al.* 2008; Taylor and Sidhu 2012). Children's accounts, such as those of Sheik[7] (a Somali boy from the minority Brava community, aged 10) and Bazi (another Somali Brava boy, aged 11) below, tell of violence, courage, loss and endurance:

Sheik

> I was playing outside when somebody [thugs] came and tell me, 'Go and knock at your neighbours' door and speak Bravanese. Tell them to open the door or I am going to shoot you'. And then I went to knock. (They told me 'Go and knock at that door' because they can't speak my language.) I said, 'Don't open it, there are some robbers here'. And they [thugs] thought that I said, 'Open the door'. They didn't open the door. And I say [to the thugs], 'They don't want to open it.'
>
> The robbers say, 'Tell those people to open it'. And I say to my neighbours, 'Don't open the door because they are still here. They kill people'. They [thugs] say to me, 'You lie to us'. They hit me with a gun! The gun never had any bullets, they just use it to hit my legs. Now I've a problem with my legs.

Bazi

One day we leave by boat . . . but the boat broken in the middle of Somalia and Kenya and some of our family fell in the water and drowned – our cousin. And we just prayed to God, and God pushed us through the sea to the land. . . . It was very deep in the middle of the sea. . . . It was night and everybody was praying. The boat was slowly going down to the sand, until it got to the sand. In the sand there was nobody and one day we slept on the sand. And another day, we were scared, some people came . . . by small boats and they came to collect us and they took us to their island. We was very hungry that day. They gave us food . . . And then we stayed for week . . . After two weeks, some people say that our family sent small ship from Mombasa to that small island . . . and they took us and then we got to Kenya . . .

(Candappa and Egharevba, 2002: 158)

Other asylum-seeking and refugee children have lived through dangers and trauma of war, persecution, or periods in refugee camps; some have been at the mercy of unscrupulous agents, some have fled alone, some have had to support emotionally absent parents. Their resilience is remarkable.

Once they reach a safe country such as the UK these children's troubles are far from over. Starting a new life as an 'asylum-seeker' is hard. They face dismal poverty living on state benefits that since 1999 have been equivalent to 70 per cent of income support, and since 2002 their parents do not have the right to work while their claim is under consideration. Additional to the poverty of their existence is the insecurity of not knowing if their claim for asylum will be successful. Families have to get on with re-building their lives in the new country not knowing whether the next day, the next week, the next month, or some day in the future they will be asked to leave, putting them under great emotional stress with implications for their physical and mental health and general well-being.

Families who have been dispersed to predominantly White areas can feel even more vulnerable and unsafe because of their visibility among the local, often hostile population. Here a 10-year-old boy and a 10-year-old girl living in a new dispersal area in Scotland talk of their fears and worries:

We live in a bad neighbourhood and there are a lot of bad young people hanging around. We are not allowed to go out without supervision. We only go out with my dad. (translation)

There's no homework club in school – we are allowed to use help at the library, but it is too far. I can't stay because of drunks around. They shout, come and talk with you – I feel scared. . .

(Candappa et al. 2007: 25)

Their visibility makes asylum-seeking children particularly vulnerable to racism. The oppression and powerlessness this causes are here captured in the testimony of an unaccompanied minor youth:

> They call me [racist] names . . . I do not respond. Sometimes I feel no freedom
> because people abusing us.
>
> (Candappa *et al.*, 2007: 27)

As Arshad *et al.* (1999: 16) pointed out, to be abused in a country where one had
sought refuge from abuse seems 'a double injustice and particularly cruel'.

'Invisible' students and visible Otherness

Asylum-seeking and refugee children are often 'invisible' in schools[8] (Arshad *et al.*
1999; Pinson *et al.* 2010). Students are not required to reveal immigration status
to the school, and schools, unless officially provided this information, usually do
not see it as their business to be involved with immigration issues. In multicultural
schools therefore asylum-seeking and refugee students could blend in with the
school population; in more monocultural areas their ethnicity would make them
visible. In either school setting they might come to the attention of the average
teacher only as a new arrival, a bilingual learner, or a migrant child new to the
British education system. Sometimes, after trust has been established some
students or their parents might tell their stories to a sympathetic teacher, but they
might also choose not to talk about their experiences to anyone at the school.
Research suggests that teachers who work most closely with asylum-seeking and
refugee students respect this silence and the student's choice if and when to
disclose their experiences (Pinson *et al.* 2010). However, at times trying to cope
with memories and effects of past traumas as well as the stresses of their new life
might manifest in unruly or disruptive behaviours in the school. Kasim's account
(a Somali boy who arrived in Britain as an unaccompanied minor) demonstrates
the types of behaviour that have sometimes been misinterpreted because teachers
have not been sensitised to the experiences and needs of refugee students:

> I come to this country in 1994 [and] . . . I was a bit upset because of my
> Mum. I didn't see her . . . for seven years . . .
>   Still worried about my Mum. Can't do my homework . . . can't do nothing
> because I'm worried. When I walk [down] the street, I think about my Mum.
> Sometimes I cry, you know that? . . . Last week at school I was thinking about
> my Mum and I was crying in my head. And one boy hit my head. I was so
> angry I got him back. That's how I almost get expelled.
>
> (Candappa 2002: 232)

Too often their silence and invisibility or stereotyping have led to asylum-seeking
and refugee students being penalised rather than provided the supports they need
(Candappa 2002).
   The decision not to disclose their refugee experiences is sometimes a coping
strategy, a way of putting the past behind and getting on with their lives. More
often asylum-seeking and refugee students are aware, from the press and media,
from community experiences and from playground talk of negative images of

'asylum-seekers' and refugees, and for self-preservation, they do not wish to reveal their pasts (Pinson *et al.* 2010). Christopoulou *et al.* (2004) suggest that silence is one of the mechanisms these young people use to handle trauma, exclusion and discrimination in their present lives. But even through this silence their peers can still identify them as the Other – the outsider, whose lack of competency in English, lack of understanding of local youth cultures and modes of dress makes their Otherness visible and excludes them from membership of the peer group until they have negotiated this painful rite of passage (Candappa and Egharevba 2002; Pinson *et al.* 2010). This often takes the form of general low-level bullying and harassment directed at all newcomers (Pinson *et al.* 2010), but for an anxious asylum-seeking or refugee student such behaviour could be experienced as hostility, non-acceptance and exclusion. If they are non-English speakers these students are highly visible and particularly vulnerable, as the accounts of Rathika and Serpil, two refugee girls, demonstrate:

> That first day, they don't sit with us . . . They don't talk to us, no-one. My sister and me were just talking our language. (. . .) There was one girl, she taking us to the coat room where we had to leave our coats. (. . .) She said, like, 'You can't talk English'. (. . .) She was like . . . kicking us.
> (Candappa 2002:231)

> I had two Turkish friends, but not that close. Sometimes they helped me but most of the time they didn't. (. . .) When they translated anything, I think they were, like, embarrassed . . . They were embarrassed that other kids will say, 'Oh, don't talk to that girl, she doesn't speak English'. . .
> (Candappa and Egharevba 2002:165)

It is significant that in both cases the girls were rejected by students from their own culture, those they and the school might have expected to help them. Whilst it reveals the low status of non-English speakers within peer cultures, it also points to complexities within peer group relations that impact on developing and sustaining an inclusive school ethos.

Building inclusivity

Under the UNCRC and British law, as we have seen, asylum-seeking and refugee children have a right to an education where they can flourish and develop to their fullest potential, and under Convention rights they should be protected and supported in the enjoyment of this right. Four other pieces of legislation, the *Race Relations Amendment Act 2000*, the *Education Act 2002*, *Education and Inspections Act 2006*, and the *Equality Act 2010* place a related statutory duty upon schools,[9] and together the Convention and these Acts carry the message of respecting difference and of inclusion.

The inclusive message has special resonance for asylum-seeking and refugee children. For them the trauma of war, forced migration and loss, together with anxieties of trying to settle in a new country could affect their ability to enjoy their right to education. Children from families seeking asylum have the added worry and uncertainty of awaiting a decision on their asylum claim. If their claim is unsuccessful families have to return to their home country; sometimes they are forcibly removed from their homes in dawn raids. If this were to happen to someone in their community other families fear their turn, and this could affect the children. Mary Campbell, a teacher in a dispersal area in Scotland (interviewed for Candappa *et al.* 2007) here describes the trauma for her school when a family is removed:

> Those periods when families are sent back are very difficult for us in trying to support the children. The children are very apprehensive about what lies ahead, and it manifests itself in school, their progress becomes slightly retarded on occasions . . . You can find behaviour difficulties, emotional difficulties.
>
> (Pinson *et al.* 2010:283)

The added protection UNCRC Article 22 bestows is therefore an entitle-ment asylum-seeking and refugee students often badly need. And the school can play a pivotal role in helping re-build their lives: a restoration of normality and order through schooling can in itself act as a healing agent (Bolloten and Spafford 1998).

The most supportive environment for asylum-seeking and refugee children is a school that respects its students as individuals and tries to empathise with their experiences and needs and responds to these, showing a willingness to put themselves 'in someone else's shoes' – in other words an inclusive school. For asylum-seeking and refugee students this would mean not just seeking to respond to immediate needs, but to situate these needs in the context of their previous experiences. But these students can be 'invisible' in classrooms, so the question how to support invisible students might seem contradictory. But if a school were to provide a safe environment that seeks to address the needs of all students, identifying individual needs without resorting to stereotypes and assumptions, then many of the needs of asylum-seeking and refugee students too would be met. Indeed, as Arshad *et al.*'s (1999: 20) research indicates being inclusive means 'not being picked out as different or special, even in positive ways'. It means feeling included in the normal learning environment of a caring school.

To sustain its ethos the inclusive school will need to develop specific structures and practices. These could include a celebration of diversity and difference; exploration and debate around social justice and humanitarian issues within the curriculum; and robust equal opportunities, anti-racist and anti-bullying policies which are rigorously implemented. It could also involve seeking ways of including parents of ASR students within the school community.[10] Specific curricular and pastoral supports that could be responsive to the needs of asylum-seeking and refugee students, even without disclosure would also need to be developed. Key among these is support for language and accessing the curriculum, fostering friendships, and supporting emotional needs.

Language and curricular supports

While some asylum-seeking and refugee children may have enjoyed uninterrupted education, the war situations in their home countries could mean that many have had little formal schooling or that their education had been disrupted. Some could find UK schools significantly different from schools in the home country in terms of pedagogic practice and discipline, for others the school they join in the UK might be the first they have attended. Research suggests that young people's early school experiences in this country are central to how well and how quickly they adjust to their new lives. Many require help in schools for an extended time thereafter.

Acquiring competence in English is a key factor in asylum-seeking and refugee students' new lives, crucial both for accessing the curriculum and for developing self-confidence and aiding social interaction (Candappa and Egharevba 2000). Many asylum-seeking and refugee students are new to English on joining school in the UK and in some education authorities intensive language support is provided at the outset, with English language acquisition seen as a basic survival need (Candappa *et al.* 2007). Many schools provide English training in separate classes or with special support in mainstream classes, and the question of the relative merits of withdrawal as against mainstreaming are often debated. It has been suggested that withdrawal allows the teacher to give individual attention to the student, who could work at his/her own pace. However, the 'social turn' in second language acquisition theory (Block 2007) challenges this argument and suggests that language learning and meaning making are products of social contexts and interactions. Moreover, withdrawal could be stigmatising and inhibit building friendships with the wider peer group. Indeed, parents in Candappa *et al.*'s (2007) study queried whether if withdrawal was seen as necessary it could be done in a way that did not suggest a student's difficulties with language are synonymous with academic failure. Below are two possible approaches to effectively support asylum-seeking and refugee students' language needs without the need for withdrawal:

School A: dispersal area, Scotland

School A had been asked by the education authority to place students from asylum-seeking families on class registers, though in reality they would work in a bilingual unit providing students with intensive English language support. The school had been multi-ethnic prior to dispersal, and found this approach contrary to its usual way of working, as the head teacher explained:

> . . . we very quickly moved away from that and began to refine our thinking – we asked, what can children do that the class was doing, e.g., expressive art, environmental studies, behind that maths, then language. We've got to get teachers and children to seek ways around that. And we also began to get peer support . . .

Now . . . we work on a completely different basis . . . the two refugee support teachers with the EAL[11] teachers work in classrooms across the school, mainly at language times. Teachers work with groups of children, which include asylum-seekers and refugees, local bilingual and monolingual pupils . . . We feel that all children benefit from this . . .

We had a debate within the school about 'withdrawal' . . . for limited times in corners . . . With joint planning with the class teacher and the support teacher . . ., where the support teacher takes the group becomes irrelevant.

(Candappa *et al.* 2007:41)

School B: London borough

School B is located in a borough that has a long tradition of providing for the needs of a diverse student community, with a non-White population well above the UK average. The EAL Co-ordinator outlined the approach to inclusion within the classroom:

We have admissions day every Monday afternoon. . . very rarely a week passes when we didn't have a new child. . . Children move straightaway into [mainstream] classes . . . Assessment is carried out within the first two weeks of admission – short and sharp sessions are found to work better. . .

(*ibid.*: 2007:41)

In these two models any stigma that could attach to withdrawal is absent, and children spend class time with their peers, in a situation that is more conducive to forming friendships and socialising.

Pastoral care and fostering friendships

As we have seen, the experiences of many asylum-seeking and refugee students are certainly extraordinary, especially when compared with normative notions of childhood in the UK. Whilst these young people's strength and resilience through such experiences should be valued, it is important for schools and teachers to remember that they may also carry scars from these experiences and could need sensitive pastoral care to support their rehabilitation. Many examples of compassionate support provided to asylum-seeking and refugee students can be found within inclusive schools, such as teachers going out of their way to provide academic and cultural support underpinned by a deep level of care, and keeping watch over them at a very personal level (Pinson *et al.* 2010). The best supports are directed to the needs of the whole child, offering students the chance to gain confidence, self-esteem and a sense of agency in taking control of their future world, such as reported by Lena, a Year 11 girl from Nigeria:

The Learning Support staff's brilliant, they're really helpful . . . taught me to be more independent than always get help . . . They kind of like, when they give you work, they make you try and do it without asking for help all the time. Like, so you can depend more on yourself than other people to help you all the time.

(Pinson et al. 2010:205)

Most inclusive schools also recognise the importance of friendships in children's lives and have schemes such as 'buddying' or 'class friends' to ease new students into the life of the school, and various clubs and extra-curricular activities to encourage socialising, sometimes leading to lasting friendships. However, a tension can exist between an inclusionary school ethos and exclusionary practices within peer cultures towards newcomers, as research has shown (Candappa and Egharevba 2002; Pinson et al. 2010). A challenge for schools is how to educate students to learn how to cope and befriend strangers, to reduce xenophobia and racial prejudice whilst encouraging compassion for those who have suffered persecution. The Citizenship Education curriculum might afford teachers an opportunity to confront these issues and to develop appropriate materials, topics and activities to link refugee issues to the promotion of democracy, social justice and human rights.

Reflections on values and practices

I have contended in this chapter that the inclusive school is the most supportive for the needs of asylum-seeking and refugee students. But the continued development of academies and free schools that function as independent state-funded schools separate from the mainstream sector raises concerns about their implications for inclusive education and this already marginalised group. The market values and competitive ethos that drives them seem at odds with the inclusive ideal, and asylum-seeking and refugee students are then seemingly left with choices rejected by those who do have a choice. However, these students' right to education under the UNCRC continues, as does schools' statutory responsibilities. In these circumstances, I would urge with Cruddas (Runnymede 2010) that we re-open a debate on how to 'move from a competitive system to a collaborative one, reconnecting teaching with pedagogy. . .'.

New teachers might consider:

- Are issues of asylum and refuge given adequate place in the curriculum, and how can teachers foster compassion for the suffering of others among students?
- How can teachers' pedagogical practice support asylum-seeking and refugee children effectively without the need for disclosure?

Suggested further reading

Pinson, H., Arnot, M., and Candappa, M. (2010) Education, Asylum and the 'Non-Citizen' Child: the politics of compassion and belonging, London: PalgraveMacmillan.

Rutter, J. (2006) *Refugee Children in the UK*, Buckingham: Open University Press.
Closs, A., Stead, J., and Arshad, R. (2001) The education of asylum-seeker and refugee children, *Multicultural Teaching*, 20(1):29–33.

Resources

Bolloten, B. (ed.) (2004) *Home from Home: a guidance and resource pack for the welcome and inclusion of refugee children and families in school*, www.savethechildren.org.uk/scuk/jsp/resources/details.
Rutter, J. (2003) *Supporting Refugee Children in the 21st Century – a compendium of essential information*, www.trentham-books.co.uk.
Rutter, J. and Candappa, M. (1998) *'Why do they have to fight?' Refugee Children's Stories from Bosnia, Kurdistan, Somalia and Sri Lanka*, London: Refugee Council.

Notes

1 Asylum seeker: A person who has left their country of origin and formally applied for asylum in another country but whose application has not yet been concluded. Refugee: In the UK, a person is officially a refugee when they have their claim for asylum accepted by the government [within the definition of the 1951 UN Convention]. (www.refugeecouncil.org.uk/policy_research/the_truth.htm accessed 07.06.15)
2 This reflects a growth in numbers of refugees worldwide, linked to the end of cold war politics plus ethnic conflicts in many parts of the world towards the end of the twentieth century.
3 At the 2011 census the BME population stood at 14.1 per cent of the total in England and Wales, increasing from 7.9 per cent in 2001. In comparison to 2001 where this population was found clustered mainly in metropolitan areas, the 2011 census found more BME people living across the UK, including in the countryside and villages.
4 Otherness is defined by difference, marked by outward signs like 'race', and often associated with marginalized people living outside the dominant social group (Onbelet 2010).
5 Refugee and asylum-seeking children are protected by a number of international, European and British legal instruments, including the European Convention on Human Rights and the UK Human Rights Act 1998. However, the most comprehensive children's rights instrument is the UNCRC, which is reflected in the Children Acts 1989 and 2004, and which I discuss here.
6 In September 2008 the UK government withdrew the discriminatory reservation on immigration it had entered when ratifying the UNCRC whereby it reserved the right to apply legislation as it deemed necessary in relation to entry into, staying in, and departure from the UK and to the acquisition and possession of citizenship. Asylum-seeking and refugee children are now entitled to the same rights under the UNCRC as other children in the UK.
7 Pseudonyms have been used for research participants throughout this chapter.
8 There are no accurate demographic data on the number of asylum-seeking and refugee children in UK schools, and known cases might be less than total numbers present. Rutter's estimate was that there were at least 60,000 ASR children of compulsory school age residing in the UK in 2006.
9 Under the *Race Relations Amendment Act 2000*, a duty is placed on schools to eliminate racial discrimination and to promote equality of opportunity and good relations between people of different groups; under section 78 of the *Education Act 2002* the curriculum for all maintained schools should promote the spiritual, moral,

cultural, mental and physical development of pupils at the school and of society; the *Education and Inspections Act 2006* places a duty on schools to promote community cohesion; and under 'The Equality Duty' in the *Equality Act 2010*, maintained schools, as public authorities, have a duty to eliminate discrimination, advance equality of opportunity, and foster good relations between people who share a protected characteristic and those who do not.

10 Possible initiatives for supporting parents can be found in Ofsted (2003).

11 English as an Additional Language.

References

Armstrong, F. (2008) Inclusive education. In Richards, G., and Armstrong, F., *Key Issues for Teaching Assistants: working in diverse and inclusive classrooms*, Abingdon and New York: Routledge, pp.7–18.

Arshad, R., Closs, A., and Stead, J. (1999) *Doing Our Best: Scottish school education, refugee pupils and parents – a strategy for social inclusion*, Edinburgh: CERES.

Blinder, S. (2014, 23/07) Migration to the UK: Asylum. *Briefing*. Oxford: COMPAS, University of Oxford, www.migrationbriefing.ox.ac.uk/sites/files/migobs/Briefing.

Block, D. (2007) *The Social Turn in Second Language Acquisition*, Edinburgh Textbooks in Applied Linguistics, Edinburgh: Edinburgh University Press.

Bolloten, B., and Spafford, T. (1998) Supporting refugee children in East London primary schools. In Rutter, J. and Jones, C. (eds.), *Refugee Education: mapping the field*, Stoke-on-Trent: Trentham Books, pp.107–124.

Candappa, M. (2002) Human rights and refugee children in the UK. In Franklin, B. (ed.), *The New Handbook of Children's Rights: comparative policy and practice*, London: Routledge.

Candappa, M., Ahmad, M., Balata, B., Dekhinet, R., and Gocmen, D. (2007) *Education and Schooling for Asylum-Seeking and Refugee Students in Scotland: an exploratory study*, Scottish Government Social Research 2007, Edinburgh: Scottish Government.

Candappa, M., and Egharevba, I. (2000) 'Extraordinary Childhoods': the social lives of refugee children, *Children 5–16 Research Briefing* No. 5, Swindon: ESRC.

Candappa, M., and Egharevba, I. (2002) Negotiating boundaries: tensions within home and school life for refugee children. In Edwards, R. (ed.), *Children, Home and School*, London: RoutledgeFalmer, pp.155–171.

Chase, E., Knight, A., and Statham, J. (2008) *The Emotional Well-Being of Unaccompanied Young People Seeking Asylum in the UK*, London: BAAF.

Christopoulou, N., Rydin, I., Buckingham, D., and de Block, L. (2004) *Children's Social Relations in Peer Groups: inclusion, exclusion and friendship*, The European Commission: CHICAM.

Corbett, J. (1999) Inclusive education and school culture, *International Journal of Inclusive Education*, 3(1): 53–61.

Elbedour, S., ten Bensel, R., and Bastien, D.T. (1993) Ecological integrated model of children of war: individual and social psychology, *Child Abuse & Neglect*, 17: 805–819.

Hammarberg, T. (1995) Preface. In B. Franklin (ed.), *The Handbook of Children's Rights: comparative policy and practice*, London: Routledge, pp. ix–xiii.

Pinson, H., Arnot, M., and Candappa, M. (2010) *Education, Asylum and the 'Non-Citizen' Child: the politics of compassion and belonging*, London: PalgraveMacmillan.

Ofsted (2003) *The Education of Asylum-seeker Pupils*, London: Ofsted Publications Centre.

Onbelet, L. (2010) *Imagining the Other: the use of narrative as an empowering practice*, www.mcmaster.ca/mjtm/3-1d.htm.

Refugee Council (2015, March) 'Asylum support', *Refugee Council Information*, www.refugeecouncil.org.uk. Accessed 20 April 15.

Runnymede (2010) Vox Pop, *Runnymede Bulletin*, Issue 361, Spring: 30.

Rutter, J. (2006) *Refugee Children in the UK*, Buckingham: Open University Press.

Stanley, K. (2002) *Cold Comfort: the lottery of care for young separated refugees in England*, London: Save the Children.

Taylor, S., and Sidhu, R.K. (2012) Supporting refugee students in schools: what constitutes inclusive education?, *International Journal of Inclusive Education*, 16:1, 39–56.

The Guardian (2.6.2014) Europe faces 'colossal humanitarian catastrophe' of refugees dying at sea, www.theguardian.com/world/2014/jun/02/europe-refugee-crisis. Accessed 07 June 2015.

Vargas-Silva, C. (2011) Global international migrant stock: the UK in international comparison, *Migration Observatory Briefing, COMPAS*, University of Oxford, UK, March2011.http://www.Migrationobservatory.Ox.Ac.Uk/sites/files/migobs/briefing%20-%20global%20international%20migrant%20stock.Pdf.

Chapter 8

I feel confident about teaching, but 'SEN' scares me

Moving from anxiety to confidence

Gill Richards

Introduction

> At the end of the third year I was confident about teaching but SEN scared me.

These words, spoken by a student teacher nearing the end of her course reflect the concerns of many new teachers. Indeed, they may also reflect the views of more experienced teachers as they respond to national developments and the challenges of inclusive education. As mainstream schools increasingly include numbers of pupils identified as having special educational needs or disabilities (SEND), what is being done to increase teachers' confidence and skills?

Initial teacher education (ITE) programmes follow a national curriculum linked to regulated standards for the award of qualified teacher status. These standards were originally influenced by a national strategy 'Removing Barriers to Achievement' (DfES 2004), which held the expectation that all teachers would teach children identified as having special educational needs. These standards have been further influenced by the Children and Families Act 2014 and the associated Code of Practice in 2015. ITE programmes are now expected to: stretch and challenge pupils of all backgrounds and abilities; understand the needs of pupils identified with SEND and remove barriers to achievement; deploy differentiation, formative and summative feedback to support pupil progress; and manage behaviour effectively (HEA 2012). So, does this make a difference?

Evidence, including that from Government agencies, seems to imply that more still needs to be done. The Office for Standards in Education (Ofsted) report, 'How well new teachers are prepared to teach pupils with learning difficulties and/or disabilities' (2008: 5), identified variable experience within ITE programmes, a heavy reliance on schools to provide most of the training on special educational needs and a weakness in monitoring this. As a result, many new teachers had completed their programmes lacking confidence and feeling unprepared for teaching children seen as having *additional* or *special* learning needs. Similar evidence can be found in later studies and reports (Norwich and Nash 2010; Carter 2015; Mintz *et al.* 2015), suggesting the need for a different approach to this part of the ITE curriculum so that all new teachers can approach their classes confidently.

What are *special* educational needs?

The concept of special educational needs came from the Warnock Report (DES 1978), replacing categories previously used from the 1944 Education Act to classify children with labels such as 'maladjusted', 'delicate' and 'educationally subnormal'. With this new concept came the role of the special educational needs co-ordinator – the SENCO – who became the lead teacher in supporting children identified with special educational needs through the formal 'statementing' process. From this, a team of professionals grew to support this work; educational psychologists were required for assessing special educational needs, teaching assistants to support identified pupils and trainers started to offer focused staff development courses – arguably creating a 'Special Needs Industry'.

Subsequent legislation, policy, reports and initiatives embedded the concept of special educational needs and focused on developing teachers' practice (Special Educational Needs and Disability Act 2001; DfES 2004; House of Commons 2006; Children and Families Act 2014; DfE 2015). Although over time, government agencies' terminology changed variously to include special needs and disabilities, disabled children, learning difficulties and disabilities, the group of children given these labels remained those originally highlighted by Warnock and set out in the 1996 Education Act, i.e. those who have a learning difficulty that calls for some kind of special educational provision to be made (Education Act 1996, Section 312). This deceptively simple definition may be the cornerstone of conflicting perspectives about pupils seen as 'special' and subsequent expectations of teachers.

When one group of learners is perceived as special, it implies that they are different from other 'ordinary' pupils. This can translate into teachers expecting *special* provision to be made through additional resources and *special* skills needed to deliver these, a view further compounded by other terminology commonly heard in schools, which describes such pupils as having *additional* needs. The danger of this is clear: if 'special' children are conceptualised as needing a specialised education, how then will 'ordinary' teachers see their duty towards them? Dividing pupils in this way may lead teachers to question whether they feel competent enough to meet some children's needs and whether someone else such as a teaching assistant, or somewhere else such as a special school, could do this better. Even more confident teachers may balk at what they see as *extra* demands being made on them.

So, special educational needs, a label that was originally intended to move away from negative categorisation in the past, now raises further issues for teachers to consider. Hall's (1997) early challenging perspective of a 'Special Land' to which pupils with special educational needs may be consigned after rejection from mainstream activities, draws attention to some of the complexities found within school provision. He asks us to reflect on the actual words 'special' and 'needs' and the effect of the concepts implicit within them. He reminds us that 'special' is something usually wanted by society, for example 'special offers' or special events, but within the educational context a *special* need is not one to which pupils generally aspire, instead it is often seen by teachers as a euphemism for 'problem'. Similarly, he contests the word 'need', suggesting that this implies 'neediness' and a 'want' rather than a learning *requirement* which implies a right to schools providing for this. It is interesting to note that this perspective still resonates with much of our current terminology and practice.

Other concerns about labelling were identified in the House of Commons Special Educational Needs report (2006: 16). This described the separation of learners with and without special educational needs as fundamentally flawed, arguing that children do not fit into neat categories but exist on a broad continuum of needs, which are often influenced by social disadvantage. It suggests that as many conditions that pupils have may be 'syndromes' with different characteristics, or linked with other impairments and issues, 'diagnosis' becomes complex. Within this context, the report suggests that the use of simplistic categories can lead to false classifications and intervention strategies that do not address individuals' unique learning requirements. This has now become more complex as terminology has changed with the Children and Families Act (2014) to 'special educational needs or disabilities' (SEND). This newly created label brings 'disabilities' into the terminology and discussions within schools, without acknowledgement of the disability rights debate on medical and social models of disability, i.e. whether 'disability' is synonymous with someone's condition or a barrier created by society.

Further concerns were highlighted in later studies showing that teachers' expectations of pupils can differ in relation to the labels allocated to them (Rix *et al.* 2004; Thomas and Vaughan 2004; Ainscow 2007; Wearmouth 2009; and Freeman 2013) who reflect on the power of labels in creating teachers' perceptions and subsequent behaviour towards children. Linked to this are issues of professionals' use of power that enables them to impose particular identities (and labels) upon pupils and make subjective decisions on definitions of 'normal' or 'ordinary' (Frederickson and Cline 2009), thereby separating groups of learners within schools. This also can result in an 'over-identification' of 'special educational needs' rather than focusing on the quality of teaching: Ofsted (2010) comments on specifically this, stating that the term 'SEN' is used far too widely and that many young people with these labels have no different needs to most other pupils, but are victims of teaching that is not good enough and low expectations.

Although this consideration of language and labels may seem overstated, the impact on teachers' thinking cannot be underestimated. School staffroom discussions about pupils described as 'the SENs' and SENCOs still seen as totally responsible for 'SEN pupils' are not uncommon, and serve to distance teachers from some children. The special educational needs label also identifies the problem as being located within the child, that they have the learning difficulty and so own the problem. This does not encourage consideration of other contextual issues such as teaching styles, classroom structures and access to appropriate resources. All this can reinforce an uncritical acceptance that *special* children need to go to *special* places for a *special* education.

Moving beyond a label

So, if we look beyond 'special educational needs' towards an inclusive education system that values diversity, where does that leave us? Clearly, there are pupils who have conditions and impairments that affect the way they learn, so teachers need to become familiar with these to ensure their teaching is effective. However, from my experience, whilst there are benefits in attending courses and reading about specific conditions, a focus on individual children and how they learn in *your* classroom is much more helpful.

It has been argued that a label is needed to ensure that the right teaching strategies and resources are provided (Lauchlan and Boyle 2007), but we might like to consider why this is thought to be the case and even question the validity of such claims. Even as early as 2002, the Audit Commission criticised statutory assessment and statementing procedures that identified learners' special educational needs and created labels as 'a costly, bureaucratic and unresponsive process . . . which may add little value in helping meet a child's needs' (2002:14–17). Similar criticisms have continued to be expressed since (British Psychological Society 2005; Ofsted 2006), creating a context of 'highly contentious' and 'confusing' language (Ofsted 2010: 8) and a 'convenient label for underprivileged pupils, sentencing the most vulnerable children to a lifetime of failure' (Maddern 2012). So, how can we move beyond a reliance on labels? How do we create a situation where teachers' judgements are valued and access is routinely provided to required resources? How can teachers feel confident in their own ability to design learning activities from which *all* pupils can benefit?

I would like to suggest that although there will always be children whose learning requirements are outside of our experience and for whom we will need to seek advice from others, maintaining a focus on the process of learning is particularly helpful. Accepting that *all* pupils' participation in tasks is affected by the demands of different classroom activities rather than solely some perceived innate ability, could further clarify the teacher's role. If we return to the expectations set out in 'Removing Barriers to Achievement' (DfES 2004) and the 2012 Teachers' Standards – that all teachers are teachers of pupils with special educational needs – then a focus on what and how pupils need to learn becomes more important than a label. This isn't to argue that all pupils should be taught without regard for any specified learning requirements, but rather that designing activities for the diversity found within any classroom becomes integral to teachers' planning. This can help teachers view their class as a community of learners, rather than separated into those with and without special educational needs (or indeed any other perceived difference) for which one activity is organised for most of the class with something separate provided for those seen as 'special'.

The Code of Practice (DfE/DoH 2015) requires schools to have high aspirations for disabled children and develop and manage provision to achieve this. The Equalities Act (2010) also requires increased accessibility of provision, elimination of discrimination and promotion of equality for disabled children. Although schools did respond positively to statutory requirements, much of the early focus was on physical changes to buildings rather than accessibility related to attitudes and classroom management. This could be considered an interesting response by schools, for changes to buildings can be financially costly, whereas changes to behaviour may involve a more personal 'cost'. Perhaps this reflects some underlying concerns. Could it be that despite a growing acceptance of barriers to learning not being located 'within the child' and recognition of the impact of social contexts, acceptance of the role of individual teachers in creating and breaking down barriers is more challenging to address?

So, what is being done to prepare new teachers for the diversity they face within their classrooms and what can be done to increase their confidence and professional skills further?

Preparing for a community of learners

Over the last 40 years, there have been many developments in special and inclusive education. The concept of 'integration' as introduced by Warnock (DES 1978) intimated that pupils should be *assimilated* into mainstream classrooms. Later, this view was challenged by the 'social model of disability', inspired by disabled people who argued that it was schools and teachers that should change to accommodate the true diversity of learners. The focus then became centred on the barriers to learning constructed by school environments rather than a child's individual condition or impairment and whether s/he could fit into a mainstream school environment. Alongside this, national policy and legislation developed, producing key initiatives such as the Special Educational Needs and Disability Act (2001), 'Removing Barriers to Achievement' (2004), the Disability Discrimination Act (2005), the Inclusion Development Programme (2008–11) and National SEN Scholarships (2010–2015) to fund teachers' and teaching assistants' additional training.

During all of these developments, Initial Teacher Education struggled to keep pace, with student teachers receiving information of variable quality (Hodkinson 2009; Carter 2015), leading many to feel that they lacked confidence and were unprepared for teaching children with special educational needs, despite being mainly satisfied with the theoretical knowledge they had received (Ofsted 2008). Concern was also expressed by tutors who suggested that the increasing focus on meeting specific standards to achieve Qualified Teacher Status (QTS), encouraged student teachers and ITE providers to adopt a 'technician approach' (Pearson 2007), concentrating on auditable skills rather than underpinning pedagogical issues (Hodkinson 2009). This concern was picked up in the Carter Review of Initial Teacher Training (2015) where he acknowledged that it was challenging to address SEND within teacher training courses but recommended that the curriculum should provide all trainees with SEND practical experience and prepare them to be resilient teachers who role-modelled good practice. This reflected recommendations from earlier studies that identified the importance of a core curriculum that focused on professional values about inclusion and accepted that while it wasn't possible to prepare trainees for every context they would meet, this should not mean that they lacked the right abilities, knowledge and skills (Moran 2009; Florian and Linklater 2010).

Early developments in ITE occurred when the Government introduced new resource materials for tutors and their students and 'specialised placements' in special schools or resourced units. Funding was made available for ITE tutors to pilot these initiatives and conduct small-scale research projects so that feedback could be used to further inform teacher education programmes.

Feedback on trainee teachers' experiences of these pilot initiatives was positive. My own university was involved with a research project focusing on the 'specialised placement'. Two cohorts were provided with different experiences to compare the impact on their professional development. Both cohorts undertook the placement in addition to their ITE programme, so it was voluntary and not assessed. The first cohort was given a two-week placement in a special school, followed by a two-week placement in a mainstream school that was recognised as having excellent practice in inclusive education. The intention of this pilot was for student teachers to reflect on transferability of knowledge and skills from special school to mainstream settings. The second cohort was given a two-week placement in either a special *or* a mainstream school and provided with additional resources about inclusive practice. Both cohorts were set the same activities to complete, including a focus on children's own voice about their experiences and social inclusion. They were asked to reflect on their learning from the experience and how they had applied this to their professional practice.

The students from both cohorts universally commended the opportunity to take part in a 'specialised placement'. They stated that it had significantly increased their skills and confidence, with one commenting that,

> Knowing what I do now, and feeling as confident as I do now, will undoubtedly make me a much more informed and inclusive teacher. People I know on the BA course have the same 'awkwardness' as I felt before about special needs, but because they haven't done these placements, they will probably still feel like that when they begin teaching their own class.

Some spoke of their initial anxieties, for example,

> It was a very new experience for me and at the start I was anxious and thought 'I can't do it'. But my confidence grew and I saw how to make adaptations and that it only had to be small things.

And,

> It's about confidence – I could talk and communicate better . . .. Now if I see a child struggling I have the confidence to adapt the teaching or change the resource, looking at what they were doing instead of just working with the better ones to push them on.

When describing the effect the placement had on their professional development, students from both cohorts identified similar key learning experiences from working with teachers skilled in inclusive education:

You can't identify children with SEN by looks or behaviour. You have to get to know children.

I really enjoyed my placement. Very positive outlook on the part of the staff, they didn't make a 'big deal' out of a child's learning difficulty. They didn't tend to label children. All the children benefited from the strategies put in place for SEN.

One student teacher powerfully described how the placement had changed her:

The placement has really changed me as a teacher. It has afforded me the confidence to work, teach and plan with children who have complex needs, alongside giving me more confidence when teaching all children. I am now more imaginative with my planning and willing to take risks with both my planning and teaching . . . it has prepared me for a life of teaching, where anything could happen.

Where the two cohorts did differ was in relation to the way that they spoke about the children. Whilst the language of both groups of student teachers still suggested that the concept of special educational needs as a separate group was already deeply ingrained, those who had experienced 'excellent' practice of inclusion indicated a growing awareness of issues of labelling and separating some learners from their peers. This led them to question the need for special schools or why teaching assistants withdrew children from classes and why ability grouping was so popular, when they had seen alternatives work so successfully. They started to think about their own practice and the impact this had on pupils' learning. In comparison, student teachers that had only experienced a special school placement did not question the impact of labels or whether pupils could have been alternatively accommodated in a mainstream school.

Whatever the length or setting of the placement, both cohorts concluded that all student teachers should have this experience. To return to the student teacher's comment at the start of this chapter, the reason for this is clear:

At the end of the third year I was confident about teaching but SEN scared me. Without the experience of the placement I would have been thinking, 'How will I cope with my own class and SEN?' Now I am more confident and think why should a child suffer whilst a teacher learns what to do . . . I can now see that SEN is an integral part of teaching.

Some also argued strongly that the placement should not be assessed because this allowed them to experiment without any feeling of 'failure'. As one student stated,

On a voluntary placement I felt that I could make mistakes and ask questions when I wasn't feeling confident, without people judging me. It was like being in the first year again and that was good.

These experiences raise some important questions for tutors and student teachers: the success, or otherwise, for individual new teachers may well depend on the quality of the practice they are exposed to and what the tutors themselves bring to the delivery of this part of the ITE curriculum. The reality for many ITE programmes is that there may not be large enough numbers of schools with 'excellent' inclusive practice in which to place all student teachers, so if their only placement is in special schools or they do not have access to excellent inclusive role models, this may reinforce the whole notion of pupils identified as having special educational needs needing special education. In addition, there may not be enough tutors experienced in, and committed to, inclusion available to deliver taught components on courses. This may create an over-dependence on 'off-the-shelf' resources like the Government's 'SEN and/or Disabilities Training Toolkit', raising the issue of tutor confidence in dealing with more challenging considerations such as those of personal values and attitudes, and teachers' roles in affecting the inclusion and exclusion of children.

So, despite these developments within ITE, the route to providing a high quality experience about SEND available to all student teachers is far less clear. This leaves new teachers still in a situation where many feel anxious about working with children identified as having special educational needs, seeing them as a separate group of learners. Moving from this perspective to a confident acceptance of individual learners bringing valued diversity into the classroom is a key challenge for teachers' development.

Professional responsibilities for all learners

For this final section I would like to return to my suggestion of classrooms having a 'community of learners'. In such a community, individuality is recognised and teaching is planned to take account of this as a core part of planning rather than an 'add-on' for different groups of (labelled) children. Awareness of learners' individual diversity is important. With increasing pressure on schools to 'Close the [achievement] Gap' between disadvantaged young people and their peers (Ofsted 2013), the focus has moved onto a range of labelled 'vulnerable' children. What is rarely addressed, is any intersectionality between these groups. In a real community of learners, the multiple barriers experienced by some young people whose personal circumstances intersect, reinforce and exacerbate each other are recognised and taken account of by teachers to ensure their inclusion (Rollock and Gillborn 2011; Mereish 2012; Thiara and Hague 2013). This raises a range of issues for teachers to consider that may provide a useful starting point for you to consider:

- What are the experiences and personal circumstances of the children in your class? Might these create multiple barriers to learning?
- Does any label given to children influence or adversely affect how they are taught? What happens if a child could have more than one label applied – what takes priority and is this beneficial for the *child*?

- How do staff share their knowledge and experiences of vulnerable children to provide a 360° view that enables all needs can be met?

These questions suggest that pupils have different experiences, based on a range of external factors. Whilst teachers may not be able to do anything about some of these, they can certainly affect change in relation to inaccessible environments and unwelcoming attitudes. From my experience, people often focus only on expensive adaptations like ramps and lifts when 'inaccessible' environments are discussed, when often really small things can make a significant difference. This is where a 'can-do' flexible attitude is important, linked to a willingness to learn from others. Seeking support from colleagues should be seen as a strength; effective teams are built on interdependence, where skills and knowledge are shared. Parents that I work with particularly mention that it is the welcome their child receives and the teacher's willingness to learn about him/her as an individual that is the most important factor for successful inclusion. This is something that all teachers can achieve.

Teachers can also ensure that pupils who have been identified as having special educational needs still receive equitable amounts of their time, rather than expecting a TA to replace this. This would help to avoid situations where learners become separated from their peers through well-intended support structures, leaving them socially and educationally isolated (Blatchford *et al.* 2012). A further way to support school-wide development includes teachers examining the way that policies and practices contribute to the inclusion or otherwise of particular learners. Many schools have, for example, a 'Special Needs Policy', but how are these learners accounted for within other school policies? Teachers may increase their confidence through taking up staff development opportunities. Whilst this may involve useful 'strategies and tips' for teaching, these alone may not bring about the 'attitudinal shift' that comes from reflecting on personal values and challenging ideological positions.

Understanding differing perspectives, particularly those of people who have experienced living with labels imposed upon them, can provide teachers with a strong professional foundation for the way in which they view and respond to all learners. Listening to a range of people's views helps teachers to make balanced judgements about how they work with learners. It can be tempting to only listen to those seen as 'experts' rather than others such as parents and the children themselves, but all have a valuable contribution to make so that you receive the whole picture. Clearly there is much to be gained from the experience of your SENCO and external advisers, but an over-dependence on 'specialists' can make you feel deskilled (Alliance for Inclusive Education 2009). Much advice that is offered relies on good teaching and learning techniques, which could be practised by *all teachers*.

Within this wider picture of teaching and learning lie more specific strategies for new teachers to engage with. Mixed ability groupings, balanced groups, peer learning and differentiation are all strategies that work successfully (Cole 2008; Hattie 2009; Higgins *et al.* 2014). Teachers can also benefit from observing each others' practice, team teaching and national initiatives like the Inclusion

Development Programme. Key to all of these is the belief in all children's ability to learn and progress. Cole (2008) and others (Hart *et al.* 2004) refer to this as 'learning without limits'; their challenge to any group being seen as of 'fixed ability' or placed within a 'no hope' category centres on the belief that teachers are fundamental in transforming pupils' learning capacity.

Conclusion

The Lamb Inquiry Report (2009) focused on securing accountability within schools for the quality of the learning experience provided to pupils identified with having special educational needs and this was extended by Ofsted (2014; 2015). Teachers' responsibility within this is clear; they state that pupils with SEND do best when they are taught by good teachers who have high aspirations for them, just as they have for all other pupils. Support to achieve these aspirations must be organised in a way that enables every pupil to have a high quality learning experience. For teachers committed to inclusive education, this will involve a *shared* learning experience, rather than one where different groups identified by one of their characteristics spend significant time away from the rest of the class.

Teachers' attitudes towards diversity within their classrooms will be a key component in setting the context for the quality of pupils' learning experiences. How they think about individual learners and the way that they engage with them will be important. Teachers are role models: children observe closely how their teachers treat other children and note the language they use. References to the 'SEN group' and problematising changes needed to facilitate particular children can be quickly picked up and replicated by pupils. A welcoming attitude and commitment to solving difficulties encountered can become a positive whole-class ethos.

Many of us become anxious when faced with new situations for which we feel unskilled, but if we focus on how these link to situations in which we do feel confident, then solutions are more easily identified. This does not mean that we ignore individual differences, just that we do not get sidetracked on the many labels children are given within our education system. If we focus on teaching and learning, then this is what teachers are trained for and should continue to develop skills in, throughout their career. New teachers will take time to learn the skills that will enable them to work confidently with all learners in their classrooms. Removing labels from the context in which they work will enable them to focus on what is important, the learners themselves.

Reflection on values and practice

Think about the children that you know have been identified as having special educational needs.

1   What has been written about them and said about them by others? How much of this presents a positive perspective and how much seems negative? What impact has this had on your own views?

2   What is their classroom experience? Do they receive a similar amount of time with teachers as that given to other pupils? Do they routinely work *with* their peers or does their support system replace this?

3   How much do you know about their lives? What 'intersectional' experiences do they have that may result in multiple barriers that affect their behaviour and learning?

4   How can you explicitly demonstrate a commitment to valuing diversity in your classroom? What welcome do you give to learners?

Suggested further reading

Mason, M. (2005 2nd edition) *Incurably Human*, London: Working Press.

Inclusion Now (Journal of Alliance for Inclusive Education) www.allfie.org.uk. The website also has a wide range of other free resources.

The Sutton Trust Education Endowment Foundation Teaching and Learning Toolkit www.suttontrust.com.

Wearmouth, J. (2009) *A Beginning Teacher's Guide to Special Educational Needs*, Maidenhead: Open University Press.

References

Ainscow, M. (2007) Taking an inclusive turn, *Journal of Research in Special Educational Needs*, 7(1):3–7.

Alliance for Inclusive Education (2009) *Inclusion Now*, vol. 22.

Audit Commission (2002) *Policy Focus Statutory Assessment and Statements of SEN: in need of a review?*, London: Audit Commission Publications.

Blatchford, P., Russell, A. and Webster, R. (2012) *Reassessing the Impact of Teaching Assistants. How research challenges practice and policy*, Abingdon: Routledge.

British Psychological Society (2005) Submission to House of Commons Select Committee Inquiry (5.4: 4).

Carter, A. (2015) Carter Review of Initial Teacher Training (ITT), Manchester: DfE.

Cole, M. (2008) Learning without limits: a Marxist assessment, *Policy Futures in Education*, 6(4), 453–463.

DES (1978) *Special Educational Needs. Report of the Committee of Enquiry into the Education of Handicapped Children and Young People*, London: HMSO.

DfE/DoH (2015) *Special Educational Needs and Disability Code of Practice: 0 to 25 years*, Manchester: Department for Education.

DfES (2004) *Removing Barriers to Achievement: the government's strategy for SEN*, Nottingham: DfES.

Florian, L. and Linklater, H. (2010) Preparing teachers for inclusive education: using inclusive pedagogy to enhance teaching and learning for all, *Cambridge Journal of Education*, 40(4):369–386.

Frederickson, N. and Cline, T. (2009) *Special Educational Needs, Inclusion and Diversity*, Maidenhead: Open University Press.

Freeman, G. (2013) Classroom practice: why labels are a dead end, not a short cut, *Times Educational Supplement Magazine* 01/11/2013.

Hall, J. (1997) *Social Devaluation and Special Education. The right to full mainstream inclusion and an honest statement*, London: Jessica Kingsley.

Hart, S., Dixon, A., Drummond, M.J. and McIntyre, D. (2004) *Learning without Limits*, Maidenhead: Open University Press.

Hattie, D. (2009) *Visible Learning. A synthesis of over 800 meta-analyses relating to achievement*, Abingdon: Routledge.

Higher Education Academy (HEA) (2012) *Working with the Teachers' Standards in Initial Teacher Education*, York: HEA.

Higgins, S., Katsipataki, M., Kokotkasi, D., Coleman, R., Major, L.E. and Coe, R. (2014) *The Sutton Trust Education Endowment Foundation Teaching and Learning Toolkit*, London: Education Endowment Foundation.

Hodkinson, A. (2009) Pre-service teacher training and special educational needs in England 1970–2008: is government learning the lessons of the past or is it experiencing a groundhog day?, *European Journal of Special Needs Education*, 24(3):277–289.

House of Commons (2006) *Special Educational Needs. Third report of sessions 2005–6.* Vol.1., London: The Stationery Office.

Lamb, B. (2009) *Special Educational Needs and Parental Confidence*, Nottingham: DCSF Publications.

Lauchlan, F. and Boyle, C. (2007) Is the use of labels in special education helpful? *Support for Learning*, 22:36–42.

Maddern, K. (2012) SENtenced to failure? *Times Educational Supplement Magazine*, 04/05/2012.

Mereish, E. (2012) The intersectional invisibility of race and disability studies: an exploratory study of health and discrimination facing Asian Americans with disabilities, *Ethnicity and Inequality in Health and Social Care*, 5(2): 52–60.

Mintz, J., Mulholland, M. and Peacey, N. (2015) *Towards a New Reality for Teacher Education for SEND. DfE SEND in ITT project report and roadmap for SEND*, London: UCL Institute of Education.

Moran, A. (2009) Can a competence or standards model facilitate an inclusive approach to teacher education? *International Journal of Inclusive Education*, 13(1): 45–61.

Norwich, B. and Nash, T. (2010) Preparing teachers to teach children with special educational needs and disabilities: The significance of a national PGCE development and evaluation project for inclusive teacher education, *Journal of Research in Special Educational Needs*, 11(2): 2–11.

Ofsted (2006) *Inclusion: does it matter where pupils are taught?*, London: HMSO.

Ofsted (2008) *How Well New Teachers are Prepared to Teach Pupils with Learning Difficulties and/or Disabilities*, London: HMSO.

Ofsted (2010) *The Special Educational Needs and Disability Review. A statement is not enough*, Manchester: Ofsted.

Ofsted (2013) *Unseen children; access and achievement 20 years on*, Manchester: Ofsted.

Ofsted (2014) *Schools. The Report of her Majesty's Chief Inspector of Education, Children's Services and Skills, 2013–14*, Manchester: Ofsted.

Ofsted (2015) *The Framework for School Inspection*. Online: available at www.ofsted. gov.uk/resources/120100. Accessed 16 April 2015.

Pearson, S. (2007) Exploring inclusive education: early steps for prospective secondary school teachers, *British Journal of Special Education*, 34(1): 25–32.

Rix, J., Sheehy, K., Simmons, K. and Nind, M. (2004) *Starting Out*, Milton Keynes: Open University Press.

Rollock, N. and Gillborn, D. (2011) *Critical Race Theory (CRT), British Educational Research Association online resource.* Available at www.bera.ac.uk/researchers-resources/publications. Accessed 18 February 15.

Thiara, R. and Hague, G. (2013) Disabled women and domestic violence: increased risk but fewer services. In Roulstone, A. and Mason-Bish, H. (eds.) *Disability, Hate Crime and Violence*, Abingdon: Routledge, pp.106–117.

Thomas, G. and Vaughan, M. (2004) *Inclusive Education. Readings and reflections*, Maidenhead: Open University Press.

Wearmouth, J. (2009) *A Beginning Teacher's Guide to Special Educational Needs*, Maidenhead: Open University Press.

Chapter 9

Challenging students, challenging settings

Jackie Scruton

Introduction

The purpose of this chapter is to help you understand and explore some of the complex issues surrounding challenging situations and behaviour that you may experience in your classroom. In doing so, it aims to help you develop effective classroom behaviour management strategies, which in turn will help you to extend your inclusive pedagogy.

The behaviour of students in a range of settings seems to be a topic that is constantly discussed by the media. It is often the extreme behaviours such as violence and aggression that the media report and it is these that *'capture the attention of the public'* (Hart 2010:353) and I suggest help to demonise some of our children and young people. This is not a new phenomenon; in 1996 the Ridings School hit the national headlines and more recently programmes such as *Educating Yorkshire* (2013) gave viewers a 'snapshot' of the state of behaviour in classrooms. As far back as the Elton report (1989) it was recognised, 'bad behaviour on schools is a complex problem which does not lend itself to simple solutions' (Elton 1989:25).

And more recently Charlie Taylor, the government's expert advisor on behaviour in schools, also articulated that managing a class effectively was both complex and essential if the children and young people were to feel safe, happy and as a result demonstrate good behaviour (Taylor 2011a). The link between managing behaviour and achievement is one that has long been recognised (Elliott *et al.* 2001; Hattie 2009; O'Neill 2011; Taylor 2012) and the experience and ability of teachers to manage the classroom is the key factor in enabling children and young people to access the learning and teaching on offer.

So, what can you do to meet such a challenge and help foster improved behaviour? This chapter will explore the historical perspectives, together with examining the latest debates and research. It will move on to identify some of the current strategies that can be used to help you develop your inclusive classroom practice. It will also suggest ways that you can reflect on your practice and in so doing compile a set of 'tips' for yourself. A key way of achieving an inclusive classroom is to ensure that you are developing an inclusive pedagogical approach.

Taylor (2011a) suggested that children are more likely to 'push boundaries' if schools do not have a 'simple' approach to managing challenging behaviour and in doing so recognise the importance of consistently applying that approach. I believe it is worth remembering Elton's (1989) suggestion that 'reducing bad behaviour' was realistic, but eliminating it completely was not. This seems to me to be as pertinent today as it was then. At the end of this chapter I hope that you will feel more confident in your own skills and abilities in order to provide a learning environment that fosters positive behaviour and learning.

What do we mean by 'challenging' students?

Trying to define this term can be problematic for a number of reasons, some of which will be explored later. However, it is worth noting that what one teacher would deem to be challenging behaviour, another would not. A few years ago I was teaching a group of adult learners, all of whom worked in educational settings. I asked each member of the group to make a list of behaviours that they found most difficult to work with. As an example I indicated that the 'clicking' of pens caused me to become frustrated and indeed created a challenge for how I dealt with the situation. A member of the group said that he found students who sat on desks the most difficult to 'deal' with. At that time I was talking to the group perched on a desk! In subsequent weeks, if I sat on a desk he would 'click' his pen – all in the spirit of humour! It seems to me this anecdote illustrates just how behaviour can be viewed quite differently and may depend on different levels of tolerance and the subjective experience of the teacher. Indeed, Roffey and O'Reirdon (2004) also comment on the fact that it is the 'constant niggles' or low level disruption that cause teachers frustration, rather than the more extreme aggressive or violent behaviours.

Thus, I suggest that defining the term 'challenging' children and indeed challenging behaviour is difficult. Moreover, often in the classroom the two can be seen as interchangeable. Behaviour may be challenging because it prevents the teacher from providing an inclusive learning environment. The challenge may also be for the teacher to alter the ways in which they approach teaching in order to ensure that learning takes place. In doing so, they may have to spend time and energy 'containing' and controlling the class rather than teaching. Particular disruptive behaviour may be aimed at challenging the teaching but could be as a result of other factors such as difficulties with curriculum content, resources and use and understanding of language and vocabulary.

Some behaviour is aimed at disruption and at undermining the authority and control of teachers. Rogers (1990) suggests that this may be a challenge to the teacher's right to exercise 'leadership' in the classroom. In such cases it may be difficult for the teacher to determine the causes of the challenge as these may be very complex. Additionally, in schools today there is an added pressure caused by the need to raise achievement in order to look good in the league tables. So as a result engaging children and young people in learning becomes even more important for you to develop your skills.

A number of definitions identify possible contributory factors to challenging behaviour, including the social and emotional aspects of learning; possible low self esteem; and specific special educational needs such as Attention Hyperactivity Deficit Disorder (ADHD) or Autistic Spectrum Disorder (ASD). In order to further develop our understanding of some of these complexities and to provide an inclusive approach in the classroom we need to explore the two main models of disability; the medical and social models. The medical model has ensured that the 'blame' lies with the child, that there is something wrong with them, that they could be described as dysfunctional or 'ill' and as a result, need to be cured. This model brings with it a particular use of language, which perpetuates the 'blame' approach and may lead to teachers seeking a solution or cure and in doing so may result in exclusionary practices (Parry *et al.* 2010 in Trussler and Robinson 2015), creating the opposite approach to the one I would advocate. The social model, which stems from the disability rights movement, takes a much more inclusive approach, removing the 'blame' from the child to suggesting that it lies with society. It is society that creates barriers that may prevent children from accessing learning opportunities. The use of the social model enables the teacher to explore what factors might create difficulties or lead to exclusion, which is beyond the child's control.

I am advocating a move from a medical model to one where we aim to change the behaviour and not the child; one that has a stronger inclusive approach. Trussler and Robinson (2015) describe this as a Transactional model where the focus is on how the environment may impact on a child's ability to access the learning and teaching. They suggest that there is need to focus on the child's potential and capability in order to remove barriers to learning. In attempting to achieve this, we may also need to examine our own behaviour and we must pay attention to the voice of the child. Increasingly, practitioners across Children's Services are being required to elicit children's views as a fundamental part of their work. This agenda was driven by government through a number of initiatives such as Every Child Matters: Change for Children (2003), the Children Act 2004 and the Children Act 2014. The most recent Act was described by Timpson (2014), the then Children and Families Minister, as key to reforming services and to give every child an 'equal chance' to make the best of themselves (https://www. gov.uk/government.news). Topping and Maloney (2005) and Taylor (2011a) draw on children's experiences where they have indicated a teacher's behaviour affects their own. For example, they argue that if a teacher treats children with respect and has a sense of humour, for example by taking time to meet and greet children at the door of the classroom, then children's commitment would increase. They also suggest that a teacher who praises good work is much more likely to be working with a class of children who are not disruptive and who engage with the learning process. The lesson for us is that our own behaviour is very likely to have an impact on our classes.

Behaviour and learning

How do we ensure that we provide an inclusive classroom that enables all children to access the learning and teaching opportunities? We could start by developing our understanding of the links between behaviour and learning.

Hadyn (2007) and Wallace (2007) suggest that there is an assumption that all children and young people come to school or college wanting to learn. This is, however, not always the case. Hadyn (2007) also suggests that many outside the world of education view learning and behaviour as two entirely separate activities, entertaining the notion that a teacher with a new class will 'sort out' behaviour in the first few weeks. Developing and understanding children's 'learning agendas' (Elliott *et al.* 2001) can be viewed as an important and essential part of a teacher's role in providing an environment that facilitates learning. Steer (2008), Taylor (2011a) and Shepherd and Linn (2015) suggest that the relationship between behaviour and learning is now widely accepted and there is an expectation that schools should not only monitor the impact of this connection, but develop a foundation of positive behaviour development through the proactive use of behaviour policies that help support strong consistent strategies.

A significant approach to managing 'challenging' children is 'Behaviour for Learning'. This theory is based on the idea that a set of three relationships should be in place which will enable the desired outcome of effective and worthwhile learning (Evans *et al.* 2003). These three relationships are:

- child and self;
- child and other;
- child and curriculum.

This theory suggests that when there is balance between the three components, a child will learn and behave appropriately. However, if there is an imbalance, learning and behaviour may be affected.

In 2004, the Behaviour 4 Learning initiative was established and used as a major component of teacher training, aimed particularly at helping new teachers to develop and foster an environment in the classroom that promotes Behaviour for Learning. This initiative was 'cut' due to funding constraints in 2011 and the associated web resource was no longer available as a tool for teachers and schools to use. As a result, a valuable resource was lost. However, in 2012 the initiative was relaunched as a social enterprise under the title of Behaviour 2 Learn (B2L). This new web-based resource aims to give teachers access to a range of materials that are helpful in developing their skills and understanding of managing challenging behaviour.

Policies, initiatives and debates

It is important to recognise the effect history has had on the ways in which we perceive behaviour and work to promote Behaviour for Learning.

The 1944 Education Act aimed at ensuring that post-war Britain had an education system that all learners could access. This laid the foundation of our current education system. The Warnock Report (1978) was ground breaking in that it marked a move away from a deficit medical model to one that could be described as positive and empowering. This report formed the backbone of various policies and legislation, including the 1981 Education Act, the 1989 Children Act and the 1989 Elton Report.

The Elton Report (1989), which has become a seminal piece, was established to examine and make recommendations regarding what was seen at the time as disruptive behaviour in schools. It made the link between behaviour and learning much more explicit and as a result, the report has relevance today. This report laid the foundations for the Steer Report (2005) and subsequent review (2008). Elton (1989) suggested a whole school approach to behaviour management through which an atmosphere would be created that would foster and promote learning. This approach would necessitate schools having clear policies and procedures not only for when things went wrong but also to highlight and reward 'good behaviour'. It recommended the development of a school wide ethos with regard to positive approaches to behaviour management. The significant difference in the recommendations when compared with previous behaviour management ideas was that of a proactive approach to teaching and learning.

National initiatives concerned with supporting children who may experience problem behaviour include Every Child Matters: A Change for Children (ECM) (2004) and the subsequent Children's Plan (2007). ECM arose following the tragic death of Victoria Climbié in 2000. It highlighted five key areas /outcomes that every child had a right to expect and that would enable all learners to fulfil their potential. The outcomes were, be healthy, stay safe, enjoy and achieve, make a positive contribution, and achieve economic well being. It is worth noting that these five outcomes helped guide the conclusions and recommendations of the subsequent report by Steer (2005).

As a teacher you will not be alone in helping children to achieve these outcomes. The focus of the initiative is to develop a multi professional Team Around the Child (TAC). Such a team has the school at the centre and as a teacher you will play an important part in helping your children, drawing on support from other members of the TAC such as the Youth Offending Team (YOT) and learning mentors. We need to be a group – all stakeholders helping children to access education and succeed.

Steer's review (2005) at the time was the centrepiece of the Government's plans for tackling what was perceived to be problem behaviour and in doing so suggested some useful strategies. These include highlighting effective practice that allows for the right conditions for good behaviour and offering practical examples of how to achieve this e.g. parental involvement and effective school leadership. Steer's later report (2008) identified what progress had been made and a further 47 recommendations were identified. The report's purpose and ideology can perhaps best be summed up by Steer's own observations:

> Consistent experience of good teaching promotes good behaviour. But schools also need to have positive strategies for managing pupil behaviour that help pupils understand their school's expectations, underpinned by a clear range of rewards and sanctions, which are applied fairly and consistently by all staff. It is also vital to teach pupils how to behave – good

behaviour has to be learned – so schools must adopt procedures and practices that help pupils learn how to behave. Good behaviour has to be modelled by all staff all of the time in their interaction with pupils. For their part, staff need training and support to understand and manage pupil behaviour effectively.

(Steer 2005:12)

More recently, Taylor (2011a) developed key principles for schools to help improve behaviour. We explore some of these later on, but it is interesting to note the title 'Getting the simple things right', may be a lesson for us all! This may raise the question for you as a teacher: what approach do you take and which of the myriad of behaviour management books and resources do you use? However, it is important to remember when you are trying to support your children and young people in managing their behaviour that: 'Effective pedagogy can reduce problematic behaviour but cannot eliminate it' (O'Neill 2011:44). It is helpful for you to be aware of your own beliefs and value sets. These may be different to those of the children you are working with due to cultural and environmental factors. You will need to be able to identify what behaviours cause you the most difficulty. Once you have identified these, it is important to try and reflect on why these behaviours cause you difficulty and you may begin to change your own behaviour. At this stage, it is also very important to focus on children's positive behaviours and to reflect on how you reward them. Above all, be prepared to embark on a journey that does not have an ending!

In general terms, there are a number of strategies you could consider using in the classroom to ensure you continue to develop your inclusive pedagogy and as a result, include all your children. These are best used within a framework, which could comprise the approaches below:

- Good communication – this should include positive body language, avoiding long complex instructions, communicating with other professionals, and listening to learners and their parents.
- Being well prepared. Elton (1989), Hadyn (2007) and Taylor (2011b) amongst others, recognised that good preparation of lessons is essential. I would also argue that having a good knowledge of the subjects you are teaching will also help your preparation.
- Establish a few simple 'ground' rules that everyone can understand and achieve; they need to be firm and fair – do not set the bar so high that achievement is impossible. Also, ensure the other adults in your classroom are fully aware and support you in implementing them.
- Use the schools policies to support your work. Ensure you know what the behaviour policy is and apply it consistently with your children.
- Remember that you are in charge in your classroom; how you meet and greet your children, how you establish and maintain routines and how you celebrate success and good behaviour will all have an impact on your children's motivation and desire to learn.

- Use the TAC. Steer (2008) indicated that the development of collegiate professionalism and the sharing of good practice should have a significant impact on behaviour.
- Use assessments to check on a children's level of achievement especially in the area of social and emotional development. Try and ensure that the activities you provide are appropriate – that they match the level at which the child is functioning. In over stretching and indeed under stretching a child you may find it exacerbates problematic behaviour.
- Involve parents wherever you can – sharing responsibility and planning can be most effective.
- Decide which behaviours to focus on and which to ignore.
- Develop your own strategies, based on our developing inclusive practice.
- Use the Social and Emotional Aspects of Learning (SEAL) initiative.

This list is by no means exhaustive but should give you a starting point.

In the final part of this section I will briefly examine two strategies, SEAL and peer mentoring, together with two types of provision: Inclusion Units and Pupil Referral Units (PRUs), the latter now also described as Alternative Provision (AP). A number of writers (Goleman 1998; Shepherd and Linn 2015) have identified that meeting children's social needs plays an important part in nurturing and fostering an environment that enables them to access the teaching and learning that is on offer and to succeed as a result. Gardner (1984) discussed the concept of 'multiple intelligences', which identified the importance of being intelligent about our own emotions. Further work was explored by Goleman (1995) who used the phrase 'emotional intelligence' and suggested that emotional and social skills could be seen as more important in developmental terms than raw intelligence. More recently, Shepherd and Linn (2015) advocate the importance of social skills in ensuring children are not rejected by their peers and are able to develop relationships with both them and staff in order to decrease challenging behaviour.

As we have already identified, there has been concern, sometimes media driven, about young people's antisocial behaviour. This, together with perceived problematic behaviour in schools (Steer 2005), has prompted the Government to develop a programme that would support nurturing learner's social and emotional skills. This has been translated into the SEAL initiative, which can be viewed as being of particular importance for children who are seen as both challenging for schools and at risk of educational failure.

SEAL is based on five broad areas: self-awareness, managing feelings, motivation, empathy and social skills. In supporting and nurturing these five areas it is envisaged that children will become more effective learners. In terms of challenging behaviour, it is intended that the initiative will enable children to build a foundation for managing their own emotions and hence a greater understanding of their behaviour and how it might affect others – in other words, that each child will develop a social conscience. A vast range of materials, which can be used flexibly, are available for teachers to support their work with this initiative.

SEAL is not the only programme available to tackle these issues; other strategies that might help support children's development are nurture groups, circle time, buddy systems, and peer mentoring. It is peer mentoring we are going to explore in a little more detail.

Over the past 20 years there has been a growth in the availability and use of peer mentoring schemes in the UK (MBF 2010; Houlston *et al.* 2009). The original focus of such schemes was to reduce bullying in schools. They are based on non-judgemental one-to-one relationships that enable children and young people to tackle other issues such as bereavement or isolation (Blake and Parson 2004), all of which can lead to challenging behaviour and possible exclusion. A clear definition of peer mentoring is provided by Houlston *et al.* (2009):

> Peer support involves school programmes which train and use students themselves to help others learn and develop emotionally, socially or academically. These may also be referred to as peer-counselling (or peer-listening), befriending, buddy or mentoring schemes. These schemes may be used in addition to more traditional adult-based pastoral support systems.
>
> (Houlston *et al.* 2009:328)

Evidence from MBR (2010) also indicates that there are a number of further benefits of running peer mentoring schemes, such as:

- Staff believe that the 'climate' in schools has changed for the better.
- The promotion and development of both self confidence and self esteem has improved.
- There is a clear fit with policy initiatives such as participation, early intervention and volunteering.

It is worth remembering that your school may run initiatives such as classroom mentors and buddy schemes, all of which could be described under the umbrella term peer mentoring. It is something you might like to consider on a small scale in your classroom or encourage your school to adopt a more widely used scheme.

Whilst considering inclusive strategies it is important that we should also recognise that educational placement has a part to play. By this I mean some children may be placed, or perceived as 'dumped', within an inclusion/exclusion unit that is part of a mainstream school or in a PRU. Inclusion units are a specific type of provision and you may find them called other things such as Learning Support Unit, seclusion room or some schools give them a more specific name like The Base Room. In essence they provide a physical environment with particular staff and short-term tailored programmes aimed at meeting individual needs. There is little guidance on how this type of provision should be run, as a result schools are left to work out what they believe is right for their particular school. Whilst the aim is to keep pupils in school, it could be argued that the units themselves internally exclude and stigmatise pupils, thus becoming a dumping ground for young people seen as 'problems' and as such are not inclusive in the wider sense.

Unlike inclusion units, PRUs are an older provision and were established in 1996 in order that local authorities became compliant with their statutory duties, providing suitable education for pupils of compulsory school age who had been excluded from mainstream provision. This type of setting is based within local areas rather than within schools. The aim is to provide short-term intervention and re-inclusion into mainstream provision. During the 1980s a number of critical reports identified that these units did not enable pupils to progress and the teaching and learning pedagogy was poor. Pupils once 'sent' to a unit rarely re-entered mainstream provision. More recently, PRUs have supported pupils in following the National Curriculum, albeit differentiated, providing a flexible approach to meeting individual pupil needs. In 2013 there were 393 PRUs across the UK. These were listed under the new umbrella term Alternative Provisions (AP), that is to say, provision physically located away from 'mainstream'. In the same year, like other Local Authority schools APs were given greater freedom and control over budgets, staffing and how to meet the needs of their pupils. The provision including FE colleges is increasingly working in successful partnerships and in doing so enables pupils to develop vocational as well as academic skills. The more recent changes to how schools can be run and governed, together with the introduction of academies and free schools, has meant that APs can be free from local authority control and as a result develop their own curriculum and employ staff. This allows for a flexibility of approach and tailored programmes designed to meet individual need.

Conclusion

Sharing knowledge and enabling learners to experience success is one of the most rewarding aspects of the role of being a teacher. However, I recognise that working in a situation where you feel challenged is a difficult task.

Having examined, albeit briefly, some of the issues and strategies that surround the concept of children who may present a challenge, I would like to emphasise that prevention is better than 'cure' (Kyriacou 2001). We have all seen the teacher who makes managing a classroom look easy. It is, in fact, highly likely that they achieve this 'ease' from having put in significant preparation behind the scenes.

I also want to stress that you are not alone in developing your skills. There are a lot of published materials to help you but probably one of the best support mechanisms you can use is effective communication. This works on a number of levels – teacher to child, teacher to teacher, teacher to parent, teacher to other professionals. Listening to and asking for help is not a sign of failure, rather it indicates a willingness to learn and to nurture individuals. Indeed, the DCSF (2009) recognises that in 'Building a 21st Century School System' every school should be working in partnership because no school can do it alone. This has been further recognised in the new Special Educational Needs and Disability code of practice (2014), which has removed Statements of Special Educational Need and replaced them with Education and Health Care Plans. The aim of such a plan is to ensure that the needs of the child or young person are viewed in a holistic way. It can be seen that this together with the policies and strategies previously mentioned can help to ensure that support for all children is in place and that this support will enable them to succeed in adult life.

Some of the strategies discussed in this chapter will help you develop your own skills and enable you to become an inclusive teacher. In order to further develop your skill, keep reading, observing, listening and talking to colleagues, the children and young people themselves.

Reflections on values and practice

1   Think about your own teaching practice. What behaviour strategies have worked for you and why? Conversely, what strategies have not worked for you and why?
2   How do you deal with the 'stress' of working children whose behaviour you find challenging? Identify your support mechanisms.
3   Think about your relationship with other adults in your classroom. Do you communicate effectively with them? In terms of managing challenging behaviour are you all aware of the rewards and strategies you use? Are you all singing from the same 'song sheet'?
4   How well do you know the community in which your setting is placed? Consider how this may impact on children's values and attitudes and how these relate to your own.

Suggested further reading

Ayers, H., Clarke, D. and Murray, A. (2000) *Perspectives in Behaviour: a practical guide to effective interventions for teachers*, London: David Fulton.
Bishop, S. (2008) *Running a Nurture Group*, London: Sage.
Ellis, S., Todd, J. (2009) *Behaviour for Learning: proactive approaches to behaviour management*, Abingdon: Routledge.
Mosley, J. (1998) *Quality Circle Time in the Primary Classroom*, London: LDA.
Rogers, B. (2011) *Classroom Behaviour: a practical guide to effective teaching, behaviour management and colleague support*. London: Sage.

References

Blake, S. and Parson, M. (2004) Spotlight Briefing. Peer Support: An Overview, London: National Children's Bureau
DCSF (2007) *The Children's Plan: building a brighter future*, London: DCSF.
DCSF (2009) Your child, your schools, our future: building a 21st century, Norwich: TSO.
DfES (2003) *Every Child Matters*, London: DfES.
DfES (2004) *The Children Act*, London: HMSO.
DfES (2014) *The Children and Families Act*, London: HMSO.
DfE and DoH (2014) *The Special Educational Needs and Disability Code of Practice: 0–25 years*, London: Crown.
Elliott, J., Zamorski, B. and Shreeve, A. (2001) *Exploring the Pedagogical Dimensions of Disaffection through Collaborative Research. Norwich area schools consortium: a final report to the Teacher Training Agency*, Norwich: HMSO.

Elton. (1989) *Enquiry into Discipline in Schools,* London: HMSO.

Evans, J., Harden, A., Thomas, J., and Benefield, P. (2003) *Support for Pupils with Emotional and Behavioural Difficulties in Mainstream Primary Classrooms,* London: EPI-Centre.

Gardner, H. (1984) *Frames of Mind: the theory of multiple intelligences,* London: Heinemann.

Goleman, D. (1995) *Emotional Intelligence,* St Ives: Bloomsbury.

Goleman, D. (1998) *Working with Emotional Intelligence,* London: Bloomsbury.

Hadyn, T. (2007) *Managing Pupil Behaviour. Key issues in teaching and learning,* Abingdon: Routledge.

Hart, R. (2010) Classroom behaviour management Educational Psychologists' view of effective practice, *Emotional and Behavioural Difficulties,* 14(3):353–371.

Hattie, J. (2009) *Visible Learning. A synthesis of over 800 meta-analyses relating to achievement,* Abingdon: Routledge.

Houlston, C., Smith, P.K. and Jessel, J. (2009) Investigating the extent and use of peer support initiatives in English schools, *Educational Psychology,* 29(3), May 2009: 328.

Kyriacou, C. (2001) *Effective Teaching in Schools: theory and practice,* Cheltenham: Nelson Thomas.

Mentoring and Befriending Foundation (MBF) (2010) *Peer Mentoring in Schools: a review of the evidence base of the benefits of peer mentoring in schools,* Manchester: The Mentoring and Befriending Foundation.

O'Neill, S. (2011) Teacher classroom behaviour management preparation in undergraduate primary education in Australia: A web based investigation, *Australian Journal of Teacher Education,* 36(10):35–52.

Parry, J., Nind, M. and Sheehy, K. (2010) *Origins of the social model.* In The E214 Team (eds.), *E214: Equality, Participation and Inclusion: learning from each other; Block 1: Principles,* Milton Keynes: Open University Press, pp.101–81.

Trussler, S., and Robinson, D. (2015) *Inclusive Practice in the Primary School: a guide for teachers.* London: Sage.

Roffey, S., and O'Reirdon, T. (2002) *Young Children and Classroom Behaviour,* London: David Fulton.

Rogers, B. (1990) *You Know the Fair Rule,* Harlow: Pearson Education.

Shepherd, T., and Linn, D. (2015) *Behaviour and Classroom Management in the Multicultural Classroom: proactive, active and reactive strategies,* London: Sage.

Special Educational Needs and Disability code of practice (2014) DfE, DoH: London: Crown.

Steer Report (2005) *Learning Behaviour: the report of the practitioners group on school behaviour and discipline,* London: DfES.

Steer Behaviour Review (2008) Available at http://dera.ioe.ac.uk/8555/2/steer%20 interim%20260308final.pdf. Accessed 11 April 2015.

Taylor, C. (2011a) *Getting the Simple Things Right,* London: Department for Education.

Taylor, C. (2011b) *Improving Alternative Provision.* London: DfE.

Taylor, C. (2012) *Improving Attendance at School.* London: Department for Education.

Timpson, E. (2014) Press release. Available at: https://www.gov.uk/government/news/landmark-children-and-families-act-2014-gains-royal-assent. Accessed 11 April 2015.

Topping, K., and Maloney, S. (2005) *Reader in Inclusive Education,* London: Routledge.

Wallace, S. (2007) *Getting the Buggers Motivated in FE,* London: Continuum.

Warnock, M. (1978) *Special Educational Needs: report of the committee of inquiry into the education of handicapped children and young people,* London: HMSO.

Chapter 10

Religious and cultural diversity and inclusive practice

Michael J. Reiss

Introduction

A decade or two ago and many might have supposed that religion was increasingly becoming less important for schools in Britain. However, this has not proved to be the case. While personal religious belief and practice is unimportant for a growing number of people in Britain, there are many for whom it remains significant. Furthermore, the numbers for whom religion is personally relevant have been swelled both by immigration, including children born in such families, and by a tendency found in many religions in recent decades for some religious believers to have become more fundamentalist/literalist. In addition, religious matters now seem more evident in the public arena – whether we are talking about the wearing of religious dress (e.g. the burqa) or religious symbols (e.g. a cross), attitudes to gay marriage, the rise of militant atheism or religious terrorism. In education, the situation is complicated by new forms of faith schooling (Chapman *et al.* 2014; Parker-Jenkins *et al.* 2014).

This chapter examines such issues from the perspective of teachers working in schools. The fundamental premise is that the right to hold a particular belief, religious or secular, should be accepted as part of a wider spectrum of rights to equal participation in education, regardless of difference – and this point applies to teachers as well as to students. Inclusive schools welcome the diversity represented by members of their neighbourhood communities and regard differences as sources for enriching teaching and learning and for fostering harmonious, respectful relationships and mutual understanding (e.g. Mirza and Meetoo 2012). However, there are times when such well-intended sentiments are easier to state than to put into practice! This chapter both considers the fundamental issues at stake and suggests pragmatic ways forward for school leaders and classroom teachers.

The chapter title includes the phrase 'cultural diversity' to indicate that one way of seeing religion is as a part of culture. In *one* sense there is nothing specific to religion for a school dealing with issues of inclusion. By way of analogy (though analogies are always risky as some people treat them as if they were intended to be identities), having a religious faith is a bit like being a vegetarian. Some vegetarians believe passionately in the importance of vegetarianism and argue strongly that for anyone to eat meat is wrong – even murder (a PETA slogan as well as a hit album by The Smiths); other vegetarians, while equally passionate about not eating meat themselves, believe strongly in the right of others to eat meat if they so choose; still other vegetarians are more laid back about their own eating habits and not averse sometimes to eating fish and eggs.

The historical context in the UK

It is widely known that until the introduction of the National Curriculum in 1988, religious education was the only subject that schools in England and Wales were required to teach. Less well known is that this requirement dates back to the 1870 Elementary Education Act. Furthermore, this Act stipulated that 'No religious catechism or religious formulary which is distinctive of any particular denomination shall be taught in the school' (Section 14). At the time, the presumption was that the education would be Christian (hence 'denomination' rather than 'religion') but thus began the long tradition, distinctive to England, that religious education was not to be a nurturing of the state religion (Barnes *et al.* 2012). This contrasts with the situation that obtains in most countries where state schools promulgate the official or majority state religion, though there are countries, notably France, Turkey and the USA, where no religious education takes place in state schools. Also included in the 1870 Act was the right, which persists to this day, of parents to remove their children from religious instruction (as the subject was then called).

The legal situation concerning religious education and associated matters (e.g. collective worship) in schools is quite complicated and fast moving and there are important differences among the four UK nations and among the various types of school. In particular, the law does now allow for certain state schools with a religious character to favour one religion over others. Nevertheless, the key features of a religious education in state schools – that it is a core part of the curriculum, has provision for student withdrawal, must be part of a broad and balanced curriculum and must have regard to community cohesion – means that the position of religious education in UK schools is often held to be a much healthier one than in many other countries. This is despite quite frequent calls that religious education be either abolished or made optional, perhaps to be replaced by lessons in philosophy, in citizenship or in personal, social and health education.

The importance of religion to people

For people for whom religion is important, it can be important in two main ways: for belief and for practice. World-wide, religion remains of significance to many people, including young people; a survey undertaken in 2011 in 24 countries found that 73 per cent of respondents under the age of 35 (94 per cent in primarily Muslim countries and 66 per cent in Christian majority countries) said that they had a religion/faith and that it was important to their lives (Ipsos MORI 2011; see also Smyth *et al.* 2013).

For some people, their religious faith is absolutely the core of their being: they could no more feel comfortable acting or thinking in a way that conflicted with their religious values than they could feel comfortable not eating. Other ways of expressing this are to say that their worldview is a religious one or that religion plays a central part in their identity. For other people, religious faith is either an irrelevancy – an historical anachronism – or positively harmful with many of the ills that befall humankind being placed at its door (Halstead and Reiss 2003).

It can be difficult for those who have never had a religious faith, or have only had one rather tenuously, to imagine what a life is like that is lived wholly within a religious ordering. Anthropologists provide good accounts of what it can be like to live a life where one's religious faith integrates with every aspect of one's life. One of my favourite such accounts is that of du Boulay (2009) who studied life in a Greek Orthodox village in the late 1960s and early 1970s. Everything that happened in the village needs to be understood by reference to Greek Orthodoxy. To give just one instance, the annual liturgical and agricultural cycles intermeshed, so that after the harvest, the sowing of the seed for next year's harvest was closely related to the Christian calendar:

> The main sowing of the wheat is carried into November, and the Archangel Michael, celebrated on 8 November and seen on his icons with drawn sword, is a formidable figure associated with the darkening November days with the leaves being stripped from the trees and the smoke gusting in ashy draughts down the chimneys; but this is a month named after the preeminent agricultural task – 'The Sower' (Σποριας). And the Entry of the Mother of God into the Temple on 21 November, soon after the Christmas fast has begun, is also in the village given the character of the time as the 'Mother of God Half-Way-Through-The-Sowing' (Παναγια Μισοσπειριτσα). The task of the sowing of the wheat then continues into the time known as 'Andrew's' (St Andrew, whose day is 30 November, but who has given his name to the following month of December), and can go on up to Christmas – and even beyond, if the weather has not been fit.
>
> (du Boulay 2009: 106)

Of course, having a secular or atheistic approach to life can be as important for some people as having a religious approach to life is for others. With the humanist John White I have argued that atheism should be studied in schools (Reiss and White 2009). Young people should think about whether they live in a divine world or a godless one. This points to discussing the standard arguments for and against the existence of God and such questions as the likelihood of life after death. They also need to discuss whether human lives can have any meaning or point outside a religious framework and whether people can live a morally good life that is not dependent on religious belief.

Sensitivity and respect are required when teaching about such matters. One does not want young people to be given the impression that they are going to hell because they espouse atheism or that they are intellectually second rate because they accept the divine inspiration of scripture.

The particular place of religious education lessons

The aims and content of religious education lessons have varied far more in recent decades than has been the case for many other subjects. When I think back to my own 1960s' and 1970s' schooling, my religious education was dire. We were fed a watered-down, bible-based and historical account of Christianity. With hindsight I think there was a vague hope that this might make us better people, though the fare we were offered seemed more likely to put one off religion than attract or inspire one. (I recall regular homework where I learnt that week's Collect, and scripture, as it was called, was the one subject that I managed to come bottom in, 27th out of 27, in any school test or examination.)

The notion of confessional religious education – i.e. that teaching the subject might lead to the development or strengthening of religious faith – was abandoned in the 1970s, largely as a result of the publication by Schools Council (1971) of *Working Paper 36: Religious Education in Secondary Schools*. Two main arguments against confessional religion were advanced: first, that confessional education entails indoctrination; secondly that confessional education is inappropriate within an increasingly secular and pluralist society. The first argument has been controversial and there are those who continue to maintain that a confessional religion need not entail indoctrination, indeed that to abandon confessionalism is to submit to a form of liberal indoctrination that makes the implicit assumption that fostering any religious belief is educationally indefensible.

The second argument – that school religious education needs to take account of life in a diverse society where Christianity is much less central than it once was both because of a substantial increase in the number of people with no religious faith and because of increasing numbers of adherents of other faiths – is widely accepted (Barnes 2012). Religious education responded in a number of ways. Particularly popular was a 'world religions' approach. The expectation was that at the least students during their schooling would study what are often referred to as the six 'world religions' of Buddhism, Christianity, Hinduism, Islam, Judaism and Sikhism. Furthermore, the influential Qualifications and Curriculum Authority *Non-Statutory National Framework* recommended the study of further traditions 'such as the Bahá'í faith, Jainism and Zoroastrianism ... and secular philosophies such as humanism' (Qualifications and Curriculum Authority 2004: 12).

While well-meaning, this multi-faith approach ran into a number of difficulties. For a start, studying so many religions rarely inspired students, leading instead to shallow learning of miscellaneous facts (the five pillars of Islam, the five, eight or ten precepts of Buddhism, etc.). Other objections were that such teaching failed to connect to students' needs, gave a false impression of religion by denying diversity within religions, created a divide between how religion is experienced by adherents and presented in the classroom, failed to engage students critically with religious truth claims and underplayed the historical and contemporary importance of Christianity in British society (Watson 2012).

More recent curricula have reduced the number of religions that are studied, placing more emphasis on those that are relevant to the students in a school and in the local communities from which they come. An additional feature of successful religious education curricula is that they contain a substantial amount of material on values and ethics. While ethics can be taught in many subjects, teachers of religious education often have particular expertise in this area. At a time when much of the school curriculum is often criticised for being fact-heavy, good teaching about ethics can be both popular and educationally valuable. It can introduce students to ways in which fundamental questions about human meaning and existence have been addressed while giving students considerable autonomy to develop their own thinking. There are, for example, no single, universally agreed 'right answers' to such questions as whether abortion is permissible, whether we have duties to the environment and if/when war is morally right.

School-wide issues

There are many issues to do with religion and inclusion that exist outside of religious education lessons. For a start it remains the case, for community schools in England and Wales, that the law states that a collective act of worship must take place daily and be wholly or mainly of a Christian character. This is a requirement far more honoured in the breach than in the observance. In their efforts not to offend students and to provide for assemblies that 'work' in school terms, few secondary schools other than faith schools nowadays provide true collective worship. In one school in which I worked, an enthusiastic group of students asked for, and received, permission to hold a half-termly alternative assembly, which was overtly Christian. (This was back in the 1980s in Cambridgeshire when few other religions were represented among the student body.) Initially about 10 per cent of the students came to the alternative assembly. However, the students, nominally under my charge (I mainly tended to tone down the occasional over-enthusiastic suggestion for what might take place in the assembly), put so much time and thought into providing this alternative, often with humour, that it rapidly grew in popularity. Eventually, the majority of the students came to it and it had to be held in the main hall while the 'main' (secular) assembly was held in a smaller room. The highlight was a sketch based on the head-to-head duologue of Mel Smith and Griff Rhys Jones' *Alas Smith and Jones* about the real meaning of Christmas that brought the house down, receiving wave after wave of cheers.

More generally, the task of a school, whether of a religious nature or not, includes affirming in its ethos the value of diversity. This seems to me a key point in respect of the place of religion in a pluralist society. It is increasingly acknowledged that one cannot prove or disprove the validity or worth of religious faith. Given that both religious faith and atheism/secularism/agnosticism are widely represented in society, it is important that schools help students of all persuasions to live and work together respectively both now in school and in the future beyond school (cf. Starkey 2015).

This is not to imply that schools should accept every view about religion. Schools have a role to play in tackling extremism, including religious extremism. Savage (2013) has shown how education can move people from low to high integrative complexity. Integrative complexity is about how straightforwardly we understand issues. In everyday language, people with low integrative complexity see things as 'black or white' issues and this is more likely to be associated with violence. More generally, extremist ideologies avoid complexity.

Science education

One place within schools where religion not infrequently rears its head outside of religious education lessons is in science. Issues to do with religion seem increasingly to be of importance in school science lessons. To many science educators even raising the possibility that religion might be considered within science education raises suspicions that this is an attempt to find a way of getting religion into the science classroom for religious rather than scientific reasons. This is not the intention here. Part of the argument is that considering religion can be, on occasions, useful simply for helping better learners understand why certain things come under the purview of science and others don't (Reiss 2014).

Another argument for considering religion within science education proceeds much as an argument for considering history in science education might. While science can be learnt and studied in an historical vacuum, there are a number of arguments in favour of examining science in its historical contexts. For a start, this helps one better understand why certain sorts of science were pursued at certain times. Wars, for instance, have sometimes led to advances in chemistry, physics and information science (e.g. explosives, missile trajectories, code breaking), while certain botanical disciplines, such as systematics and taxonomy, have flourished during periods of colonisation. Then there is the observation that for many learners understanding science in historical context can aid motivation.

Similarly, while many students enjoy learning about the pure science of genetics and evolution, others are motivated and come to better understand the science if they appreciate something of the diversity of religious beliefs held by such principal protagonists as Charles Darwin, Joseph Hooker, Thomas Huxley and Gregor Mendel. Such teaching is enhanced if students come to appreciate the religious views (including the diversity of religious views) of the cultures in which such scientists lived and worked.

There are a number of places where religion and science interact. Consider first, the question of 'authority' and the scriptures as a source of authority. To the great majority of religious believers, the scriptures of their religion (the Tanakh, the Christian bible, the Qur'an, the Vedas, including the Upanishads, the Guru Granth Sahib, the various collections in Buddhism, etc.) have an especial authority by very virtue of being scripture. This is completely different from the authority of science. Newton's *Principia* and Darwin's *On the Origin of Species* are wonderful books but they do not have any permanence other than that which derives from their success in explaining observable phenomena of the material world and enabling people to see the material world through Newtonian / Darwinian eyes. Indeed, as is well known, Darwin knew almost nothing of the mechanism of inheritance despite the whole of his argument relying on inheritance, so parts of *The Origin* were completely out of date over a hundred years ago.

Then consider the possibility of miracles, where the word is used not in its everyday sense (and the sense in which it is sometimes used in the Christian scriptures), namely 'remarkable', 'completely unexpected' or 'wonderful' (as in the tabloid heading 'My miracle baby'), but in its narrower meaning of 'contrary to the laws of nature'. Scientists who do not accept the occurrence of miracles can react to this latter notion of miracles in one of three ways: (i) miracles are impossible (because they are contrary to the laws of nature); (ii) miracles are outside of science (because they are contrary to the laws of nature); (iii) miracles are very rare events that haven't yet been incorporated within the body of science but will be (as rare meteorological events, e.g. eclipses, and mysterious creatures, e.g. farm animals with two heads or seven legs, have been).

The relationship between science and religion has changed over the years (Brooke 1991; Al-Hayani 2005); indeed, the use of the singular, 'relationship', risks giving the impression that there is only one way in which the two relate. Nevertheless, there are two key issues: one is to do with understandings of reality; the other to do with evidence and authority. Although it is always difficult to generalise, most religions hold that reality consists of more than the objective world and many religions give weight to personal and/or (depending on the religion) institutional authority in a way that science generally strives not to.

For example, there is a very large religious and theological literature on the world to come, i.e. life after death, (e.g. Hick 1976/1985). However, to labour the point, although some (notably Atkins 2011) have argued that science disproves the existence of life after death, it can be objected that science, strictly speaking, has little or nothing to say about this question because life after death exists or would exist outside of or beyond the realm to which science relates.

It is clear that there can be a number of axes on which the science/religion issue can be examined. For example, the effects of the practical and ritual dimension are being investigated by scientific studies that examine such things as the efficacy of prayer and the neurological consequences of meditation (e.g. Lee and Newberg 2005); a number of analyses of religious faith, informed by contemporary understandings of evolutionary psychology, behavioural ecology and sociobiology, examine the possibility or conclude that religious faith can be explained by science (e.g. Dennett 2006); the narrative/mythic dimension of religion clearly connects with scientific accounts of such matters as the origins of the cosmos and the evolution of life (Reiss 2011); the doctrinal and philosophical dimension can lead to understandings that may agree or disagree with standard scientific ones (e.g. about the status of the human embryo); and the ethical and legal dimension can lead to firm views about such matters as land ownership, usury and euthanasia.

Sex education

Most of the world's religions have a great deal to say about sexual values. Of course, those with a religious faith also need to understand something of secular reasoning about sexual ethics: it is still too often the case that those with a religious faith assume that only they (a) really know what is good sexual behaviour; (b) can put such knowledge into effect.

In recent years there has been an increasing acknowledgement from all sex educators, whether or not they themselves are members of any particular religious faith, that religious points of view needs to be taken into account, if only because a significant number of children and their parents have moral values significantly informed by religious traditions.

The first major attempt in the UK among believers from a number of religious traditions to agree a religious perspective on sex education resulted in an agreed statement by members of six major UK religions (Islamic Academy 1991). This statement provided a critique of contemporary sex education, listed principles which it was felt ought to govern sex education and provided a moral framework for sex education. This framework 'Enjoins chastity and virginity before marriage and faithfulness and loyalty within marriage and prohibits extramarital sex and homosexual acts', 'Upholds the responsibilities and values of parenthood', 'Acknowledges that we owe a duty of respect and obedience to parents and have a responsibility to care for them in their old age and infirmity' and 'Affirms that the married relationship involves respect and love' (Islamic Academy 1991: 8).

Another early UK project to look at the importance of religion and ethnicity for sex education was the Sex Education Forum's 'religion and ethnicity project'. A working group was set up which 'was concerned to challenge the view that religions offer only negative messages around sex, wanting to explore the broader philosophy and rationale behind specific religious prescriptions' (Thomson 1993: 2). Each participant was sent a total of 28 questions (e.g. 'Are there different natural roles for men and women, if so why?' and 'What is the religious attitude towards contraception and/or "protection" for example, safe sex re: STDs, HIV?') and the project chose to present a range of views, rather than attempting to reach a consensus. The outcome was a pack that had chapters on Anglican, Hindu, Islamic, Jewish, Methodist, Roman Catholic, secular and Sikh perspectives.

At the same time as Rachel Thomson was compiling her pack, Gill Lenderyou and Mary Porter of the Family Planning Association were putting together a booklet arising from the 'Values, faith and sex education' project (Lenderyou and Porter 1994). At a four-day residential event in this project, a bill of pupils' rights was drawn up by 22 people of different religious faiths, and agreed statements on sex education were produced under the headings of: Respect and difference, Faith and change in society, Male and female equality, Relationships and marriages, Homosexuality, Cohabitation, Disability and sexuality, and Celibacy. The bill of pupils' rights is more liberal and the agreed statements are more tentative than the contents of Islamic Academy (1991). For example, included in the bill of pupils' rights are the assertions that pupils have the right to sex education that

'Provides full, accurate and objective information about growth and reproduction on topics including puberty, parenthood, contraception, child care and responsible parenthood' and that pupils have the right 'To be consulted about the manner in which sex education is implemented in the classroom in connection with issues such as whether it takes place in single sex or mixed groups or which topics can be included in the programme' (Lenderyou and Porter 1994: 37).

Subsequently, Shaikh Abdul Mabud and I edited an academic book titled *Sex Education and Religion*, which concentrated on Christian and Muslim views about sex education (Reiss and Mabud 1998), and publications resulted from projects funded by the Department of Health's former Teenage Pregnancy Unit including 'Supporting the Development of SRE [sex and relationships education] within a Religious and Faith Context' (Blake and Katrak 2002). Since that time, an increasing number of publications have considered the importance of religion for sex education (e.g. Rasmussen 2010; Smerecnik *et al*. 2010; Yip and Page 2013).

Conclusions

Schools are diverse communities yet UK schools have mostly been slow to consider religion as an inclusion issue. Done poorly, which it all too often is (Ofsted 2013), education about religion can bore students and achieve little. Done well – and not just through formal religious education lessons but in other subjects and in the life and ethos of the whole school – it can engage students, build knowledge, sharpen ethical thinking, contribute to community cohesion (Hess 2009; Woodward 2012) and make religious extremism less likely (Savage 2013).

However, this isn't always easy! In particular, teachers may find themselves holding very different views about the importance, relevance and messages of religion to those held by their students. There are various ways of dealing with this – schools typically have policies about such matters as religious dress and time for prayers. It is also important not to equate cultural practices concerning arranged marriages or female genital mutilation with religious positions. More generally, religion can be thought of as a controversial issue, namely as one where a range of positions may rationally be held. In most instances the cardinal rule is for teachers to respect students – and vice versa – even if they don't agree with them. As students grow older, they can benefit from teachers who disagree with them talking with them, helping them to think of the implications of their views, so long as this is always done in a non-confrontational manner that doesn't appear to attack religion and doesn't abuse the authority that teachers have over their students.

Reflection on values and practice

- Should schools place any restrictions on the religious symbols or articles of clothing that students wear?
- Can sex education be positive about the teachings and practices of all religions?

- How can you manage an inclusive approach to religious diversity that takes account of your own views and those of your students?
- Is it realistic to expect schools to play a role in combating religious extremism?

Suggested further reading

Barnes, L.P. (ed.) (2011) *Debates in Religious Education*, London: Routledge.
Hess, D.E. (2009) *Controversy in the Classroom*, New York: Routledge.
Mirza, H.S. and Meetoo, V. (2012) *Respecting Difference: Race, Faith and Culture for Teacher Educators*, London: IOE Press.

References

Al-Hayani, F.A. (2005) Islam and science: contradiction or concordance, *Zygon*, 40: 565–76.
Atkins, P. (2011) *On Being: a scientist's exploration of the great questions of existence*, Oxford: Oxford University Press.
Barnes, L.P. (2012) Diversity. In Barnes, L.P. (ed.) *Debates in Religious Education*, London: Routledge, pp. 65–76.
Barnes, L.P., Lundie, D., Armstrong, D., McKinney, S. and Williams, K. (2012) Religious education in the United Kingdom and Ireland. In Barnes, L.P. (ed.) *Debates in Religious Education*, London: Routledge, pp. 22–51.
Blake, S. and Katrak, Z. (2002) *Faith, Values and Sex & Relationships Education*, London: National Children's Bureau.
du Boulay, J. (2009) *Cosmos, Life, and Liturgy in a Greek Orthodox Village*, Limni, Evia: Denise Harvey.
Brooke, J.H. (1991) *Science and Religion: Some Historical Perspectives*, Cambridge: Cambridge University Press.
Chapman, J.D., McNamara, S., Reiss, M.J. and Waghid, Y. (eds.) (2014) *International Handbook of Learning, Teaching and Leading in Faith-Based Schools*, Dordrecht: Springer.
Dennett, D.C. (2006) *Breaking the Spell: Religion as a Natural Phenomenon*, London: Allen Lane.
Halstead, J.M. and Reiss, M.J. (2003) *Values in Sex Education: From Principles to Practice*, London: RoutledgeFalmer.
Hess, D.E. (2009) *Controversy in the Classroom*, New York: Routledge.
Hick, J. (1976/1985) *Death and Eternal Life*, Basingstoke: Macmillan.
Ipsos MORI (2011) *Religion and Globalisation*, London: Ipsos MORI.
Islamic Academy (1991) *Sex Education in the School Curriculum: the religious perspective – an agreed statement*, Cambridge: Islamic Academy.
Lee, B.Y. and Newberg, A.B. (2005) Religion and health: a review and critical analysis, *Zygon*, 40: 443–68.
Lenderyou, G. and Porter, M. (eds.) (1994) *Sex Education, Values and Morality*, London: Health Education Authority.
Mirza, H.S. and Meetoo, V. (2012) *Respecting Difference: race, faith and culture for teacher educators*, London: IOE Press.
Ofsted (2013) *Religious Education: realising the potential*, Manchester: Ofsted.

Parker-Jenkins, M., Glenn, M. and Janmaat, J.G. (2014) *Reaching In, Reaching Out: faith schools, community engagement, and 21st-century skills for intercultural understanding*, London: IOE Press.

Qualifications and Curriculum Authority (2004) *Religious Education: non-statutory national framework*, London: QCA.

Rasmussen, M.L. (2010) Secularism, religion and 'progressive' sex education, *Sexualities*, 13: 699–712.

Reiss, M.J. (2011) How should creationism and intelligent design be dealt with in the classroom?, *Journal of Philosophy of Education*, 45: 399–415.

Reiss, M.J. (2014) What significance does Christianity have for science education?. In Matthews, M.R. (ed.) *Handbook of Historical and Philosophical Research in Science Education*, Dordrecht: Springer, pp. 1637–62.

Reiss, M.J. and Mabud, S.A. (eds.) (1998) *Sex Education and Religion*, Cambridge: Islamic Academy.

Reiss, M. and White, J. (2009) Atheism needs to be studied in schools, *The Independent*, Education, 16 July: 4.

Savage, S. (2013) Head and heart in preventing religious radicalization. In Watts, F. and Dumbreck, G. (eds.) *Head and Heart: perspectives from religion and psychology*, West Conshohocken, PA: Templeton Press, pp. 157–93.

Schools Council (1971) *Working Paper 36: Religious Education in Secondary Schools*, London: Evans/Methuen.

Smerecnik, C., Schaalma, H., Gerjo, K., Meijer, S. and Poelman, J. (2010) An exploratory study of Muslim adolescents' views on sexuality: implications for sex education and prevention, *BMC Public Health*, 10: 533.

Smyth, E., Lyons, M. and Darmody, M. (eds.) (2013) *Religious Education in a Multicultural Europe*, Basingstoke: Palgrave Macmillan.

Starkey, H. (2015) *Learning to Live Together: struggles for citizenship and human rights education*, London: IOE Press.

Thomson, R. (ed.) (1993) *Religion, Ethnicity & Sex Education: Exploring the Issues – a resource for teachers and others working with young people*, London: National Children's Bureau.

Watson, B. (2012) Why religious education matters. In Barnes, L.P. (ed.) *Debates in Religious Education*, London: Routledge, pp. 14–21.

Woodward, R. (2012) Community cohesion. In Barnes, L.P. (ed.) *Debates in Religious Education*, London: Routledge, pp. 132–45.

Yip, A.K.-T. and Page, S.-J. (eds.) (2013) *Religious and Sexual Identities: a multi-faith exploration of young adults*, Farnham: Ashgate.

Chapter 11

Teachers working with teaching assistants

Vikki Anderson and Linda Lyn-Cook

Introduction

Effective partnerships between teachers and teaching assistants form an essential part of embracing diversity and enabling all pupils to participate fully in the classroom. However, the impact of such collaboration is highly dependent on the conditions under which teaching assistants operate and the ways in which their roles are interpreted and understood. This chapter explores the roles of teaching assistants and their effect on inclusive classroom practice, highlighting some of the key issues to consider when working with them in partnership.

The role of teaching assistants

There are around 243,700 full-time equivalent teaching assistants employed in schools across England – a figure that has more than trebled since 2000 (DfE 2014) – and this growth has been accompanied by marked changes in their roles and responsibilities (DCSF 2008). Traditionally, teaching assistants came from parent helper routes, learned on the job and functioned as classroom auxiliaries who relieved teachers of care and housekeeping-type duties (Clayton 1993). However, changes in educational policy have resulted in them taking on an array of tasks, ranging from administrative and classroom support to providing targeted academic interventions for individual pupils or small groups.

Teaching assistants have the opportunity to develop within a four-level professional career structure in which level four represents higher level teaching assistant (HLTA) status (Bedford *et al.* 2006). Under the direction of teachers, HLTAs can work with whole classes and as part of the Workforce Remodelling initiative (DfES 2003), began to perform roles that were previously undertaken exclusively by teachers, for example pastoral year leader and assistant SENCO (Goddard *et al.* 2007).

Various reports have highlighted the importance of teaching assistants in school improvement generally and in improving outcomes for pupils (DCSF 2009a; Ofsted 2010; Ofsted 2015a) and the Framework for School Inspection (Ofsted 2015b) has been influenced by the findings of these reports. The Lamb Inquiry into Special Educational Needs (DCSF 2009b) identified the need for the education of all pupils, especially those with learning difficulties, to be placed firmly within the overall framework for school inspection. Findings suggested that unless this was incorporated into the inspection process, due attention to the progress and attainment of these pupils was less likely to be a priority for school leaders. A raft of weaknesses with regard to systems of accountability, inspection and school improvement were highlighted in relation to the education of pupils with learning difficulties and the need for all inspectors to receive additional training in special educational needs and disability (SEND) was a key recommendation of the report. Ofsted expects all teachers to show evidence of the progress made by pupils with SEND, with their Subsidiary Guidance: Supporting the Inspection of Maintained Schools and Academies (Ofsted 2014) providing further advice on how they make judgements about such progress. The current framework for inspection requires inspectors to evaluate the use of and contribution made by teaching assistants: 'They should consider whether teaching assistants are clear about their role and knowledgeable about the pupils they support' (Ofsted 2015a: 58), noting whether pupils who receive additional interventions show accelerated or sustained progress as an indication of their efficacy.

The Special Education Needs and Disability Review (Ofsted 2010) found that many pupils with learning difficulties were underachieving, often because the quality of the school's mainstream teaching provision was not high enough to meet the needs of all pupils. Some pupils were also identified as having special educational needs when their underachievement was due to teaching that was not matched carefully enough to individual requirements. The responsibility for their education was then transferred to the SENCO and/or teaching assistants, a process that absolved class teachers of full responsibility for the progress of, and outcomes for all. On the other hand, where things were found to be working well for pupils, class and subject teachers retained overall responsibility for the progress and attainment of *all* pupils in their classes (Ofsted 2010). There was also evidence of careful monitoring of progress, with timely intervention and thorough evaluation of its impact by teachers. Emphasising that 'teaching assistant time should never be a substitute for teaching from a qualified teacher', the 2011 Green Paper, Support and Aspiration: A New Approach to Special Educational Needs and Disability, states: 'Within schools, support staff can make a real difference to the achievement of pupils with SEN, but they need to be deployed and used effectively in order to do so' (DfE 2011: 63). It can therefore be beneficial to take an evidence-based approach to the effectiveness of teaching assistants by examining educational research (Higgins *et al.* 2014).

The effectiveness of teaching assistants

In some cases, the effectiveness of trained teaching assistants is linked to the fact that they are likely to remain in the job. This consistency is exemplified by the deputy head teacher of an Inner London primary school:

> I would say that the vast majority of phonics teaching, quality phonics teaching was done by TAs who've been trained because they're the ones who

are consistently here. We've had five members of new staff this term, we haven't managed to get all the training in for them yet but we've got TAs who've been doing it consistently and we'll actually use them to demonstrate how to do it when it comes up to initiate new members of [teaching] staff.

(Bach *et al.* 2006: 16)

This transfer of skills forms part of the '*connecting* and *mediating*' role that teaching assistants can play between a variety of stakeholders (Howes 2003: 150). Teaching assistants have been found to improve contact between home and school, with parents regarding them as more approachable than teachers due to shared values, similar cultural backgrounds and familiarity with the local community (Collins and Simco 2006; Logan and Feiler 2006). Mansaray's (2006: 179) research illustrates the complexities and subtleties at work within inclusive schools and how a teaching assistant's work can extend to contexts that are not easily accessible to the teacher:

some of the kids we have in our school do not have breakfast. They don't have – either don't have time to have breakfast, or their parents probably don't get up, and [by] the time they get up it's just in time for them to be at school . . . I know the ones who eat, who doesn't eat, and I just make sure they have sufficient food inside of them.

(Stephanie: TA, Fenton)

This study also shows how teaching assistants from minority ethnic groups use their own cultural and social resources to foster inclusion by correcting stereotypes, developing intercultural understanding and 'creating shared spaces of meaning'. For example, Luke, a Black Rastafarian, describes the advantages of engaging with pupils of African Caribbean heritage in their own vernacular:

You know, they will try things on, but then I know like the culture, and I know how things are, and I'll be like, 'is that right, yeah?', and they'll be like, 'oh'. . . . I know exactly what they're talking about, whereas someone else might not, you know what I mean? . . . I don't know, maybe some of them might feel more comfortable coming to speak to me rather than someone else, you know.

(Mansaray 2006: 181)

A major aspect of teaching assistants' work lies in 'bridging pedagogic boundaries' by removing barriers to participation in the classroom (Mansaray 2006: 178). However, much of the research in this area is based on the views and experiences of teachers and teaching assistants, rather than objective evaluations of practice. The large-scale, longitudinal Deployment and Impact of Support Staff (DISS) project has filled this gap by providing a comprehensive assessment of the deployment and impact of teaching assistants across a range of outcomes (Blatchford *et al.* 2012). In one strand of the study, systematic observations were carried out in 49 primary and secondary schools in England and Wales in order to investigate the effects of teaching assistants on pupil and adult behaviour in class (Blatchford *et al.* 2009a). In the primary schools, all pupils appeared to benefit from the presence of teaching assistants in terms of better classroom control and more individualised attention, enabling pupils to interact more actively with adults. At secondary level, pupils identified as having special educational needs benefited from more individualised attention, together with a significant increase in on-task behaviour, and there were benefits for all pupils in terms of classroom control and the amount of teaching overall.

The DISS project (Blatchford *et al.* 2009b) also included a systematic analysis of the extent to which the amount of support from teaching assistants was related to end of year attainment in English, Mathematics and Science, controlling for factors that might be expected to explain the relationship, such as prior attainment, income deprivation, English as an additional language and whether pupils had a statement of special needs or were at School Action or School Action Plus of the then SEN Code of Practice (DfES 2001). The results revealed a negative relationship between the amount of additional support and the academic progress of pupils in Years 1, 3, 7 (English and Mathematics) and 10 (English), and Years 2, 6 and 9 (English, Mathematics and Science). In other words, the higher the amount of support, the lower the level of progress. Moreover, it was found that the effect of TA support on pupils' academic progress was more marked for pupils with statements of special educational needs (Webster *et al.* 2010).

Findings from the DISS project were mirrored in the Making a Statement (MAST) study (Webster and Blatchford 2013), which explored the teaching, support and interactions experienced by pupils with SEN attending mainstream primary schools. Forty-eight Year 5 pupils with statements for moderate learning difficulties or behavioural, emotional and social difficulties were tracked and 151 average-attaining pupils observed for comparison. It was found that compared with average-attaining pupils, those with statements spent less time in lessons with teachers and peers and were over three times more likely to interact with teaching assistants than teachers. Pupils with statements also had almost half as many interactions with their classmates compared with the other pupils. Teaching assistants were found to be largely responsible for teaching statemented pupils. Many planned and delivered alternative programmes and interventions and almost all were primarily responsible for explaining and modifying tasks set by the teacher, mainly 'in the moment', to make teaching accessible (Webster and Blatchford 2015:334), a typical comment being:

> I don't plan specifically for Greg. I kind of say [to the TA], 'This is what the class are doing; this is what my more able and less able are doing . . . Use your judgement to figure out what he can access or not.'
>
> (Teacher)

An important finding was how teachers regarded teaching assistants as the experts on the pupils and their SEN despite both having similar limitations in their knowledge and training, and in so doing, detached themselves from these pupils. Nevertheless, the results showed that pupils with statements did not differ greatly from the comparison pupils in terms of the amount of time they were off-task, reinforcing the findings of Blatchford et al. (2009a) that teaching assistants are effective in keeping pupils on-task.

Drawing upon a range of additional data gathered throughout the DISS project, Webster et al. (2011) highlight a number of 'wider factors' that could have affected the relationship between pupils' academic progress and teaching assistant support, including: insufficient paid time for joint planning and feedback; pupils becoming separated from their teachers and the broader curriculum; the ways in which teaching assistants interact with pupils and a lack of training for teachers in working effectively with support staff. These are key issues that have been identified throughout the literature and should be considered by all teachers entering into partnerships with teaching assistants.

Teachers working with teaching assistants

Ofsted (2008; 2010) reports that the quality of teaching is enhanced when teachers provide clear guidance to teaching assistants and involve them in planning. In effectively supported lessons, teaching assistants should know in advance what each pupil is expected to learn; build on prior learning; model effective approaches; enable pupils to work independently; check and review their learning at the end of the lesson and provide evidence of the impact of their support. Class and subject teachers also need to monitor the impact of teaching assistant support and interventions and feed this back to the SENCO as appropriate (Cheminais 2015).[1]

Nevertheless, a number of studies highlight a lack of paid joint planning and evaluation time (Higgins et al. 2014). An example of good practice is provided by Fox et al. (2004) who describe a situation in which a primary school teacher informed the teaching assistant about the whole day's planning, focusing on the work of the entire class, together with specific planning for a child with Down's syndrome. The teaching assistant recorded her views in the teacher's planning and assessment book at the end of the morning and afternoon sessions, and the teacher used these to differentiate the next day's lessons. Russell et al. (2013) describe a case study in which a primary school brought the start and finish times of the teaching assistants' days forward by 15 minutes in order to create guaranteed time for daily planning and sharing feedback. In another primary school, teachers and teaching assistants were allocated a weekly slot to engage in reflection and planning during whole school assembly, and in a secondary school, 'Working Together' slips were created, enabling teachers and teaching assistants to increase communication, plan collaboratively and reflect on their work (Vincett et al. 2005).

If teaching assistants do not have opportunities to share their ideas with, seek advice from, and give feedback to the teacher, the 'voice vacuum' described by O'Brien and Garner (2001: 3) will restrict the growth of a fruitful professional partnership aimed at improving the quality of teaching and learning. The responsibility for collaborative working does not therefore rest solely with the class or subject teacher but is a management issue that requires a whole school approach (Webster *et al.* 2011).

The fact that teaching assistants often focus on those who are seen to need 'extra help' may reinforce 'the peer-group label of "dumb"' (Mansaray 2006: 179) and can create dependency on the part of pupil and teacher. Gerschel (2005: 71) cautions against 'a "Velcro" model' of teaching assistants being attached to single pupils, which can result in emotional dependency on the assistant and them being less likely to be fully included in the class or form relationships with their peers. Blatchford *et al.* (2009b: 134) argue that pupils experiencing barriers to participation are likely to benefit from more, not less, of a teacher's time and that there is a danger that delegating responsibility to teaching assistants means the teacher does not feel the need: 'to consider pedagogical approaches that might benefit the whole class'. It is therefore important to rethink the ways in which teaching assistants work, for example rotating groups to allow teachers to spend more time with pupils with SEN whilst the teaching assistant monitors the rest of the class and ensuring that teaching assistants and teachers have more time to communicate and engage in professional development, especially in relation to working with pupils with SEN (Russell *et al.* 2013).

If a specific pedagogy is being used, teaching assistants should be trained so that they fully understand the principles of the approach and the techniques required to apply it. In the DISS project, teaching assistants were found to prioritise the achievement of outcomes as opposed to promoting engagement in the learning process and ownership of tasks. For example, they were observed telling pupils what to do; giving them answers or physically doing work for them rather than prompting them to think for themselves (Rubie-Davies *et al.* 2010; Radford *et al.* 2011). This approach may be influenced by messages communicated unintentionally by teachers about the need to meet targets and get through the curriculum (Higgins *et al.* 2014). Radford *et al.* (2013) stress the importance of developing more effective ways in which teaching assistants interact with pupils, such as styles of questioning that support independent learning. The Education Endowment Foundation's Guidance Report (Sharples *et al.* 2015) makes a number of recommendations for 'making the best use of teaching assistants' and includes useful resources such as a framework that teaching assistants can use for more effective questioning.

Training for non-pedagogical input is also important. With regard to managing challenging behaviour, Martin and Alborz (2014) found the focus was on interventions rather than exploring the complex factors that contribute to the emergence of such behaviour. Research indicates that the most beneficial behaviour management training equips staff with a theoretical understanding of the factors underpinning the emergence of challenging behaviour, together with an understanding of the principles behind behavioural approaches (Grey *et al.* 2007; Tierney *et al.* 2007). While certain aspects of such training need to be carried out during non-contact time, there are elements that could be provided by trainers working alongside teaching assistants and teachers on an ongoing basis to educate staff within their typical working environment (Ling and Mak 2012). Focusing on pupils with autistic spectrum conditions in mainstream schools, Symes and Humphrey (2011a) suggest arranging for experts from outside agencies to shadow a teaching assistant for the day and provide advice on how s/he can better support pupils. They also highlight the importance of providing time for teaching assistants to access SENCOs to help them develop skills and strategies, suggesting that SENCOs could arrange a weekly 'drop-in' session, in which teaching assistants can ask questions or voice their concerns. Asking teaching assistants to share their knowledge and expertise can have a positive effect on their confidence as well as the inclusive classroom (Symes and Humphrey 2011b). Teaching assistants should therefore be encouraged to contribute to daily information sharing, staff meetings, INSET days, newsletters and staff intranet sites, with knowledge-sharing targets included in their performance reviews (Malcolm *et al.* 2003).

Inclusive education involves responding to pupils from a wide range of backgrounds and cultures with different experiences, knowledge, understanding and skills. It is therefore essential for teachers to develop ways of working that will enable them to devote sufficient time and expertise to those who require it most. Drawing upon the outcomes of the Effective Deployment of Teaching Assistants project, Russell *et al.* (2013) have published guidance on how schools can review current practice and employ effective classroom-tested strategies for working with teaching assistants in primary and secondary schools. Various other innovative approaches are documented in the literature. In a primary school, Rose (2000) observed that teaching assistants played an important role in supporting whole classes rather than concentrating on individuals with statements of SEN. For example, a teaching assistant monitored the work of the rest of the class while the teacher worked intensively with a pupil who had speech and language difficulties. In both primary and secondary schools, Vincett *et al.* (2005) used the models of Zoning and Room Management for collaborative working. Zoning involves arranging the class into learning zones usually structured by the placement of groups (for example, six groups could be split 5/1, 4/2 or 3/3) and allocating these to the teacher or teaching assistant. Within Room Management, each of the adults in the classroom occupies a clear role – that of activity or learning manager. The activity manager concentrates on the larger group and the learning manager provides intensive support to particular individuals. Staff can take on either role, depending on the needs of the class and the activities to be carried out, and can switch roles during a session if required. With each model, however, the teacher has overall responsibility for the whole class. Both of these models were found to have positive effects on pupils' self-esteem and engagement in learning, and enabled teaching assistants to become more involved in the learning experiences of all pupils.

Conclusion

In placing emphasis on reinforcing teachers' responsibility and accountability for 'the progress and development of the pupils in their class, including where pupils access support from teaching assistants or specialist staff' (DfE/DOH 2014: 99), the 2014 Code of Practice is encouraging in that it should prompt school leaders and teachers to think more inclusively about pupils with SEN. Partnership working between teachers and teaching assistants is crucial and if good practice is to occur, an ongoing process of clear, constructive communication and reflective practice is needed, together with supportive organisational cultures that enable teaching assistants to work to their strengths and benefit from joint professional development. Time for joint planning is vital, together with teaching and learning strategies that ensure that all pupils receive equitable amounts of the teacher's time and do not become separated from their peers. Finally, it is important that the teaching assistant/teacher relationship is based on mutual respect and that whatever their role, teaching assistants feel valued if they are to play an optimal part in improving educational opportunities for all learners, regardless of difference.

Reflection on values and practice

1   Reflect on a relationship you have had with a teaching assistant. What was successful and what aspects could have been improved? How can you use this reflection to build positive relationships with teaching assistants in the future?
2   What joint training would you and the teaching assistant you work with benefit from and how might this be pursued?
3   How might you work with the teaching assistant so that *all* pupils receive equal amounts of your time and pedagogical expertise?
4   What could you do to help the teaching assistant use language and questioning that encourages pupils to think for themselves?

Suggested further reading

Cheminais, R. (2015) *Special Educational Needs for Qualified and Trainee Teachers*, London: Routledge.
Russell, A., Webster, R. and Blatchford, P. (2013) *Maximising the Impact of Teaching Assistants: guidance for school leaders and teachers*, London: Routledge.
Sharples, J., Webster, R. and Blatchford, P. (2015) *EEF Guidance Report. Making best use of teaching assistants*. Available online at: https://educationendowmentfoundation.org. uk/uploads/pdf/TA_Guidance_Report_Interactive.pdf.

Note

1 Cheminais (2015:199) recommends 'an excellent monitoring table' that can be downloaded from *Maximising Progress: Ensuring the Attainment of Pupils with SEN* (2005) and used by class and subject teachers working with teaching assistants.

References

Bach, S., Kessler, I. and Heron, P. (2006) Changing job boundaries and workforce reform: the case of teaching assistants, *Industrial Relations Journal*, 37(1): 2–21.

Bedford, J., Goddard, G., Obadan, F., Mowat, P. (2006) How gaining higher level teaching assistant status impacts on the teaching assistant's role in English schools, *Management in Education*, 20(1): 6–10.

Blatchford, P., Bassett, P., Brown, P. and Webster, R. (2009a) The effect of support staff on pupil engagement and individual attention, *British Educational Research Journal*, 35(5): 661–686.

Blatchford, P., Bassett, P., Brown, P., Koutsoubou, M., Martin, C., Russell, A. and Webster, R. (2009b) *Deployment and Impact of Support Staff in Schools: the impact of support staff in schools (Results from Strand 2, Wave 2)*, London: DCSF.

Blatchford, P., Russell, A. and Webster, R. (2012) *Reassessing the Impact of Teaching Assistants. How research challenges practice and policy*, Abingdon: Routledge.

Cheminais, R. (2015) *Special Educational Needs for Qualified and Trainee Teachers*, London: Routledge.

Clayton, T. (1993) From domestic helper to 'assistant teacher' – the changing role of the British classroom assistant, *European Journal of Special Needs Education*, 8: 32–44.

Collins, J. and Simco, N. (2006) Teaching assistants reflect: the way forward?, *Reflective Practice*, 7(2): 197–214.

DCSF (2008) *School Workforce in England*. Available online at: www.dcsf.gov.uk/rsgateway/DB/SFR/s000787/index.shtml. Accessed 18 January 2010.

DCSF (2009a) *Identifying and Teaching Children and Young People with Dyslexia and Literacy Difficulties. An independent report from Sir Jim Rose to the Secretary of State for Children, Schools and Families*, Nottingham: DCSF.

DCSF(2009b) *Lamb Inquiry Special Educational Needs and Parental Confidence*, Nottingham: DCSF.

DfE (2011) *Support and Aspiration: a new approach to special educational needs and disability*, Norwich: TSO.

DfE (2014) *School Workforce in England: November 2013.*Available online at: https://www.gov.uk/government/statistics/school-workforce-in-england-november-2013. Accessed 16 April 2015.

DfE/DOH (2015) *Special Educational Needs and Disability Code of Practice: 0 to 25 years*. Available online at: https://www.gov.uk/government/uploads/system/uploads/attachment_data/file/398815/SEND_Code_of_Practice_January_2015.pdf. Accessed 14 April 2015.

DfES (2001) *Special Educational Needs Code of Practice*, London: DfES.

DfES (2003) *Raising Standards and Tackling Workload: a national agreement*, London: DfES.

Fox, S., Farrell, P. and Davis, P. (2004) Factors associated with the effective inclusion of primary-aged pupils with Down's syndrome, *British Journal of Special Education*, 31: 184–190.

Gerschel, L. (2005) The special educational needs coordinator's role in managing teaching assistants: the Greenwich Perspective, *Support for Learning*, 20: 69–76.

Goddard, G., Mowat, P. and Obadan, F. (2007) One year on: The impact of obtaining HLTA status on teaching assistants and schools, Paper presented at the British Educational Research Association Annual Conference, Institute of Education, University of London, 5–8 September. Available online at: www.leeds.ac.uk/educol/documents/165904.doc (accessed 18 January 2010).

Grey, I. M., Hastings, R. P. and McClean, B. (2007) Staff training and challenging behaviour, *Journal of Applied Research in Intellectual Disabilities*, 20: 1–5.

Higgins, S., Katsipataki, M., Kokotsaki, D., Coleman, R., Major, L.E., and Coe, R. (2014) *The Sutton Trust-Education Endowment Foundation Teaching and Learning Toolkit.*

Available online at: www.suttontrust.com/about-us/education-endowment-foundation/teaching-learning-toolkit/. Accessed 17 April 2015.

Howes, A. (2003) Teaching reforms and the impact of paid adult support on participation and learning in mainstream schools, *Support for Learning*, 18(4): 147–153.

Ling, C. Y. M. and Mak, W. W. S. (2012) Coping with challenging behaviours of children with autism: effectiveness of brief training workshop for frontline staff in special educational settings, *Journal of Intellectual Disability Research*, 56(3): 258–269.

Logan, E. and Feiler, A. (2006) Forging links between parents and schools: a new role for teaching assistants?, *Support for Learning*, 21(3): 115–120.

Malcolm, J., Hodkinson, P. and Colley, H. (2003) The interrelationships between informal and formal learning, *Journal of Workplace Learning*, 15(7/8): 313–318.

Mansaray, A.A. (2006) Liminality and in/exclusion: exploring the work of teaching assistants, *Pedagogy, Culture &Society*, 14(2):171–187.

Martin, T. and Alborz, A. (2014) Supporting the education of pupils with profound intellectual and multiple disabilities: the views of teaching assistants regarding their own learning and development needs, *British Journal of Special Education*, 41(3): 310–327.

O'Brien, T. and Garner, P. (2001) Tim and Philip's story: setting the record straight. In O'Brien, T. and Garner, P. (eds.) *Untold Stories: learning support assistants and their work*, Stoke-on-Trent: Trentham Books, p.3.

Ofsted (2008) *The Deployment, Training and Development of the Wider School Workforce*, London: Ofsted.

Ofsted (2010) *The Special Education Needs and Disability Review: a statement is not enough*, Manchester: DfE.

Ofsted (2014) *Subsidiary Guidance: supporting the inspection of maintained schools and academies*. Available online at: www.ofsted.gov.uk/resources/110166 (accessed 16 April 2015).

Ofsted (2015a) *School Inspection Handbook*. Available online at: www.gov.uk/government/uploads/system/uploads/attachment-data/file/391531 (accessed 18 May 2015).

Ofsted (2015b) *The Framework for School Inspection*. Available online at: www.ofsted.gov.uk/resources/120100 (accessed 16 April 2015).

Radford, J., Blatchford, P. and Webster, R. (2011) Opening up and closing down: comparing teacher and TA talk in mathematics lessons, *Learning and Instruction*, 21(5): 625–35.

Radford, J., Bosanquet, P., Webster, R., Blatchford, P. and Rubie-Davies, C. (2013) Fostering learner independence through heuristic scaffolding: a valuable role for teaching assistants, *International Journal of Educational Research*, 63: 116–126.

Rose, R. (2000) Using classroom support in a primary school: a single school case study, *British Journal of Special Education*, 27(4): 191–6.

Rubie-Davies, C., Blatchford, P., Webster, R., Koutsoubou, M. and Bassett, P. (2010) Enhancing learning? A comparison of teacher and teaching assistant interactions with pupils, *School Effectiveness and School Improvement*, 21(4): 429–49.

Russell, A., Webster, R. and Blatchford, P. (2013) *Maximising the Impact of Teaching Assistants: guidance for school leaders and teachers*, London: Routledge.

Sharples, J., Webster, R. and Blatchford, P. (2015) *EEF Guidance Report. Making best use of teaching assistants*. Available online at: https://educationendowmentfoundation.org.uk/uploads/pdf/TA_Guidance_Report_Interactive.pdf (accessed 16 April 2015).

Symes, W. and Humphrey, N. (2011a) School factors that facilitate or hinder the ability of teaching assistants to effectively support pupils with autism spectrum disorders (ASDs) in mainstream secondary schools, *Journal of Research in Special Educational Needs*, 11(3): 153–161.

Symes, W. and Humphrey, N. (2011b) The deployment, training and teacher relationships of teaching assistants supporting pupils with autistic spectrum disorders (ASD) in mainstream secondary schools, *British Journal of Special Education*, 38(2): 57–64.

Tierney, E., Quinlan, D. and Hastings, R. P. (2007) Impact of a 3-day training course on challenging behaviour on staff cognitive and emotional responses, *Journal of Applied Research in Intellectual Disabilities*, 20: 58–63.

Vincett, K., Cremin, H. and Thomas, G. (2005) *Teachers and Assistants Working Together*, Maidenhead: OUP.

Webster, R., Blatchford, P., Bassett, P., Brown, P., Martin, C. and Russell, A. (2010) Double standards and first principles: framing teaching assistant support for pupils with special educational needs, *European Journal of Special Needs Education*, 25(4): 319–336.

Webster, R., Blatchford, P., Bassett, P., Brown, P., Martin, C. and Russell, A. (2011) The wider pedagogical role of teaching assistants, *School Leadership and Management*, 31(1): 3–20.

Webster, R. and Blatchford, P. (2013) *The Making a Statement Project Final Report*. Available online at: www.nuffieldfoundation.org/sites/default/files/files/mastreport%281%29.pdf (accessed 17 April 2015).

Webster, R. and Blatchford, P. (2015) Worlds apart? The nature and quality of the educational experiences of pupils with a statement for special educational needs in mainstream primary schools, *British Educational Research Journal*, 41(2): 324–342.

Chapter 12

Including parents with disabled children

Michele Moore

Introduction

In this chapter I look at how parents of disabled children can be allies in the new teachers' project of advancing inclusion. I draw on insider perspective as a parent of two children with impairments to encourage new teachers to recognise the invaluable role parents can play in helping new teachers include children they may find difficult to support. The literature includes many similar parent-led analyses of how new teachers can support families with disabled children including Benson (2014), Hodge and Runswick-Cole (2008), Rix and Matthews (2014) that new teachers will find helpful. These sources give much evidence of parent-professional relationships as problematic for both parents and professionals but also show how maximising involvement of parents in a new teacher's work can prove enabling and empowering for all concerned. Ideally, parents can be viewed as allies, able to support new teachers seeking to optimise inclusion. I also draw for this chapter on years of professional work to support teachers building best practice in inclusive education, which means I can see the task of building relationships between new teachers and parents from both perspectives. My approach has been developed over the years from both academic research-based knowledge *and* experience as a parent of disabled children so that I am combining a strong theoretically based view of how teachers can support parents of disabled children with a passionate commitment to persuade new teachers of its necessity. I have found close relationships between teachers and parents reduce risk of exclusion, not just for children with impairments, but for *all* children. So in this chapter I am offering an idea for enhancing teaching and learning through closer relations with parents of a disabled child that can be applied to parents of *any* child, emphasizing that inclusive practice is good for everyone.

Learning through Disability Studies

Ideas and that which have evolved through the work of disabled people offer new teachers useful practical strategies for involvement of parents. Disabled people's own ideas offer a rich resource to any teacher willing to take seriously inclusive teaching and learning. At the centre of a strategy to help new teachers work with parents of disabled children lies application of the *social model of disability* which, once understood, quickly helps a new teacher move past any constraints to the participation of disabled children and their parents. The *social model of disability* was developed by disabled people who came together to create a theoretical framework that would enable non-disabled people to understand that difficulties people with impairment face in their lives are not a product of their impairments, but the outcome of the experience of living in a disabling world (UPIAS 1976; Oliver 2009, 2013). The *social model of disability* calls for recognition of material, attitudinal, cultural and other socially constructed barriers that limit the lives of people with impairments. Once social barriers to inclusion are identified they can be dismantled so that children need not encounter disabling schools, communities and identities. If new teachers apply social model thinking to their discussions with parents of disabled children then the focus of intervention falls on dismantling any barriers that potentially inhibit inclusion. The social model of disability enables parents and teachers to stop worrying about a child's impairment and concentrate instead on the child's experience. This is highly facilitative since neither teachers nor parents can typically alter the fact of impairment but both can have a deep moment by moment impact on changing a child's experience.

'Social model thinking'

'Social model thinking' allows teachers and parents to work together on shared projects for reducing exclusion of disabled children and can equally be applied to dismantling barriers compounding risk of exclusion due to wider politics of inequality such as poverty, membership of a cultural, faith or linguistic minority groups, complexities relating to migration status and so on. This is how it works.

'Social model thinking' involves focusing directly on barriers encountered by children; it enables teachers to take a creative approach to dismantling the barriers that create segregation, exclusion and disablement, rather than worrying about specific questions of impairment. To effectively include a child who has hearing impairment in teaching and learning, for example, it is not necessary to have an in-depth knowledge of paediatric audiology but it is essential to work tirelessly to understand and remove the day-to-day disabling barriers a child faces and this is greatly assisted through working closely with parents (Case 2000; Hodge and Runswick-Cole 2008). A parent can tell you where their deaf child would like to sit to benefit from light in the classroom, how many voices they can comfortably access in group activities, the distance in paces at which they can lip-read, whether subtitles will help follow a film or confuse and so on (Beazley *et al.* 2012). An enabling teacher, concentrating not on 'the child's problem' but on 'dismantling barriers that create difficulty' can capitalise on huge willingness of parents to be part of the project of enabling their child's education. Where an individualised deficit approach is taken to talking to parents about their disabled children confidence and trust breaks down (consider being told at every parent's evening year-in-year-out 'your daughter isn't a good listener'); social model thinking promotes a shared and creative approach to foster positive relationships and inclusion (the liberation offered by a teacher who asks 'what can I do to communicate more effectively with her?').

The website of the Centre for Studies of Inclusive Education (http://www.csie.org.uk) evidences widespread commitment amongst parents to support the participation of their disabled children in mainstream settings but parents know:

> Inclusion is not an easy option. It is difficult because it requires people to examine their deepest held prejudices and fears; it asks people to learn new skills; it means people have to think creatively . . . it means doing things differently.
>
> (Mason 2009)

The imperative for teachers and parents to work together as allies in support of inclusive education for children with impairments is plain. Social model thinking, in which we are always focused on breaking down barriers, strengthens parent-teacher relations because discussions are never child-blaming and are always solution-oriented.

It is not discretion, pity or specialist knowledge of impairment that a new teacher needs when involving parents in responses towards their disabled children, but simply an enabling attitude towards inclusion. The idea that it is not impairment that creates disability but experience, lies at the heart of 'social model' thinking for inclusive practice; focus on this idea provides an assured way to enhancing relationships between teachers and parents. Any teacher who can make plain social model thinking gives parents tangible insight into how they as the teacher will actively seek to tackle barriers that create disablement and exclusion. A parent who hears a teacher talking about 'unblocking the blocks' to their child's participation in school and classroom life starts to feel disablement fall away from their child's experience of education and opportunities for parent-teacher collaboration take firm root.

On the other hand, a parent who hears a teacher worry about what they do or do not know about the specifics of a child's impairment, hesitate about 'problems' associated with particular impairments or stress numerous difficulties a child may face in the classroom, knows for certain that in this teacher's class their child is on a trajectory leading to construction of disablement. I find time and time again that teachers who are social model theorists – and many intuitively are because they focus intently on their own teaching difficulties rather than a child's learning difficulties – these teachers instil confidence in parents for working in partnership to dismantle difficulty. When a parent hears a teacher take the locus of responsibility for their disabled child's education and development away from the child, and place enablement within their own practice, then the distance between teachers and parents is quickly reduced; then parents feel themselves to be allies in the new teacher's project of inclusion.

A premise of consultation

There have been policy shifts towards consulting with and maximising participation of parents in order to improve services for vulnerable children and support families (Lamb Inquiry 2009; Children and Families Act 2014). Emphasis is on trying to give parents a strong voice, acknowledging close involvement of parents in their child's education can make a positive difference to how parents feel and is advantageous because parents know a great deal about what will benefit their children. Nonetheless, having formal legal rights to involvement does not necessarily mean parents can realise these rights in school (Tveit 2009). In the UK, at the time of writing, evidence is found daily of parents with disabled children struggling to make their voices heard: 'Mums are the most knowledgeable but professionals won't listen, are patronising' (Morgan 2015a); 'Mums told "not to bite the hand that feeds" – how to challenge when you are in the system, what sort of starting point?' (Morgan 2015b).

Research already cited in this chapter shows many parents face a battle to get into a close relationship with professionals but also reveals that those in close contact with teachers feel best supported and have children who make optimum progress. Consequently, new teachers will wish to continually review their own relationships with parents.

Parents' voices

The more difficult it is to have a close relationship with parents the more important it will be to find a way so to do. In the following example the long-lasting deleterious effects of poor communications between a teacher and a parent of a disabled child can be seen – in this case the teacher is not a new teacher but the significance of the story will hopefully stay in the mind of any new teacher reading about it.

The mother of a disabled teenager – Ruth – I worked to support recently had been accused by a non-disabled child of giving Ruth black eyes. Ruth's mother asked me to support her in discussions with teachers because inconclusive medical explanation for the frequently occurring black eyes led teachers to doubt her protestations of innocence. As Ruth has learning and speech difficulties her teachers concluded her own declarations that her mother did not injure her were unreliable. It is always the case that not hearing, overriding and silencing a child's own voice is unacceptable, and compounding this with avoidance of contact with Ruth's mother, meant communication rapidly broke down. A decision was taken to discuss Ruth's injuries with her estranged father but not with her, or her mother. Now I can see in these entanglements many reasons why teachers were wary of involvement with Ruth's mother; they suspected she was protesting her innocence too loudly, seeking to deflect the conclusions they were drawing about her. The more intently Ruth's mother reasoned she was not the perpetrator of injuries the more teachers formed the view she was clever and trying to ward off suspicion; the more they decided she was trying to ward off suspicion the more they pathologised her and the less willing they were to involve her in discussions about Ruth. Ruth's father, on the other hand, who rarely saw or spent time with his daughter and refused to speak to her mother on account of the accusations, did not learn of Ruth's disclosure to her mother that she had long been the victim of a homophobic bullying campaign. In school – where this information was not known because teachers had closed down conversations with both Ruth and her mother – Ruth became more and more isolated and withdrawn, occurrence of black eyes did not cease and she started to frequently be absent from school. Her exclusion was constructed not because of impairment but because teachers could not find a way to reduce the distance between themselves and her mother. It was not until Ruth received a further bruised eye, this time recorded on the school's CCTV, that the inevitability that distance between parents and teachers would intensify exclusion – and in this case allow for continued physical harm – was fully realised by the school. Undoubtedly, it is difficult for teachers to involve parents in discussions about a child when there are safeguarding issues; the point is simply the more difficult it is for a teacher to have a conversation with a parent the more important it is to have it – even more so where teachers do not have skills for comfortable and effective communication with a disabled child. Pahl (2010) stresses the importance of listening to the stories and experiences of parents 'for things that might be missing' so that as practitioners we might 'hear them'. The need for delineation of legitimate voices of teachers, pupils, and parents requires immensely careful attention and I hope the true story of the marginalisation of Ruth's mother will alert new teachers to the importance of seeking the widest possible conversation with parents and keeping minds open as widely as possible too.

Wilde and Hoskin-Clark (2014) remind us of the importance of guarding against assumptions about parents that can mean important issues will be misread or go unaddressed. Tveit (2009) found diversity among parents an inadequately addressed issue in schools; ensuring parents have access to teachers includes making sure all parents can participate equally. This extends to inviting interpreters when there is no shared spoken or signed language for example, or thinking creatively about how disabled parents can participate. Within early years settings involvement of parents is easier to establish as fewer teachers are involved with a child. It is important to think about keeping parents centrally involved in secondary schools where many teachers come into contact with a child. At a typical UK secondary school carousel style Parent-Teachers Evening, for example, where every teacher across a year group sits at desks in rows and parents rush about queuing for short discussions with subject teachers the communication environment is likely to be prohibitive for deaf parents, inhibiting for parents who use mental health services or simply inaccessible for a parent who cannot physically dash about to find one teacher in the dining room and another upstairs on the mezzanine. If such events comprise the main occasion for teachers to talk to parents it is very easy to see how parents can find themselves outside of the conversation. New teachers can support parents of any child by taking a social model approach to the practical dismantling of organisational barriers that might limit opportunities for a parent to come to school.

There is hard work involved for new teachers committed to bringing parents into a closer relationship but the legislative context does assert that all parents, including those with disabled children, should have a strong voice in their child's education. Where they do not, we hear terrible stories from parents as already described. The manner in which disabled children and their parents are brought into consultation with teachers working to support them is crucial. Although the focus of the illustrations coming next in this chapter is on inclusion of disabled children, it is evident that any teacher who can apply social model principles to their work has skills that will facilitate the inclusion of *any* child at risk of exclusion. The skills of social model thinking quickly inscribe an aptitude for inclusive thinking and practice upon teachers. Moreover, disability can be reduced when teachers are willing to involve parents as allies.

Involving parents

My son's impairment involves limb reconstruction through external fixation of bones, typical for children with limb discrepancies, as well as for those with restricted growth. His situation is interesting to any new teacher because he moves in and out of 'disabled child' status depending on where we are up to in terms of surgery. His experience of impairment provides a clear example of how impairment may be a fixed determinant of identity but disability is not. At the beginning of Michael's journey into disabled child status teachers understood disability as a social practice and connected the minimising of disablement to commitment to inclusion and valuing of parental involvement. His head teacher's response was:

> Michael is a Rowan [school] boy. We want to keep him in our Rowan school. We will do whatever we have to do to keep him in. If we have to move Year 5 classrooms downstairs or put in a stair lift we will . . . and we'll just be making provision for other children who come our way in the future . . .

Michael's inclusion was seen as an opportunity for the school and its wider community and inclusion would be the key through which disablement would be minimised. The head teacher remembered her own daughter's medical history as once having jeopardised her inclusion, which brings to mind the observations of Sharma *et al.* (2008) that the more contact teachers have with children with impairments and their parents the more confident they are likely to feel about including them in their classrooms.

The school's response to me as a parent seeking inclusion was made easier because I had privilege and power in my relations with teachers that not all parents have. Since first knowing of Michael's impairment I had been shamelessly manufacturing positive relationships with teachers, building my chances of being seen as the school's ally. I conducted some free research to assist governors for example, and started helping with literacy assessments because I needed teachers talking to me and on my side. These efforts paid dividends and Michael's ongoing inclusion was relatively seamless. His class teacher arranged wheelchair access, children were taught the difference between the consequences of impairment and the consequences of exclusion. Obstacles that couldn't be overcome, such as an accessible children's toilet, were circumvented by allowing use of staff toilets. Where there were no ramps the caretaker improvised with boards; often ordinary everyday solutions to dismantling barriers that create exclusion. Inclusive attitudes and close involvement of parents enabled a disabled child to be included. I was even able to encourage risk knowing that disabled children like their non-disabled peers are entitled to encounter risk and this offers many benefits and Michael was included in tennis lessons in his wheelchair (Moore and Dunn 2005).

Yet Hasan, who occupied the next hospital bed to Michael, having identical impairment and surgery, attended a school at which the head teacher expressed fear of disability and ensured Hasan was excluded. For months every time we saw Hasan and his parents at outpatient clinics they told us his teacher 'couldn't manage him back yet'. The obstacle to Hasan's inclusion resided in the lack of power his parents could wield in their relationship with teachers. They were made to feel they should be passive in discussions over which teachers asserted a dominant voice; this closed down the possibility of discussing Hasan's return to school, precluded his parents from advocacy of his entitlement to be in school and impacted upon the way they felt about subsequently trying to make their son's case for returning to school with obvious and inevitable bearing upon the child's learning. The danger of disempowering, alienating and excluding parents with subsequent damage to a child's development is clear.

The importance of a close relationship between parents and teachers to enable inclusion of disabled children is marked in the different experiences of Michael and Hasan. My own positive experience was facilitated by a particular kind of resource I could offer to the brokering of a strong parent-teacher relationship. Crabtree (2009), also the mother of a disabled child, noticed this when she wrote '[teachers] did talk to me because I made myself a nuisance' adding, 'I'm a journalist, I'm used to ferreting and checking. I cannot imagine how those with English as a second language cope.' For Hasan's mother, who did not speak English and who had five younger children at home, a teacher would need to take an entirely proactive approach to bring her in to a conversation about how her disabled son might best be included. She was not in a position to engineer her own involvement. It is easy to see how application of social model thinking would have been assistive: rather than obsessing over the complexities of Hasan's impairment teachers could have focused on what they needed to do to break down the barriers of his inclusion; finding ways to communicate with his mother would have offered immediate ways forward.

I have seen time and time again, in very different schools and communities across the world, that close relationships between teachers and parents is key to inclusion of disabled children (Moore 2010). The more teachers and parents share the detail of their joint commitment to a disabled child's inclusion the more enablement becomes possible. Over the weeks when Hasan was still not in school I watched an initially hesitant teacher begin to include Michael in everything his peers were doing. Sometimes she referred to me, particularly seeking assurance that the level of risk she was taking was acceptable. In these ways, a teacher who was at pains to say she 'had no special needs training' first evolved, and then cascaded, the kind of inclusive practice that diminished disablement. She did it through social model thinking and by sustaining a close relationship with a disabled child's parents. The teacher constantly asked herself not, 'what are the problems with Michael?' but 'what do I have to do to reduce problems for Michael?' and if she didn't know, she asked me. All teachers can facilitate the inclusion of disabled children when they are willing to apply this kind of social model thinking to their involvement with parents: this approach enables teachers and parents to be co-constructors of inclusion. My child struggled with impairment but this was not turned into disability by processes of exclusion. Hasan, whose mother was not brought into close contact with his teachers, missed school for six months. His parents became resigned to disempowerment regarding their own involvement in their son's education as problematic and unwanted in spite of the fact that they had legitimate perspectives on the matter of his exclusion. Hasan became isolated and unsurprisingly setback in learning and self-esteem – not because of impairment – we have already seen his impairment, age and stage were the same as Michael's, but excluded because teachers did not cultivate a close relationship with his parents. As in the case of Ruth cited earlier, actual physical harm ensued when following months stuck at home Hasan's physical recovery was compromised by immobility and pressure-sores. These true stories show there is no room for complacency over the way teachers involve parents of disabled children; where relationships with parents are neglected or underestimated the consequences are immensely detrimental for children.

I often hear parents of children with impairments express reluctance to seek out close contact with teachers. They fear being a nuisance or putting their child's problems too closely under scrutiny. A mother told me, 'I was too scared to go in about Katy's reading because I'm probably a bit dyslexic too and I'm worried I won't really understand what they're saying.' An observant teacher, willing to embed social model thinking into their practice, thinking always 'how can I get to tackle Katy's reading progress more effectively?' will spot barriers to involvement of parents and find ways of circumventing them. Later, the same mother was asked to help with her younger son's class lettuce planting. 'One of the teaching assistants', she said, 'was really friendly and I started asking her a bit about what they do about dyslexia.' I have written elsewhere about how teaching assistants can bring parents into closer relationship with schools and their role in supporting new teachers is well worth maximising (Moore 2008).

Positive stories of teachers working with parents of disabled children to promote inclusion offer new teachers good practice pointers (Moore 2010). Rix and Matthews (2014) observed how the father of a disabled boy who attended over 40 formal meetings with staff at nursery and school settings developed many important relationships with a range of practitioners and 'despite some disagreements along the way' was able to report mutual benefits for teachers and the child's family as each meeting was associated with strengthening mutual understanding of the wider support context which could have impact upon the child and the support he received. Rix and Matthews point out that focus of teacher-parent conversation doesn't have to be on an individual child or teacher but can usefully be about who else in the school system can help support inclusion. With this social model perspective in hand, new teachers can easily recognise the wider role played by parents of disabled children and even divergent perspectives need not become obstacles to inclusion.

Conclusions

In these stories the focus has been on working with the social model of disability to maximise inclusion of parents in the education of disabled children. Involving parents of disabled children is not always easy for new teachers but it has been shown how social model thinking helps teachers keep options for reducing distance open. Inclusion lies in the willingness of teachers to facilitate close involvement of parents and to focus on dismantling whatever barriers may create disablement. I hope the chapter conveys how considerable benefits accrue when teachers privilege involvement of parents and inscribe their work with the principles of a social model approach to dismantling barriers surrounding inclusion of children and parents alike. This approach unifies the parent and teacher's agenda, focusing on how *any* child is to be welcomed and included in school. We can think of inclusion of *all* children as simply a decision and a practice immensely facilitated by good relationships between teachers and parents.

Reflection on values and practice

1   For any new teacher the presence of disability in your own life may not be too far away. What can you learn from your own experience that would encourage and enable you to involve parents of disabled children in your work?
2   The chapter ends by asking new teachers to think of inclusion of disabled children and their parents as 'a decision and a practice'. What is the decision required and what are the practice requirements for you as a new teacher?
3   If you are struggling to make contact with the family of a disabled child who can help?

References

Beazley, S., Merritt, R. and Halden, J. (2012) *Working with Deaf Children*. In Kersner, M. and Wright, J. (eds.) *Speech and Language Therapy*, London: Taylor & Francis, pp.126–134.
Benson, D. (2014) *Education – School*. In Colin Cameron (ed.) *Disability Studies: a student's guide*, London: Sage, pp.50–52.
Case, S. (2000) Refocusing on the parent: what are the social issues of concern for parents of disabled children? *Disability & Society*, Volume 15, Issue 2, pp.271–292.
Children and Families Act (2014) The Stationery Office. Available online at: www.tsoshop.co.uk. Accessed 12 May 2015.
Centre for Studies of Inclusive Education (CSIE) (2015) Website: http://www.csie.org.uk. Accessed 12 May 2015.
Crabtree, S. (2009) 'I came to see the school as a little corner of paradise', *The Observer*, Sunday 20 December 2009.

Hodge, N. and Runswick-Cole, K. (2008) Problematising parent–professional partnerships in education, *Disability & Society*, 23(6): 637–647.

Lamb Inquiry (2009) Special educational needs and parental confidence, Reference: DCSF-01143-2009, Nottingham: DCSF Publications.

Mason, M. (cited 2009) http://www.michelinemason.com/topics/inclusion.htm. Accessed 1 May 2012.

Moore, M. and Dunn, K. (2005) Research on developing accessible play space, *Children, Youth and Environments*. Vol. 15 (1): 331–353.

Moore, M. (2008) Inclusive relationships: insights from teaching assistants on how schools can reach parents. In Richards, G. and Armstrong, F. *Key Issues for Teaching Assistants. Working in diverse and inclusive classrooms*, London: Routledge, pp.84–95.

Moore, M. (2010) Inclusion, narrative and voices of disabled children in Trinidad and St Lucia. In Lavia, J. and Moore, M. *Cross-Cultural Perspectives on Policy and Practice*, London: Routledge, pp.101–115.

Morgan, H. (2015a) Twitter @HannahnagroM 18 May 7:46 am.

Morgan, H. (2015b) Twitter @HannahnagroM 18 May 7:46 am.

Oliver, M. (2009 second edition) *Understanding Disability: from theory to practice*, London: Macmillan.

Oliver, M. (2013) The social model of disability: thirty years on, *Disability & Society*, 28(7): 1024–1026.

Pahl, K. (2010) Changing literacies. In Lavia, J. and Moore, M. *Cross-cultural Perspectives on Policy and Practice*, London: Routledge, pp.58–71.

Rix, J. and Matthews, A. (2014) Viewing the child as a participant within context, *Disability & Society*, 29(9): 1428–1442.

Sharma, U., Forlin, C., and Loreman, T. (2008) Impact on training on pre-service teachers' attitudes and concerns about inclusive education and sentiments about persons with disabilities, *Disability & Society*, 23(7): 773–785.

Tveit, A. D. (2009) A parental voice: parents as equal and dependent – rhetoric about parents, teachers, and their conversations, *Educational Review*, 61(3): 289–300.

UPIAS (1976). *Fundamental Principles of Disability*, London: Union of the Physically Impaired Against Segregation.

Wilde, A. and Hoskin-Clark, A. (2014) *Families*. In Colin Cameron (ed.) *Disability Studies: a student's guide*, London: Sage, pp.56–58.

Chapter 13

Why did he do *that?* Evidence-based teaching and learning

Gill Richards

Introduction

> Why did he do *that?*
> How can I do that better?
> Why isn't this working for her?

As a new teacher working in an 'Observation and Assessment Centre' for young people who had been sent there by the UK court system to determine their future education needs, I spent a lot of time wondering why the young people with whom I worked behaved in the ways that they did. As I gained more teaching experience, I then started to wonder why some of my sessions didn't work for particular individuals and what I could do differently. I also became more aware of groups within education who seemed to struggle, with their needs clearly not being met or understood by staff. Later, as a part-time youth leader working in an area in which I also taught, I regularly met pupils in other contexts and started to realise that we only see part of young people's lives in school and much that affects them is unknown or even deliberately hidden from us.

Over the years I became used to new national education developments that required me to teach differently. Some of these excited me, but I was sceptical about others. There was usually some 'evidence' produced to explain why teachers should take on these new developments – such as impressive statistics – but as a busy practitioner, I didn't have time to consider the quality of this. It was only later, when I took part in postgraduate studies that I became enthusiastic about research and understood the importance of using robust evidence to underpin teachers' practice.

After a lifetime of teaching in schools, colleges and universities, there are still many things that I 'wonder' about and this curiosity has been the basis of my continuing interest in research and work supporting teachers – trying to find out 'why?', particularly where this could make a difference for young people who were finding education settings and learning difficult. Teachers rightly place a high level of importance in professional knowledge and skills, but research should not be seen as an isolated activity that detracts from daily classroom practice: excellent research can underpin excellence in teaching and pupils' learning.

It is this belief – that research should be an integral part of teachers' professional practice – that provides the context for the chapter, exploring the role of evidence-based practice within schools and the importance of teachers' contribution in generating this. It focuses on the benefits for individual teachers in understanding more to help them respond to the diverse learners within their own classrooms. Increasing inclusion and responding positively to diversity can make significant demands on all teachers. Identifying what works and why within their own setting can enable busy professionals to more effectively personalise their practice to meet pupils' specific needs. So, to return to the start of this chapter, what happens in your classroom and school that you 'wonder' about?

Evidence-based practice: why is it important for teachers and pupils?

The idea of teachers as researchers has a long history both within the UK and internationally. For example, in the 1960s–1970s, Stenhouse introduced the view that research-based teaching was required to generate new pedagogical knowledge (Stenhouse 1975) and later, Hargreaves (1996) identified the importance of 'evidence-based' practice within schools and called for teaching to be a researched-based profession. In the US, the National Council of Teachers of Illinois, drew attention to the increasing complexity within such developments, arguing that despite the relationship between teaching and research either being assumed or ignored, the emphasis on research-based practice has made it

> imperative that teachers understand not only how to use research to help their students learn but also how to critique the claims made by researchers and policy-makers outside the classroom who use research as means of influencing or even over-riding teacher decision-making.
>
> (National Council of Teachers 2005: 4)

In Australia, Victoria's Department of Education and Early Childhood Development's report, *Teachers as Researchers*, made similar claims, describing the need for teachers to 'attempt to better understand their practice, and its impact on their students, by researching the relationship between teaching and learning in their world of work' (DEECD 2006: 3).

As the profile of research in schools was raised, teachers' unique 'insider knowledge' became increasingly respected within the research community (Burke and Kirton 2006). Despite this recognition, many teachers remained unconvinced about the application of research to the realities of their world: academic writing about research studies was seen as inaccessible and unrelated to school core priorities (Hulme *et al.* 2009). Although teachers accepted that there were benefits in using research evidence to inform their choices about classroom practice, most preferred this to be provided at conferences and workshops, where research had already been translated into practice for them (Nelson and O'Beirne 2014). The difficulty with this was that they then received research evidence filtered by others and so were unable to form their own views based on an overview of the whole research process and different kinds of data which emerged. An example of this was when the media created a storm with headlines about the negative impact of teaching assistant support. The actual report (Blatchford *et al.* 2012) did provide significant evidence to support this claim but also clarified where support was successful – additional information that many teachers did not access. When taking this approach, teachers are not encouraged to become confident users of research evidence themselves and their reliance on receiving 'second-hand evidence' may result in rejection of information that does not fit with their own experiences. Teachers need to believe in the value of evidence if an evidence-based teaching profession is to become a reality (Nelson and O'Beirne 2014). Without this belief, there is a danger that 'outsider' research can disenfranchise teachers and exclude them from debates about professional knowledge, leaving them vulnerable to increasing external intervention (Hulme *et al.* 2009).

National developments within education have attempted to embed research into core school activity and teachers' professional learning (Hulme *et al.* 2009; Harris and Jones 2012; Nelson and O'Beirne 2014; Cordingley 2015). Research is increasingly seen as having a vital role to play in not only enriching the work of educational professionals, but also in informing policy-making processes (BERA and UCET 2012). Department for Education funding has enabled Teaching School Alliances and other teacher groups to engage in research activity on locally identified priorities as well as nationally led projects. Initial concerns about schools' capacity to produce high quality research evidence were followed by calls for teacher training courses to further develop trainees' skills in this (Nelson and O'Beirne 2014) and increased collaboration and support from academic researchers to help create a 'democratisation of research relationships' (Hulme *et al.* 2009: 19). This latter point was further developed by Cordingley (2015: 236) who argued that 'a shared language between teachers and researchers' was needed to increase research-informed professional development and embed findings into everyday practice. All of this supports teachers' understanding of the different interpretations about what constitutes 'evidence' and the different methods and tools that can be used to collect this. Increased understanding increases confidence in identifying the quality of claims made and robustness of evidence collection – all of which can enable teachers to make choices that can enhance their own practice and benefits for all students.

Even with these changes, tensions are still evident on the relevance of teachers' research. Teacher research is often dismissed as small-scale, anecdotal and non-replicable. Goldacre (2013) in particular argues for the need of large-scale randomised testing approaches, similar to those used by the medical profession, but this is challenged by others who argue that research does not have to produce objective and generalisable national knowledge bases (Burke and Kirton 2006; Hulme *et al.* 2009; Smith 2013; Nelson and O'Beirne 2014). They suggest that contextualised small-scale research recognises institutional constraints on diverse experiences and practices, and in deepening understanding at local level, 'wider connections can be made to shed light on broader educational policy and practice'

(Burke and Kirton 2006: 2). This is particularly relevant for teachers who want to understand what research evidence means for them in their own situation. They know that what works in one school will not necessarily work in another, so claims made by large-scale research for universal benefit across diverse contexts can do more damage than good. Teachers are less likely to engage with the findings of these or critique the quality of the evidence presented where such studies fail to address the nuances and complexities of local level practice. While proponents of large-scale studies claim that these provide evidence that is value-free and decontextualised, Burke and Kirton (2006: 2) disagree, arguing that such studies are 'unable to say much about how difference and diversity is lived out and often reinforces educational exclusions and inequalities'. This argument highlights the importance of further investigation to increase achievement and inclusion for the diversity of learners found in every classroom today.

Diversity, achievement and inclusion

'Diversity is a multi-dimensional, broadly inclusive concept that embraces the richness of human difference' (Coleman *et al.* 2011: 20). It is not an ambiguous term that is a 'code' for specific groups, although it is important to consider 'differences' when ensuring equitable experiences and outcomes for all pupils. A significant amount of international research suggests that diversity within learning environments provides benefits for all students through improved academic achievement, inculcation of democratic values and collaborative learning (Fine and Handleson 2010; Coleman *et al.* 2011). This association of diversity with educational excellence reflects a major shift in the way that education leaders think and act about diversity issues. Previously, schools responded to diverse groups of learners either by not recognising differences between students or – particularly in the case of those identified as having learning or behavioural difficulties or disabilities – by establishing separate provision for them. Now, although barriers do still remain for some young people, we can see 'a shift from externally imposed set obligations to institutional choice associated with educational goals' (Coleman *et al.* 2011: 15), creating an opportunity for schools to prioritise inclusive responses to meeting diverse learning needs.

Research studies into diversity, achievement and inclusion have identified several issues important for teachers to be mindful of in their work with young people: pupils from 'working class' backgrounds are still the lowest achieving group within schools, and girls from this group have the greatest fear of failure and are more likely to benefit less from 'equality' initiatives (EHRC 2009; Ofsted 2011); pupils in care often have lower aspirations and educational outcomes, and despite feeling cared for still feel unconnected to others (Duncalf 2010); aspirations are formed at an early age but are sometimes clouded by concerns about the discrimination and disadvantage (Hutchinson *et al.* 2011); and pupils who have been identified as having special educational needs and Black boys are still more likely to be excluded from school (Atkinson 2013).

Inequality in educational attainment has been the focus of national policy and school developments to 'Narrow the Gap' (Ofsted 2007). Evidence shows that inequality is strongly associated with socio-economic background and that 'current provision still has inadequacies in opening up opportunities and challenging low expectations and aspirations based on stereotypes' (Hutchinson *et al.* 2011: p.ii). Particular groups, such as those identified with special educational needs, certain minority ethnic groups and young people within the care system, have long been identified as vulnerable to underachievement (Ofsted 2007; Ofsted 2013), even within seemingly high performing schools:

> They are found even within seemingly prosperous communities where the majority achieve well ... labelled, buried in lower sets, coasting through education until at the first opportunity they can sever their ties with it.
>
> (Wilshaw 2013: 5)

Wilshaw's perspective highlights a fundamental problem about the way that some schools respond to initiatives to close the achievement gap. If schools view diversity and an inclusive ethos as unconducive to a high quality learning environment, they may react with selection criteria that appear unwelcoming to some families and internal arrangements that separate 'problem' learners from their higher achieving peers. This can result in different pupils receiving very different experiences from the same teachers, policies and practices (Hattie 2009). Other 'gaps' may also be present in schools, but receive less attention: gaps between young people who engage with school life and those who do not; those who feel included and those who do not; and those whose voices are heard and those whose are not. While these gaps may be clearly observed within a school community, others may sometimes be hidden by young people who do not want to share their lives for a wide range of reasons, or whose outward behaviour masks internal disengagement.

Although research evidence informs us of what is happening nationally and internationally, there is much we do not know, especially at a local level. Goodman and Gregg, (2010) make it clear that despite significant research evidence about attainment, much is still left unexplained. Other researchers in this field agree, stating that we do not understand the more complex inter-relationship between aspirations and educational outcomes (Kintrea *et al.* 2011) or the effects home and school factors have on educational achievement (Cole 2012). It is these gaps in knowledge that teachers can fill through localised research evidence collection.

Teachers can use national and international research as the basis for a further collection of evidence on their own pupils' experiences. Large-scale research often focuses on diversity within separate 'equality strands', producing collective evidence rather than acknowledging pupils' intersectional identities that may compound experiences of inequality and exclusion (Hutchinson *et al.* 2011; Sherry 2013; Tomlinson 2014). A more individualised approach to investigation enables a focus on pupils' very specific experiences to inform teaching, evaluate the impact of strategies such as those used for Pupil Premium funding and provide personalised solutions to increase achievement and inclusion. This provides the opportunity for teachers to reappraise existing practices, challenge assumptions and reframe perceived problems, fostering greater capacity to meet learner diversity (Miles and Ainscow 2011).

An evidence base for diversity and inclusion

The monitoring of pupil progress and achievement through analysis of data evidence is a standard requirement for schools, with national league tables, the Data Dashboard and more localised comparisons providing a basis for parental choice of school and Ofsted inspections (Ofsted 2015). Within this, particular groups must be reviewed in relation to their 'labels' – for example, those targeted for the Pupil Premium, pupils who receive free school meals or have been identified as having special educational needs. What may be less rigorously analysed is the achievement and wider experiences of two groups of young people – those who may be less easily identifiable by 'labels' but still on the margins of school life and those whose personal circumstances create several disadvantages that intersect, reinforcing and exacerbating each other. Knowledge about this is limited because evidence from such experiences is rarely collected through national research studies (Frederickson and Cline 2010; Rollock and Gillborn 2011; Mereish 2012; Thiara and Hague 2013), but this is a key area for teachers to review at their own school level to help them understand the impact of multiple aspects of disadvantage on pupils' lives (Joseph Rowntree Foundation 2014). Taking an in-depth approach to collecting and analysing evidence of a wider range of young people's experiences has long been recommended by researchers to identify 'in-school factors that can entrench wider social inequalities' (Dunne *et al.* 2007: 9), monitor equality issues and aspirations (Hutchinson *et al.* 2011) and focus on 'pedagogical approaches and strategies that go beyond teacher-led 'differentiation' to learner-centred, personalised classroom practice . . . that raise achievement and develop resilience (European Agency for Development in Special Needs Education 2012: 17).

Since research evidence has demonstrated that many funded initiatives for closing the attainment gap have actually been successful in increasing achievement for all learners – thereby maintaining rather than narrowing the gap between vulnerable learners and their peers – questions remain about what can actually close the gap and how evidence can demonstrate this (Save the Children 2012; House of Commons 2014; Sosu and Ellis 2014; Centre for Social Justice 2015; Australian Government 2015). One of the problems teachers face is the lack of robust evidence about the impact of these initiatives. Reports by the Joseph Rowntree Trust (2014) and Kendall *et al.* (2008) criticised the highly variable quality and quantity of data currently available, suggesting that this has contributed to a lack of reliable knowledge, particularly where this involved 'intersectional' social inequalities. Similar concerns were expressed by the European Agency for Development in Special Needs Education (2012) within its report, *Raising Achievement for All Learners – Quality in Inclusive Education*, where it stated that developments were inevitably failing because they were 'over-laid' or bolted-onto an inherently flawed and unfair education system. All of these reports called for improved accountability mechanisms in schools to provide concrete evidence of effective strategies that meet 'vulnerable' young people's needs and increase their inclusion. Undertaking this would require more in-depth interrogation and cross-analysis of data, and collection of evidence from a wider range of sources than routinely available, to discover the 'story' behind the data. In particular, the voices of the young people themselves should feature prominently, so that understanding is increased about their 'world', what barriers they face and what matters to them.

Making research evidence work in 'real' classrooms

Teachers engage in forms of research every day. They regularly pose questions, investigate and gather information, analyse it and use this to decide what needs to change (Anderson 2015). This process may not be as systematic as is described earlier in this chapter or be recognised as more formal 'action research', but does provide a sound foundation for a more in-depth approach to seeking evidence about diversity and inclusive practice. What is important is that the focus should be on what makes a difference for young people: what improves their experiences of learning, their achievement and sense of belonging?

Research and evidence collection can be seen by busy teachers as yet another thing to include in an ever-expanding list of duties, further intensifying their workload and potentially impinging on the core job of teaching (Hulme *et al.* 2009). By keeping the focus on gaining a better understanding of pupils' experiences to increase their participation and achievement, research activity can be effectively linked to teachers' everyday work and key priorities. There will always be practical challenges in doing this. Capacity may be a constraint, with time being the main concern. Skills in carrying out rigorous research activity and evidence collection may also be a concern for some teachers if they have had limited prior experience. Accessing external evidence can be time consuming and at times impenetrable. Studies on teachers carrying out research found that success was affected by a few key factors – their own beliefs, values and priorities; working in small support groups with the opportunity to discuss activity, share and critique findings; and selecting methods that fit within the time available and their skills (McLean and Mohr 1999; Hulme *et al.* 2009; Nelson and O'Beirne 2014; Cordingley 2015).

So where does a busy teacher start? School data and professional knowledge are obvious places to identify pupils who are creating concern, but to return to earlier parts of this chapter – what about those whose personal circumstances intersect more than one potential disadvantage or who appear to be engaged, but on closer scrutiny are possibly masking disengagement. In today's diverse society, nothing can be taken for granted. While the national focus may be on young people with a range of familiar 'labels', others who are apparently more successful may also be struggling, affected by situations of divorce, redundancy, health, abuse or cultural tensions. This means that school data can only be the starting point, as no single source can give us the whole accurate picture. Cross-analysis of this can highlight further issues and where pupils may be at risk of multiple disadvantage, but then other perspectives are needed to give deeper information – the story behind the 'numbers' – drawing out underlying problems or pinpointing initiatives that do/ do not work and why? These can be gained through a range of investigative methods such as interviews, observations and researching wider information. This leads teachers into considerations of their ethical responsibilities as a teacher-researcher (BERA 2011), requiring careful attention to collecting informed consent where needed, avoiding abuse of teacher 'power', diligence about confidentiality and shielding pupils from any controversy resulting from evidence collected.

Once additional information has been collected, it should be analysed critically to identify assumptions, look for the 'unexpected' and identify evidence that can inform professional practice. Research is not about finding a perfect answer or 'proving a point'. It can be 'messy', often creating more questions and uncomfortable answers, but it can also provide evidence that helps to meet a localised need for specific pupils in specific classrooms. Confident use of research evidence by teachers, whether generated by themselves or others, will enable them to better understand the experiences of young people in their classes, and in doing so increase their participation, achievement and inclusion. New teachers will have a lifetime career of wondering 'why', those who embrace this way of working may find answers that benefit them and their pupils.

Reflection on values and practice

What is going on in pupils' lives?

1   Take the time to stand back and really look at your pupils. What do you *assume* and what do you actually *know* about their 'world', their individual experiences in your classroom, their friends and what happens outside of school?
2   Are there any pupils that cause you concern? What do *you* wonder about?
3   What can you do to find out more about individual pupils' lives?

Suggested further reading

Burton, D. and Bartlett, S. (2005) *Practitioner Research for Teachers*, London: Paul Chapman.
Harris, A. and Jones, M. (2012) *Connecting Professional Learning: leading effective collaborative enquiry across teaching school alliances*, Nottingham: National College for School Leadership.
Miles, S. and Ainscow, M. (eds.) (2011) *Responding to Diversity in Schools*, Abingdon: Routledge.
Ofsted (2013) *Unseen Children: access and achievement 20 years on*, Manchester: Ofsted.

References

Anderson, A. (2015) *An Introduction to Teacher Research*. Learn NC. Available at: www. learnnc.org. Accessed 31 May 2015.

Atkinson, M. (2013) *Inquiry into Social Exclusion. They never give up on you.* London: Office of the Children's Commission.

Australian Government (2015) *Closing the Gap. Prime Minister's report*, Australia: Australian Government.

BERA (2011) *Ethical Guidelines for Educational Research*, London: British Educational Research Association.

BERA/UCET Working Group on Education Research (2012) report – *Prospects for Education Research in Education Departments in Higher Education Institutions in the UK*, London: UCET.

Blatchford, P., Russell, A. and Webster, R. (2012) *Reassessing the Impact of Teaching Assistants: how research challenges practice and policy*, Abingdon: Routledge.

Burke, J. and Kirton, A. (2006) The insider perspective: teachers-as-researchers, *Reflecting Education*, 2(1): 1–4.

Centre for Social Justice (2015) *Closing the Divide. Tackling inequality in England*, London: Centre for Social Justice.

Cole, M. (ed.) (2012) 3rd edition, *Education, Equality and Human Rights*, Abingdon: Routledge.

Coleman, A., Negron, F. and Lipper, K. (2011) *Achieving Educational Excellence for All: a guide to diversity-related policy strategies from school districts*, Virginia, USA: National School Board Association (NSBA).

Cordingley, P. (2015) The contribution of research to teachers' professional learning and development, *Oxford Review of Education* 41(2): 234–252.

Department of Education and Early Childhood Development (2006) *Teachers as Researchers*, Victoria: D of Education and ECD.

Duncalf, Zachari (2010) *Listen up! Adult Care Leavers Speak Out: the views of 310 care leavers aged 17–78*, Manchester: Care Leavers' Association.

Dunne, M., Humphreys, S., Sebba, S., Dyson, A., Gallannaugh, F. and Muijs, D. (2007) *Effective Teaching and Learning for Pupils in Low Attaining Groups*, Nottingham: DfES Publications.

Equality and Human Rights Commission (EHRC) (2009) *Staying On*, London: Equality and Human Rights Commission.

European Agency for Development in Special Needs Education (2012) *Raising Achievement for All Learners – quality in inclusive education*, Odense, Denmark: European Agency for Development in Special Needs Education.

Fine, E. and Handleson, J. (2010) *Benefits and Challenges of Diversity in Academic Settings*, Madison, USA: WISELI.

Frederickson, N. and Cline, T. (2010) *Special Educational Needs, Inclusion and Diversity*, Maidenhead: Open University Press.

Goldacre, B. (2013) *Building Evidence into Education*. Available at: www.tactyc.org.uk/pdfs/Goldacre-paper.pdf. Accessed 20 April 2015.

Goodman, A and Gregg, P. (eds.) (2010) *The Importance of Attitudes and Behaviour for Poorer Children's Educational Attainment*, York: Joseph Rowntree Foundation.

Hargreaves, D. H. (1996) *Teaching as a Research Based Profession: possibilities and prospects,* London: Teacher Training Agency.

Harris, A. and Jones, M. (2012) *Connecting Professional Learning: leading effective collaborative enquiry across teaching school alliances*, Nottingham: National College for School Leadership.

Hattie, D. (2009) *Visible Learning. A synthesis of over 800 meta-analyses relating to achievement*, Abingdon: Routledge.

House of Commons (2014) *Underachievement in Education by White Working Class Children*, London: The Stationery Office.

Hulme, M., Lowdes, K. and Elliot, D. (2009) Teachers as researchers: initial experiences within the Scottish 'Schools of Ambition', *Journal of Teacher Education and Teacher's Work*, 1(1): 18–30.

Hutchinson, J., Rolf, H., Bysshe, S. and Bentley, K. (2011) *All Things Being Equal? Equality and diversity in careers education, information, advice and guidance*, Manchester: EHRC.

Joseph Rowntree Foundation (JRF) (2014) *Closing the Attainment Gap in Scottish Education*, York: Joseph Rowntree Foundation.

Kendall, S., Straw, S., Jones, M., Springate, I. and Grayson, H. (2008) *Narrowing the Gap for Vulnerable Groups. A review of the research evidence*, Slough: NFER.

Kintrea, K., St Clair, R. and Houston, M. (2011) *The Influence of Parents, Places and Poverty on Educational Attitude and Aspirations*, York: Joseph Rowntree Foundation.

McLean, M. and Mohr, M. (1999) *Teacher – researchers at work*, Berkeley, CA: Natle writing project.

Mereish, E. (2012) The intersectional invisibility of race and disability studies: an exploratory study of health and discrimination facing Asian Americans with disabilities, *Ethnicity and Inequality in Health and Social Care*, 5(2): 52–60.

Miles, S. and Ainscow, M. (eds) (2011) *Responding to Diversity in Schools*, Abingdon: Routledge.

National Council of Teachers (2005) *Understanding the Relationship between Research and Teaching*, Illinois, USA: National Council of Teachers.

Nelson, J. and O'Beirne, C. (2014) *Using Evidence in the Classroom: What works and why?* Slough: NfER.

Ofsted (2007) *Narrowing the Gap, the Inspection of Children's Services*, London: Ofsted.

Ofsted (2011) *Girls' Career Aspirations*, Manchester: Ofsted.

Ofsted (2013) *Unseen Children: access and achievement 20 years on*, Manchester: Ofsted.

Ofsted (2015) *Inspecting Schools: a handbook for inspectors*, Manchester: Ofsted.

Rollock, N. and Gillborn, D. (2011) *Critical Race Theory (CRT)*, British Educational Research Association online resource. Available at: www.bera.ac.uk/researchers-resources/publications. Accessed 18 February 2015.

Save the Children (2012) *Closing the Achievement Gap in England's Secondary Schools*, London: Save the Children.

Sherry, M. (2013) International perspectives on disability hate crime. In Roulstone, A. and Mason-Bish, H. (eds.) *Disability, Hate Crime and Violence*, Abingdon: Routledge, pp.80–91.

Sosu, E. and Ellis, S. (2014) *Closing the Attainment Gap in Scottish Education*, York: Joseph Rowntree Foundation.

Stenhouse, L. (1975) *An Introduction to Curriculum Research and Development*, London: Heinemann Educational.

Thiara, R. and Hague, G. (2013) Disabled women and domestic violence; increased risk but fewer services. In Roulstone, A. and Mason-Bish, H. (eds.) *Disability, Hate Crime and Violence*, Abingdon: Routledge, pp.106–117.

Tomlinson, S. (2014) *Repeat Performance: special education, lower attainers, race and class*, Social Justice SIG BERA.

Smith, M. (2013) *Evidence-based Education: is it really that straightforward?* Available at www.theguardian.com/teacher network/2013. Accessed 20 April 2015.

Wilshaw, M. (2013) *Unseen Children*, HMI's speech 20 June 2013.

Chapter 14

Global approaches to education, disability and human rights

Why inclusive education is the way forward

Richard Rieser

> From now on the new paradigm of inclusive education must mark the institution of education, understanding that the traditional education system, as it was conceived and designed, is not only opposed to diversity, but also works against the rights and interests of populations historically excluded.
>
> (Vernor Munoz Villalobos 2007, UN Special Rapporteur on the Right to Education)

Introduction

This chapter examines some of the main issues you will face in thinking about the values and practices that underpin inclusive education from a global perspective. This is not an academic but a practical concern as in every mainstream school and class there are a diversity of pupils including those from different social classes, cultures, ethnic backgrounds and with different impairments. A firm understanding of the issues involved in responding to, and celebrating, difference will help you develop effective inclusive teaching.

Inclusive education is a buzzword. However, many who use it, or who oppose it, do not understand that it involves a process of structural change throughout the education system. Inclusive education requires the transformation of much common practice in schools and colleges, to ensure all learners can achieve their social and academic potential. Historic inequalities have existed throughout human history. A human rights' perspective, which has gained support in the years since the UN Declaration of Human Rights (1948), demands that the world move forward to embrace a collaborative future where people and environments are placed before profits. We all have a right to grow up and receive our education together. Breaking down the barriers that prevent this is an important part of human progress and the development of a sustainable future. Educating all children together is the most effective means of achieving this, requiring changes in theory and practice.

The international context

The 2006 United Nations Convention on the Rights of Persons with Disabilities ratified by the UK, requires us to develop new thinking about disabled pupils, moving away from a special educational needs' deficit view to an empowering rights' based view:

> An evolving concept (. . .) that disability results from the interaction of persons with impairments and attitudinal and environmental barriers that hinder their full and effective participation in society on an equal basis with others.
>
> (Article 1)

Countries ratifying the Convention must address disabling barriers such as lack of accessible transport and buildings, rigid grade related curriculum and assessment fixed by national government, teachers untrained in inclusive pedagogies, attitudes that are based on identifying what people cannot normally do, lack of social acceptance and opportunity for employment and denial of human rights (United Nations 2006).

Previously, in 1994, 92 countries and 20 NGOs came together under the auspices of UNESCO in Salamanca, Spain, and adopted the Salamanca Statement, giving the world community a clear steer towards a more inclusive education system.

- Education systems should be designed and educational programmes implemented to take into account the wide diversity of these characteristics and needs.
- Those with special educational needs must have access to regular schools, which should accommodate them within a child-centred pedagogy capable of meeting these needs.
- Regular schools with this inclusive orientation are the most effective means of combating discriminatory attitudes, creating welcoming communities, building an inclusive society and achieving education for all; moreover, they provide an effective education to the majority of children and improve the efficiency and ultimately the cost-effectiveness of the entire education system.

(UNESCO 1994)

Salamanca set an inclusive education framework for the world but needed clarity. This was one of the key themes at the 2009 Global Conference on Inclusive Education, *Confronting the Gap: Rights, Rhetoric, Reality? Salamanca 15 years On*. This Conference adopted a resolution that sees inclusion as a process of transforming existing education systems by giving support to all pupils to achieve their potential and the removal of barriers. It stated:

> We understand inclusive education to be a process where mainstream schools and early year's settings are transformed so that *all* children/students are supported to meet their academic and social potential and involves removing barriers in environment, attitudes, communication, curriculum, teaching, socialisation and assessment at all levels.
>
> (Inclusion International 2009)

This is in line with a wider definition adopted by UNESCO (2006), which sees inclusive education as a:

> . . . process of addressing and responding to diversity of needs of all learners through increasing participation in learning, cultures and communities, and reducing exclusion within and from education. It involves changes and modifications in content, approaches, structures and strategies, with a common vision which covers all children of appropriate age range and a conviction that it is the responsibility of the regular system to educate all children.

At a recent Day of General Discussion (April 2015), by the Convention on the Rights of Persons with Disabilities Committee (the elected body overseeing the implementation by State Parties of the Convention) submissions showed that there was slow progress towards inclusive education in the 152 countries that have ratified the Treaty. There were many examples of children and young people with all types of impairments being included but there was a failure by States to understand, plan and bring to scale the necessary transformations (OHCHR 2015).

In 2011/12, I examined a wide range of examples of inclusive education across the 53 Commonwealth countries (Rieser 2012). Most examples were more to do with *placement* of disabled pupils in mainstream schools, i.e. *integration*, but there were some examples of teachers and schools restructuring to accommodate disabled pupils. From these, the following criteria at National, Regional, District and School level were drawn up.

What needs to be done to ensure all children are included successfully in school?

Requirements at a national level

- A flexible National Curriculum with the means of making the curriculum accessible to all.
- Assessment systems that are made flexible and meaningful to include all learners.
- Active encouragement to disabled pupils and their parents to enrol in their local school.
- Sufficient school places and adequate numbers of support staff and specialist teachers, including those with expertise in visual, hearing, physical, communication, learning or behavioural impairments.
- All teachers trained in inclusive teaching and learning.
- Sufficient specialist teachers for the development of a pupil-centred pedagogy where all can progress at their optimum pace.
- Sufficient capital for school building and modification.
- The reduction of class sizes.
- A media and public awareness campaign to establish rights based approaches to disability and inclusive education.

- The mobilisation of communities to build new schools or adapt existing environments.
- Sufficient specialist teachers for those with visual hearing, physical, communication, learning or behavioural impairments work with a range of schools.

Requirements at regional/district levels

- The strengthening of effective links between Education, Health, and Social Services so that they work collaboratively on a joint inclusion strategy.
- The developments of links between schools and local authorities with the support of disabled advisors.
- Support for ongoing inclusion training for teachers, parents, and community leaders.
- The development of Centres with equipment and expertise on techniques that support inclusive education, e.g. Sign, Braille and augmented and alternative communication.
- Ensure all disabled children identified are able to enrol in their local schools.
- Draw on the knowledge and experience of members of the local community who can support the cultural and experiential interests of pupils.
- Regular training on inclusive teaching and learning, for teachers, parents and community leaders.
- Support for parents of disabled children to empower their children.
- The sharing of best practice in the region.

Requirements at school level

- Sufficient staff and volunteers are in place to provide support for disabled children and that teachers are trained and support each other in planning and developing inclusive practice.
- All staff understand and know what is required of them to include *all learners,* including disabled children.
- Curricula and pedagogies are accessible to all with a range of learning situations, styles and paces.
- Inclusion is audited regularly and barriers tackled systematically.
- School environment and activities are accessible and information is available in alternative forms as required e.g. Braille, audio, pictures, signing.
- Create a school that welcomes difference, and in which pupils support each other – collaboration rather than competition should be the ethos.
- Assessment is continuous, flexible and used formatively to assess what children have learnt.
- The school is the hub of the community and encourages the involvement of all its members, regardless of difference.

From medical model to social model – implications for education provision and teaching

In the UK we have moved some way towards inclusive education, but 'medical model' attitudes still lie behind Government thinking. This identifies children with different impairments as having varying educational needs and then provides a range of provision to meet those needs. In some local authorities, parents can choose mainstream schooling for their children with significant impairments. However, it is assumed those labelled with 'profound or complex needs' will attend special schools and many professionals encourage this view. This is classic 'medical model' thinking, where children's needs are identified by their Special Educational Needs assessment based on what they 'can't do' and different levels of provision are made for them. The medical model sees the problem in the person and their impairment rather than in the system and its need for restructuring (Mason and Rieser 1994).

In my book on *Implementing Inclusive Education* throughout the Commonwealth (Rieser 2012) I drew up the following table contrasting different ways of thinking about disability and education:

Table 14.1 Types of thinking about disabled people and forms of education

Thinking/model	Characteristics	Form of education
Traditional	Disabled person a shame on family, guilt, ignorance. Disabled person seen as of no value.	**Excluded** from education altogether.
Medical 1	Focus on what disabled person cannot do. Attempt to normalise or if cannot make to fit into things as they are keep them separate.	**Segregation** Institutions/ hospitals Special schools (with 'expert' special educators).
Medical 2	Person can be supported by minor adjustment and support, to function normally and minimise their impairment. Continuum of provision based on severity and type of impairment.	**Integration** in mainstream a) At same location but in separate class/ units b) Socially in some activities e.g. meals, assembly or art. c) In the class with support, but teaching and learning remain the same. **What you cannot do determines which form of education you receive.**
Social model	Barriers identified – solutions found to minimise them. Barriers of attitude, environment and organisation are seen as what disables and are removed to maximise potential of all. Disabled person welcomed. Relations are intentionally built. Disabled person achieves their potential. Person centred approach.	**Inclusive education** – schools where all are welcomed. Staff, parents and pupils value diversity and support is provided, so all can be successful academically and socially. This requires reorganising teaching, learning and assessment. Peer support is encouraged. **Focus on what you can do.**

Source: Rieser (2012)

In a previous study I carried out for the Department for Education and Skills (DfES 2006) in the UK to identify best practice in making reasonable adjustments for disabled pupils, we visited 40 mainstream schools, and filmed and observed much inclusive practice. We carried out more than 300 interviews with heads, SENCOs, teachers, parents and pupils. They identified the following:

Factors that support the development of good inclusive practice (DfES 2006)

- vision and values based on an inclusive ethos
- a 'can do' attitude from all staff
- a pro-active approach to identifying barriers and finding practical solutions
- strong collaborative relationships with pupils and parents
- a meaningful voice for pupils
- a positive approach to managing behaviour
- strong leadership by special educational needs co-ordinators or management and governors
- effective staff training and development
- the use of expertise from outside the school
- building disability into resourcing arrangements
- a sensitive approach to meeting the impairment-specific needs of pupils
- regular critical review and evaluation
- the availability of role models and positive images of disability

Despite these findings there are many detractors of inclusive education who may confuse integration with inclusion. A brief examination of the development of special education will help illuminate other reasons.

Policy making in a historical context

Disabled people were traditionally invested with meanings from different cultures that saw us as evil, penitent sinners, objects of charity, holy, incapable, a figure of fun or unworthy of life. From the Enlightenment, we became subject to fledgling medical science, so if we did not conform to 'normal' development of body and mind we had to be rehabilitated, 'made normal', or locked away from society. This process was extended by the false science of Eugenics, wishing to breed superior human beings, which held sway from the 1880s to 1950s and led to the sterilisation, incarceration or death of millions of disabled people throughout Europe and North America. Psychological testing was often used to justify these practices, with dubious psychometric procedures (Rieser 2000a).

Mass primary education was introduced in England in the 1870s. Blind and deaf children in the late nineteenth century acquired a right to education; other disabled children were deemed in-educable. Until the Second World War, a series of measures were introduced that allowed selected groups of disabled children to receive education, usually in separate settings designated for particular categories of impairment and isolated from their non-disabled peers. There was a strong rehabilitative and medical emphasis, underpinned by highly medicalised and impairment-led perceptions of disabled children and young people, as illustrated by the labels used to describe them, e.g. 'physically handicapped', 'mild educationally subnormal'.

The Warnock Inquiry (1978) recommended that disabled children should no longer be categorised by their impairments (or 'handicaps'), but by their special educational needs and, wherever possible, should be integrated into mainstream or ordinary schools. However, Warnock had no conception of inclusion, rather *integration* was to be locational (on the same campus in different institutions), social (mixing for assemblies, play) or functional (in the same class with some support, the overall approaches to teaching and learning remaining unchanged). This Inquiry led to the 1981 Education Act, which allowed for the *integration* of disabled children in ordinary schools, unless they fell under one of three caveats: it was deemed that their needs could not be accommodated, their 'special educational needs' would interfere with the education of other children or the costs involved were considered to be an inefficient use of resources.

In practice, as there was no new funding put in place to support this policy, a slow increase in the proportion of the education budget in each local authority went into supporting disabled pupils, usually by the employment of unqualified teaching assistants, as specified through the newly introduced Statements of Special Educational Needs. Some local authorities, such as Newham and Barnsley, took the 1981 Act at face value, started dismantling special schools and setting up resourced schools and experienced teams of support teachers. In more rural areas, such as Cumbria, Cornwall, North Yorkshire and Norfolk, a higher proportion of disabled children were already attending their local schools in a process of piecemeal integration. However, for the majority of local authorities it was business as usual and increasingly the caveats were used, often against the wishes of pupil and parent, to assess disabled children as needing special schooling. There were many arguments, so a later Education Act (1993) introduced an independent Special Educational Needs Tribunal and a much more codified process of assessment and placement, with a statutory Code of Practice (Rieser 2000b; DfES 2001).

In 1997, New Labour came to power with a stated commitment to human rights for disabled people, as exemplified in both the Green Paper *Excellence for All* (DfEE 1997) appearing to offer support for 'inclusion', and in the 2001 Special Educational Needs and Disability Act, passed after some strong lobbying from disabled people and parents. This removed two of the caveats, leaving only 'interfering with the efficient education of other children' and gave parents a right to choose either mainstream or special schools for their disabled child's education. The 2001 Act also set up a new duty for all schools, not to treat disabled pupils 'less favourably' than other pupils and to make 'reasonable adjustments' in admissions, education and associated services. The special educational needs assessment and statementing system was left intact to provide the resources, and the school environment had to be made gradually more accessible under the Schools' Access

Planning Duty. A similar duty was placed on all post-school provision. All education settings had to meet learners' needs and remove physical barriers to participation as part of making reasonable adjustments. However, an increasing reliance on market principles in the design and culture of education systems as well as notions of 'choice' have undercut New Labour's stated intentions regarding inclusive education (Dyson 2005).

Recent policy developments and the international context

Between 2003 and 2006 a backlash towards the presumption of inclusion as a desirable and achievable goal occurred. Baroness Warnock (2005) decided she had changed her mind and the opposition, particularly David Cameron, argued for a moratorium on special school closure. This shift appears to have been motivated by two groups. Firstly, by some parents who felt their children were not getting the support they needed and secondly special school head teachers, fighting to maintain the position of special schools. This led the government to build a new generation of special schools and to talk of a 'continuum of need to be met in a continuum of provision' (Ashton 2003). This missed the point that inclusive schools need to be resourced and staff trained, to meet the diverse needs of all. Not 'one size fits all' as inclusion has been parodied, but 'all sizes fit in here' (Barton 2005; DEE 2005). This became Conservative Party policy (2010) in 'terms of opposing the bias to inclusion'.

Currently, UK policy is contradictory. The Disability Discrimination Act with its protection from discrimination has been incorporated into the 2010 Equalities Act. Under this legislation disabled children, students and disabled staff, defined as those with a 'physical or mental impairment that has a substantial and long term impact on their ability to carry out normal day to day activities' (judged without the impact of medicines, aids and appliances), are protected from direct discrimination, indirect discrimination (arising inadvertently from policies, procedures and practices), discrimination arising from disability and are entitled to an anticipatory duty of making reasonable adjustments and elimination of harassment. All publicly funded bodies, including maintained schools and colleges, academies and free schools, have to enforce this legislation, and are under a general duty to promote equality. Disabled children, students and a large proportion with special educational needs will also be covered by this legislation. However, enforcement relies on parents taking cases to SENDIST, which very few do.

Children and Families Act 2014 (Part 3)

In 2014, the Children and Families Act, Part 3, whilst maintaining a presumption of mainstreaming, made it harder for parents who want mainstream education for their child to get it, introducing more reasons for a school to reject a child with an Education, Health and Care Plan (EHCP), previously a Statement of Special Educational Needs. The Act got rid of School Action/School Action Plus, which covered over 1.3 million school pupils and replaced it with School Support.

Where children (about 232,000) get a statutory assessment leading to an EHCP parents can express a preference for where they want their child educated. A large and increasing minority still want a segregated education in special schools (47.3 per cent DfE 2014), up from 89,390 in 2006 to 99,760 in 2014, a result of increasing pressure on schools to deliver results and a lack of training/preparation for inclusion. Other reasons for the increase in numbers of parents wanting segregated education for their children include: failure to properly staff and equip schools, lack of a welcoming inclusive culture, pressure on performance, which impacts on staff feeling able to meet diverse needs, large inhuman schools and fears about bullying. Parents generally choose mainstream but when these factors are not adequately addressed in a majority of mainstream schools parents become refugees from the mainstream. There is a ten-fold difference in rates of inclusion across English local authorities (Norwich 2014), some local authorities and individual schools offering more capacity and support for inclusive education than others, and a much wider range of disabled children are successfully included. These schools demonstrate that where there is a strong inclusive ethos, a willingness to address barriers and find solutions, all children benefit socially and academically. Recent films of inclusion working show that with the right attitudes and values inclusion is possible and beneficial to all (World of Inclusion 2015).

In England, the Children and Families Act (Part 3) was the culmination of a three-year period of consultation and pilots to try to remove the difficulties parents had, having to battle for support for their disabled children and students. It is doubtful that there will be improvements for young disabled people and their families, despite the rhetoric, as local authority cuts continue and schools have more freedom in their admissions. A total of 70 per cent of schools in England now set their own admissions policy and in the main do not favour enrolling disabled children with more complex needs.

Part 3 puts disabled children, students, those with special educational needs and their families at the centre of being consulted and having their concerns met (Section 19); requires local authorities to publish a local offer and for health and social care agencies to collaborate in assessing and making an Education, Health and Care Plan; these plans now cover children and young people from 0 to age 25 and are based on outcomes including transition and preparation for adult life. (The introduction of this system is phased over 40 months from September 2014.) The presumption of mainstreaming has been maintained, but now has so many caveats that it will be possible for any school/college not to admit a child/student with an EHC Plan.

Under Section 40.3:

> The local authority must secure that the EHC plan names the school or other institution specified in the request (from parents or young person) unless
>
> (a) the school or other institution requested is unsuitable for the age, ability, aptitude or special educational needs of the child or young person concerned, or

(b) the attendance of the child or young person at the requested school or other institution would be incompatible with

   (i) the provision of efficient education for others, or
   (ii) the efficient use of resources.

These caveats are based on the opinion of the school. Schools are encouraged by Ofsted and the Government to be very conscious of their results and league tables. Many will not want disabled children who develop at a different or slower pace. The local authority has to consult the school or college and if necessary revise the EHC plan. It would still be open for the local authority to place the child or young person at the school or college, but on current practice they would be unlikely to do so. The SEN and Disability Code of Practice (DfE 2015), which provides statutory guidance on implementing this legislation and to which schools must pay regard, tries to bring the disability and SEN aspects together. In this it appears unsuccessful, as the first is based on a human rights position and the second on a 'deficit' medical model. The medical model approach predominates in all chapters apart from Chapter 1. Little attempt has been made to integrate the two approaches. For example, under the Equalities Act there is an anticipatory duty to make reasonable adjustments, which means prior to the disabled child/young person being in the school. Under the Schools' chapter this is hardly mentioned, and instead all pupils are meant to go through a series of assessment cycles without reasonable adjustments – 'assess, plan, do, review' (Chapter 6, DfE 2015).

Contradictions with the global human rights' position

The United Nations Convention on the Rights of Persons with Disabilities (UNCRPD) (2006) is the first human rights' treaty of the new Millennium and extends to disabled people the human rights proclaimed for all in the 1948 Universal Declaration of Human Rights. Disabled people were not specifically left out of this declaration but were not mentioned, so it was not seen that human rights should apply to us. This was not malign in the main, but based on traditional and medical model thinking. We were seen as exceptions, as less than human.

   The ambiguity of the UK Government's position on inclusive education is demonstrated by the fact that it was the only country in the world to register a reservation and an interpretive declaration against inclusive education, Article 24 of the UNCRPD, when they ratified in June 2009, and still is.

   Article 24 requires state parties to ensure:

* All disabled children and young people can fully participate in the state education system and that this should be an inclusive education system at all levels
* The development by persons with disabilities of their personality, talents and creativity, as well as their mental and physical abilities, to their fullest potential
* This right is to be delivered in local schools within an inclusive primary and secondary education system, from which disabled people should not be excluded

- Reasonable accommodations should be provided for individual requirements and support provided in individualised programmes to facilitate their effective social and academic education.

(United Nations 2006)

The Millennium Development Goal 2 – that all children will complete primary education by 2015 – has not been achieved, with some 40 per cent of the 58 million out of school being disabled. A large proportion of the 240 million who drop out are also disabled children. As the Global Campaign for Education (2015) argues, it will not be possible to ever achieve this goal, without a fully inclusive education system in every country.

It is clear what needs to be done to ensure all children are included successfully in school, but it appears to suit many governments to maintain confusion rather than embrace the task at hand. Hopefully, the forthcoming General Comment of the CRPD Committee on Article 24 will encourage the development of genuine inclusive systems around the world.

Given that parents, disabled people, teachers and academics have been demonstrating the efficacy of inclusive education for more than 30 years, one may be tempted to ask why such fundamentally good educational practice is taking so long to be implemented throughout the education systems of the world. Many arguments have been put forward by those who do not understand inclusive education. These are all answered by the evidence and principles demonstrated by the Centre for Studies on Inclusive Education (CSIE).

Conclusion

We now have the human rights framework. We have the experience around the world to know how to develop and build inclusive education. We have exemplars of how to make inclusive education work. Yet negative attitudes, fear, the inertia of existing education systems and professionals remain the major reasons why inclusive education is not developing. It is vital that existing teachers and those entering the profession understand that developing their practice to accommodate all learners, where diversity is valued in the curriculum and in the methods of teaching and learning, underpins a human rights' approach, with inclusive educational practice the best way of ensuring this. All teachers should familiarise themselves with the practice and principles of inclusion in general (UNESCO 2009). They also need to familiarise themselves with the adjustments necessary to accommodate those with different forms of impairment in regular schools and classrooms. A good outline to these is provided by UNESCO Bangkok (2009).

Surely now is the time for the development of an inclusive education system, emphasising collaboration rather than competition, involving all children, based on fundamental human values. It is time to recognise we are each interdependent and a shared understanding and commitment of human rights for all is crucial to the development of a more just and harmonious society. There is no better place to start than through the collaborative work of teachers, schools and communities.

Reflections on values and practice

1   Examine the wording of Article 24 of the UNCRPD and then think of a local authority you know and list the changes that would have to occur for Article 24 to be fully implemented.
2   A parent of a child who has a physical impairment and low vision wants their child to attend their local mainstream school. Imagine you are a) the head teacher and b) the class teacher. Describe how you will find out about the changes that may be needed. What might these changes be and how will you implement them?
3   You are in the role of an Ofsted inspector and you are inspecting a school known to you. How would you assess the progress disabled children make, how safe they are and whether they have full equality?

Resources

Rieser, R. (2012) *Implementing Inclusive Education: A Commonwealth guide to implementing Article 24 of the UN Convention on the Rights of People with Disabilities*, second edition, London: Commonwealth Secretariat. Available at: http://worldof inclusion.com/v3/wp-content/uploads/2014/01/Implementing-Inclusive-Education-promo-copy1.pdf.
World of Inclusions (2015) *Inclusion Working in 2015*. The organisation *World of Inclusion* has made a series of films to demonstrate that inclusive education of disabled children is possible in 2015 in schools with the right policies and attitudes. These can be accessed on the *World of Inclusion* website: http://worldofinclusion.com/
UNICEF (2013) *Take us Seriously! Engaging Children with Disabilities in Decisions Affecting their Lives*. Available at: http://www.unicef.org/disabilities/files/Take_Us_Seriously.pdf.

References

Ashton, Baroness (2003) Press release of report of Special Schools Working Group. Available at https://www.tes.com/article.aspx?storycode=379948.
Barton, L. (2005) A Response to Warnock, M. 2005: Special Educational Needs – A New Look. Available at: http://www.leeds.ac.uk/disability-studies/archiveuk/barton/Warnock.pdf. Accessed 18 August 2015.
Children and Families Act 2014 (Part 3) Available at: http://www.legislation.gov.uk/ukpga/2014/6/part/3/enacted. Accessed 18 August 2015.
Conservative Party (2010) Education Manifesto. Available at: http://issuu.com/conservatives/docs/drafteducationmanifesto. Accessed 19 August 2015.
CSIE-Centre for Studies on Inclusive Education (2002/1989) 'The Inclusion Charter' CSIE, Bristol http://www.csie.org.uk/resources/charter.shtml. Accessed 18/08/15.
DfE (2014) Special Education Statistics. Available at: https://www.gov.uk/government/collections/statistics-special-educational-needs-sen. Accessed 18 August 2015.
DfE (2015) Special educational needs and disability code of practice: 0 to 25 years. Available at: https://www.gov.uk/government/uploads/system/uploads/attachment_data/file/398815/SEND_Code_of_Practice_January_2015.pdf. Accessed 18 August 2015.
DfEE (1997) *Excellence for All Children: meeting special educational needs*, London: DfEE.

DfES (2001) SEN Code of Practice. Available at: http://webarchive.nationalarchives.gov. uk/20130401151715/https://www.education.gov.uk/publications/eorderingdownload/ dfes%200581%20200mig2228.pdf. Accessed 18 August 2015.

DfES (2006) Implementing the Disability Discrimination Act in Schools and Early Years. DfES, London: Prologue. Films available online at: http://worldofinclusion.com/v3/wp-content/uploads/2014/01/RAP-document-with-youtube-links.pdf. Accessed 18 August 2015.

Disability Equality in Education (DEE) (2005) Warnock challenges the rights of disabled children to inclusion (an open letter, signed by over 600 people and organisations, as an advert in the TES issue 8th July 2005). Available at: http://worldofinclusion.com/res/ warnock/Warnock_Ad.pdf. Accessed 18 August 2015.

Dyson, A. (2005) Philosophy, politics and economics? The story of inclusive education in England. In Mitchell, D. (ed.) *Contextualizing Inclusive Education: evaluating old and new international perspectives*, London: Routledge, pp.63–88.

Equalities Act 2010, UK Government. Available at: http://www.legislation.gov.uk/ukpga/ 2010/15/contents. Accessed 19 August 2015.

Flavey, M. (2004) Reviewing inclusive education, USA: TASH Journal.

Inclusion International (2009) Global Conference on Inclusive Education. October 21–23, 2009, Salamanca, Spain. Available at: http://www.inclusion-international.org/en/extras/ 4.html. Accessed 5 January 2014.

Global Campaign for Education (2015) Global Campaign for Education Submission to the Committee on the Rights of Persons with Disabilities: Day of General Discussion (DGD) on the right to education for persons with disabilities. Available at: http://www. ohchr.org/Documents/HRBodies/CRPD/DGD/2015/GlobalCampaignEducation.doc. Accessed 19 August 2015.

Mason, M., and Rieser, R. (1994) Altogether Better, London: Comic Relief. Available at: http://worldofinclusion.com/res/altogether/AltogetherBetter.pdf. Accessed 19 August 2015.

Munoz Villalobos, V. (2007) The Right to Education of Persons with Disabilities, Report of the Special Rapporteur on the Right to Education to the UN Human Rights Council A/HRC/4/29, Geneva. Available at: www.unesco.org/education/gmr2008/annexes/ annex8.pdf. Accessed 19 August 2015.

Norwich, B. (2014) *Contrasting responses to diversity: school placement trends 2007– 2013 for all local authorities in England*, Bristol: CSIE.

Office High Commissioner on Human Rights CRPD Committee (OHCHR) (2015) CRPD Committee General Day of Discussion. Available at: http://www.ohchr.org/EN/ HRBodies/CRPD/Pages/DGDontherighttoeducationforpersonswithdisabilities.aspx. Accessed 19 August 2015.

Rieser, R. (2000a) Disability discrimination, the final frontier: disablement, history and liberation. In Cole, M., *Education Equality and Human Rights*, London: Routledge. Available at: http://www.worldofinclusion.com/res/edeqhr/Rieser1.pdf. Accessed 19 August 2015.

Rieser, R. (2000b) Special educational needs or inclusive education: the challenge of disability discrimination in schooling. In Cole, M., *Education Equality and Human Rights*, London: Routledge. Available at: http://www.worldofinclusion.com/res/edeqhr/ Rieser2.pdf. Accessed 19 August 2015.

Rieser, R. (2012) *Implementing Inclusive Education: A Commonwealth guide to implementing Article 24 of the UN Convention on the Rights of People with Disabilities*, second edition, London: Commonwealth Secretariat. Available at: http://worldof

inclusion.com/v3/wp-content/uploads/2014/01/Implementing-Inclusive-Education-promo-copy1.pdf. Accessed 19 August 2015.

United Nations (1948) Universal Declaration of Human Rights, New York. Available at: http://www.un.org/en/documents/udhr/index.shtml. Accessed 19 August 2015.

United Nations (2006) Conventions on the Rights of People with Disabilities. Available at: http://www.un.org/disabilities/default.asp?id=150. Accessed 19 August 2015.

UNESCO (1994) *The Salamanca Statement on Principles, Policy and Practices in Special Needs Education*, Paris: UNESCO. Available at: http://www.unesco.org/education/pdf/SALAMA_E.PDF. Accessed 19 August 2015.

UNESCO (2006) Guidelines for Inclusion Access for All. Available at: http://unesdoc.unesco.org/images/0014/001402/140224e.pdf. Accessed 19 August 2015.

UNESCO (2009) Policy Guidelines on Inclusive Education. Available at: http://unesdoc.unesco.org/images/0017/001778/177849e.pdf. Accessed 19 August 2015.

UNESCO Bangkok (2009) Embracing Diversity: Toolkit for Creating Inclusive Learning-Friendly Environments. Teaching Children with Disabilities in Inclusive Settings. Available at: http://unesdoc.unesco.org/images/0018/001829/182975e.pdf. Accessed 19 August 2015.

Warnock Inquiry (1978) *Special Educational Needs: the Warnock Report*, London: HMSO.

Warnock, M. (2005) 'Special educational needs: a new look' (No. 11 in a series of policy discussions Philosophy of Education Society of Great Britain).

World of Inclusion (2015) Films of Inclusion Working – The Wroxham Primary, Emersons Green Primary, Priestnall Secondary. Available at: http://worldofinclusion.com/inclusion-working-in-2015/. Accessed 19 August 2015.

Index

Printed in Great Britain
by Amazon